Dorm Room Dealers

DORM ROOM DEALERS

Drugs and the Privileges of Race and Class

A. Rafik Mohamed and
Erik D. Fritsvold

LYNNE
RIENNER
PUBLISHERS

BOULDER
LONDON

Published in the United States of America by
Lynne Rienner Publishers, Inc.
1800 30th Street, Boulder, Colorado 80301
www.rienner.com

and in the United Kingdom by
Lynne Rienner Publishers, Inc.
3 Henrietta Street, Covent Garden, London WC2E 8LU

Library of Congress Cataloging-in-Publication Data
Mohamed, A. Rafik.
 Dorm room dealers : drugs and the privileges of race and class /
A. Rafik Mohamed & Erik D. Fritsvold.
     p. cm.
 Includes bibliographical references and index.
 ISBN 978-1-58826-667-5 (hc : alk. paper)
 ISBN 978-1-58826-721-4 (pb : alk. paper)
 1. College students—Drug use—United States—Case studies.
2. Drug dealers—United States—Case studies. 3. Criminal behavior—
United States—Case studies. I. Fritsvold, Erik D. II. Title.
 HV5824.Y68M63 2009
 363.45084'20973—dc22
                                                           2009016415

British Cataloguing in Publication Data
A Cataloguing in Publication record for this book
is available from the British Library.

Printed and bound in the United States of America

    The paper used in this publication meets the requirements
 ∞ of the American National Standard for Permanence of
    Paper for Printed Library Materials Z39.48-1992.

Contents

Acknowledgments

We would like to offer our warmest appreciation to everyone who supported us in both the research and writing phases of this project. First and foremost, this book would not have been possible without the encouragement of Andrew Berzanskis at Lynne Rienner Publishers. Also, it would have been far less interesting if not for the help of our devoted team of research assistants, including but not limited to Terressa Benz, Athena Krell, and Jen Neill. Naturally, we would be remiss if we did not thank all of the dorm room dealers who willingly shared their stories with us and, in many cases, allowed us to be flies on the wall as they conducted their business. We are particularly grateful to Brice and Cecilia for their willingness to use their rapport within this network to advance this project. In addition, we are both extremely fortunate to have benefitted from the expertise and guidance of Kitty Calavita. We would also like to thank John Dombrink and the rest of the Criminology, Law, and Society Department at the University of California, Irvine, for their training and their inspiration.

A. RAFIK MOHAMED: To my father, mother, and grandmother, thanks for the indescribable role you played in shaping my life and mind. Thanks to my sisters, Rena and Shalisa, for your support over the years. And of course, I must acknowledge my wife, Beverly, for her encouragement and for tolerating and understanding my many idiosyncrasies. Thanks to my lifelong friends in Maryland and DC, and to those friends and colleagues whom I have picked up along the way. To everyone at the University of San Diego, and particularly the

Department of Sociology, thanks for bringing me on board and for being great colleagues over the years. To my friend and coauthor, Erik Fritsvold, thanks for all you did in bringing this project together and for always making me look good. Finally, this book and my career never would have happened if it were not for Bill Chambliss. Bill, thanks for pulling me, a wayward would-be attorney, aside and giving me a sense of purpose by talking me into graduate school.

ERIK D. FRITSVOLD: I would like to thank Brad Schneider of 454 Tattoo and my coauthor and friend, Rafik Mohamed, for a decade of life-changing mentoring. In another vein, as a parent now myself, I more fully understand the decades of diligence and sacrifice that my own parents invested in my education, and I appreciate that tremendously. I would also like to acknowledge David Drew for his academic advice with the rare twist of practicality. Lastly, I want to thank my wife, Fabiola, and my daughter, Kayla, whose love and support are awe inspiring.

1

Overlooked Illegal Markets: Dealing Dope, College Style

The scene is stark: an odious drug-dealing partnership comes to a head with a dispute over money and threats of severe, even fatal violence. Dallas—until recently a drug dealing associate and good friend—arrived at Brice's house early in the morning, unannounced.[1] He woke Brice and began demanding "fuckin' compensation." Brice asked his girlfriend to leave while he confronted a visibly irate Dallas. Brice was disgusted with his long-time partner. "I told him, 'I don't ever want to see you again. If I ever see you again I will do something drastic.'" Brice suggested that he had a gun nearby and iterated his demand that Dallas leave immediately. But Dallas—perhaps because he felt a true sense of injustice or perhaps due to the influence of the stimulants he had likely taken earlier—would not leave.

Brice, in turn, refused to acknowledge that he owed Dallas anything.

"Fuck it," said Dallas. He reached into his pocket and, rather than a weapon, brandished the business card of Brice's father. Dallas said, "Let's just see what your dad thinks about your newfound interests."

This moment, in both its genesis and outcome, not only challenges the archetypal portrayals of drug dealers, but also serves as a defining moment in the approximately six years of fieldwork that went into this research.[2] Unlike the stereotypical drug-related conflicts often depicted in popular media, this dispute did not take place on the mean streets of Baltimore, Harlem, Detroit, or South Central, but rather in the shadow of the ivory tower. This conflict did not take place between marginalized youth struggling to survive, between

1

ghetto superstars struggling to get a rep, or between junkies looking for their next fix, but rather between educated, white college students of relative privilege. This conflict was less about desperation and social disorganization and more about the themes that emerge in undergraduate business economics courses. A few years after the above-described exchange, instead of ending up as yet another collateral consequence of the US war on drugs—permanently disabled, in prison, disenfranchised, or dead—both Brice and Dallas had reinvented themselves as successful young professionals, members of the legitimate white-collar workforce.

What follows is a firsthand account of Brice, Dallas, and roughly fifty others that might accurately be described as part of the silent majority of US drug dealers,[3] an off-the-radar collection of middle- and upper-class drug pushers whose deviant behaviors are largely unknown beyond the limits of their social networks; whose dealings are typically not directly associated with violence; and whose often flagrant illegal activities are generally carried out without the hindrances of police scrutiny and without the stigma of being labeled a criminal. Here is an insider account of a college drug-dealing network that existed essentially unmediated, hidden in plain sight. Welcome to the silent majority of the collegiate drug-dealing world; welcome to *Dorm Room Dealers*.

Anti-Targets

STOPPER (COLLEGE DRUG DEALER): Where I'm from, stoners were kids who wore hemp. We have a kind of granola culture. But these kids [at this university], you weren't looking at the 4.0 students, but they were normal, they were involved, good majors—business majors—they didn't fit the stereotype of what a drug user would look like. These kids were pretty upstanding kids to most people. They just smoked a lot of weed.

Currently, more than 7 million people in the United States are under what criminologists and criminal justice professionals refer to as "correctional supervision." This means that on any given day more than 3 percent of the US adult population, or one in every thirty-one persons eighteen years of age or older, is living on probation, parole, or in one of the country's thousands of jails and prisons.[4] At the beginning of 2008, approximately 2.3 million of these people under correctional supervision were locked up in state and federal prisons or in local jails, amounting to an incarceration rate in the United States of 762 per 100,000.[5] To put these figures into a global context, in both total population and rate, the United States incarcerates more of its citizens than any other industrialized, democratic nation. Further, the number of people behind bars in the United States and the rate of incarceration are substantially higher than those of many nations, including China, Russia, and Iran, whose citizens have fewer freedoms and are lorded over by despotic regimes.[6]

While these figures are startling in and of themselves, they only tell part of the US criminal justice story in the new millennium. These data fail to show the extent to which the present-day girth of our criminal justice system has been fed by excessively punitive drug policies enacted during the Reagan and George H. W. Bush administrations and enhanced during the subsequent Clinton and George W. Bush administrations continuation of the "war on drugs." Over the course of these administrations,' the number of incarcerated drug offenders rose by more than 1,000 percent, primarily as a result of increased law-enforcement scrutiny and not as a result of increased rates of offending.[7] Currently in the United States, approximately 20 percent of state prisoners and more than 50 percent of federal prisoners are incarcerated for drug-law violations as their most serious offense. By way of pre–drug war context, in 1980 only 6.5 percent of state and 25 percent of federal prison inmates were sentenced to prison for drug-law violations. Additionally, despite the hearty rhetoric behind the get-tough antidrug laws that characterized the era, those incarcerated for drug-law violations since the war on drugs began have tended to be users and low-level dealers rather than major dealers and drug kingpins.

Perhaps the most widely commented upon and ethically problematic outcome of the war on drugs has been the disproportionate negative impact these policies have had on poor and minority communities, particularly African Americans. While comprising only 13 percent of the US population, African Americans make up nearly one-half of the more than two million people behind bars in the United States, more than 35 percent of all persons arrested for drug abuse violations, and approximately 45 percent of state prison inmates serving time for drug offenses. This is despite the fact that drug-user data suggest that racial and ethnic groups in the United

States tend to have rates of drug use close to their representation in the US population. For example, federal government drug-use surveys indicate that African Americans make up about 15 percent of the total drug user population while whites comprise over 70 percent of all drug users.

According to criminologist Elliot Currie, author of the award-winning *Confronting Crime,* "Nationally, there are twice as many Black men in state and federal prison today as there were men of all races twenty years ago. More than anything else, it is the war on drugs that has caused this dramatic increase."[8] Adding to Currie's drug policy assessment, Yale law professor Steven B. Duke writes, "By almost any measure, Blacks suffer disproportionately from drug prohibition . . . racial minorities suffer from drugs and drug prohibition vastly out of proportion to their representation in the population."[9]

These glaring disparities have even garnered the unlikely attention of high profile politicians who typically steer clear of questioning the rationality of drug policy for fear of being labeled soft on crime. For example, in 2007 while vying for the Republican Party nomination during a PBS-sponsored presidential debate, Republican candidate Ron Paul spoke out against the drug war saying, "For instance, blacks make up 14 percent of those who use drugs. Yet 36 percent of those arrested are blacks. And it ends up that 63 percent of those who finally end up in prison are blacks. This has to change. We don't have to have more courts and more prisons. We need to repeal the whole war on drugs. It isn't working."[10]

Clearly then, poor and minority populations along with the other "low hanging fruit"[11] upon whom the drug war primarily has been focused have faced disproportionate consequences for their participation in illegal drug activities. But this book is not directly about the targets of the war on drugs and those who have borne the greatest brunt of its criminal justice scrutiny since the early 1980s. Rather, this book is about one specific group of *anti-targets,* a network of drug dealers who have operated with relative impunity while making little effort to conceal their illicit activities. In spite of the "zero tolerance" zealotry driving the drug war, for these boys and girls next-door who are comfortably shielded from criminal justice scrutiny by race- and class-based privileges woven into the fabric of US society, the drug war has apparently made no discernable difference in how they construct their drug distribution networks or carry out their routine dealing activities.

Over a period of approximately six years beginning in 2001, we were provided with uncommon access to a drug-distribution network that publicly thrived largely off of the criminal justice system's radar. This network was almost entirely comprised of affluent current and former college students, and its members provided an array of illegal drugs to several colleges in Southern California.[12] What began as an examination of what we speculated would be somewhat low-level and benign drug peddling between college students turned out to be an exploration of a much more extensive and serious drug-dealing network—a collection of college drug dealers loosely subdivided into several primary strains of fluid, informally organized distribution channels servicing one common user base.

From the number of network dealers we spoke with and the substantial access barriers to the user community without legitimate entrée, it stands to reason that the members of this network supplied the majority of marijuana consumed at one university. The network also was responsible for supplying significant amounts of marijuana to students at several other local colleges and universities. In fact, over the course of this research, one of our key informants had emerged as one of the area's foremost pot dealers, moving anywhere from five to ten pounds of marijuana per week and grossing between $80,000 and $160,000 per month in ill-gotten revenue. This particular dealer was a large-volume wholesaler selling marijuana primarily in pound or multi-pound increments and almost never selling quantities of less than one-quarter pound; therefore his profit margins were less than if he were to stretch out the product by selling pot in smaller increments. Nonetheless, when his operation was at its peak, this particular dealer hauled in total weekly profits ranging from $2,500 to in excess of $5,000, certainly more cash than he could hide under his mattress.

This network's larger dealers blew a substantial amount of their profits on partying with friends, supporting the drug use of friends and other hangers-on, high-tech media equipment, "pimped out" accessories for their cars, and other whimsical expenditures. In fact, Brice, one of the primary dealers profiled throughout this study, used some of his drug sale profits to fund a three-month excursion to Asia. Not only was he able to comfortably bankroll his entire Asian adventure with drug proceeds, but was also able to pay rent and utilities for himself and his roommate who remained at home. Similarly, Weasel, another wholesale supplier to dealers in the network, was unable to make a scheduled interview with us because he decided to take an impromptu European vacation. At the height of his dealing, LaCoste, one of our network's most interesting characters, was selling approximately one pound of marijuana per week to his fellow students. When asked what he bought with his estimated profits of $1,200 per week, he replied:

LaCoste: Whatever I want. I used to go on shopping sprees first semester a whole bunch, like, whatever I want. I want to buy these rims for my car [a $50,000 Cadillac purchased for him by his parents] that are tight . . . the ones that spin . . . yeah, those are sick. Ah, I just buy shit. I spend lots of money.

Additionally, a handful of dealers channeled some of their proceeds into legitimate business ventures. Since most of the dealers we observed and interviewed were already children of privilege, these material excesses and investment capital almost never drew them any unwanted attention from law enforcement or university officials.

Over the course of our observations and interviews with the network's dealers, users, and several people charged with policing their behaviors, we also uncovered relatively robust markets for cocaine, "party" drugs, and prescription drugs, all servicing the same college populations. And, while the scope, depth, and wealth to be gained from wheeling and dealing in this market were often remarkable, there were several other discoveries that proved more noteworthy. Among the more startling of our findings were the near absent or, perhaps more accurately, pathetic risk-minimization strategies employed by most of the dealers with whom we came into contact. Given their families' affluence and their place at an expensive private university, these dealers stood to lose a great deal if caught selling drugs, a seemingly irrational choice.

We also found ourselves intrigued by our dealers' motivations for selling drugs, motives that were generally different in many ways from those associated with stereotypical street-drug dealers popularized by mainstream news and entertainment media. These impetuses were quite revealing and demonstrated the angst, insecurities, greed, and often arrogance of the dealers we observed and interviewed. They were also often accompanied by a variety of rationalizations and "techniques of neutralization" that served, at least in the minds of many of our dealers, to mitigate what they knew to be illegal activity.

Finally, while not entirely surprising—given the well-documented tendency of the criminal justice system to closely monitor the illegal activities of the poor while simultaneously turning a blind eye to similar activities carried out by the non-poor—we were still taken aback by the lack of criminal justice and university administration attention paid these dealers, despite the brazenness, incompetence, and general dearth of street smarts that tended to characterize the dealers' daily practices. For the most part, members of the network managed their extensive drug-dealing activities virtually immune to law enforcement scrutiny, and we theorize that our dealers' racial, ethnic, and socioeconomic backgrounds allowed them and their clientele to exist freely as anti-targets in the US drug war and to maintain a nondeviant public status despite their flagrantly illegal behavior.

The findings we report upon in this book are based on hundreds of hours of observation and dozens of formal interviews with current and former dealers and their clients. The past experiences and rapport that we and our research assistants had with participants in this network allowed us to provide a detailed sociological description of the individual and collective behaviors of these "law-abiding lawbreakers." As drug researcher Patricia Adler has noted, this unusual view from the inside is one of the very few perspectives from which social science can learn about inherently secretive criminal organizations.

Location, Location, Location

Once again, the network we explored operated primarily in Southern California. More specifically, our dealers principally sold their wares in a coastal and near-coastal metropolitan area also situated within reasonable driving distance to the US-Mexico border. This location offered both geographic and cultural advantages to drug dealers of all backgrounds, including those who operated in our network. Given the vastness of the US-Mexico border and the fact that most of the world's cocaine is produced in South America, quite logically the southwest US border serves as the primary point of entry for cocaine smuggling into the United States, with an estimated 65 percent of all illegal cocaine imports traversing this land route. In addition, marijuana produced in Mexico remains the most widely available to US consumers, and California supplies much of its own consumer demand as the leading producer of both indoor and outdoor domestically grown marijuana.[13] In fact, agricultural staples like lettuce, tomatoes, oranges, strawberries, and even grapes trail behind marijuana as California's number-one cash crop. As part of a statewide drug eradication campaign that has been in existence for twenty-five years, in 2007 alone state authorities seized 2.9 million marijuana plants worth an estimated $10 billion from backyards, public lands, and forests.[14] In spite of this and other federal, state, and local eradication efforts, in 2006 an estimated $15 billion dollars of marijuana was grown in the state.[15] By way of comparison, the state's total farm sales in 2006 generated $31.4 billion.[16]

In addition to the land routes, maritime routes from Mexico to the United States make this metropolitan area an ideal point of entry for drugs, and evidence of illegal drug shipments is routinely found in the nearby coastal waters. For example, in April 2008, the US Coast Guard discovered an 18-foot boat loaded with 362 pounds of marijuana a few miles up the coast from our network's home turf. This vessel had crashed into rocks during a pre-dawn drug-smuggling run and was one of several drug-smuggling boats that authorities had come across in recent weeks along the same several-mile stretch of shoreline.

On the demand side, this particular Southern California location offers distinct cultural advantages to drug dealers. Proportionally, people living in metropolitan areas, either small or large, are more likely to use illicit drugs than those in more rural parts of the country. Also, the rate of illicit drug use in the western United States is higher than that of any other region in the country, leading to a larger market for illegal drug sales.[17] Finally, the beach communities in this metropolitan area are dominated by what could be called a "surfer culture" as well as transient and other nonpermanent populations. Characteristics of these communities include a reputation for tolerance of personal freedoms and a general acceptance of soft drug use.

Method and Access

Ethnographic investigations of criminal organizations, groups inherently clandestine to some extent, mandate rapport and trust between researcher and subject. And even though we were completely forthcoming with our research agenda, it often took months of relationship building for us to secure key dealer interviews and otherwise gain the access necessary to physically observe drug transactions and the day-to-day activities of the dealers in our study. Primarily, we gained entry to this community of drug dealers and users largely through what Patricia Adler defined as "peripheral membership."[18] In this role, we maintained relatively close relationships and regularly interacted with many of our study's key dealers. However, consistent with Adler's description of this particular approach to research, in order to maintain objectivity and a balance between participant and observer, at no time did we actually engage in the central activities that defined group membership and group identity.

Even with this as our research philosophy and strategy, it would be reasonable to ask why these dealers would trust us enough to tell all of the details of their illicit activity and, in several cases, allow us into their homes while they conducted their business. In both instances—interviews and observations—our personal backstories and reputations as established, "down," trustworthy, and visible members of the local community directly facilitated the requisite confidence necessary to carry out this study. By way of example, one researcher not only existed as a peripheral member of this group for several years, but also had a longstanding personal relationship with Brice, a key dealer in the study, and Cecilia, another of the study's linchpins. This same researcher was active in the local surfing and environmentalist community, was a member of several local bands, worked at a local surf shop, and was a surfing instructor on a popular stretch of beach frequented by members of this drug-dealing network.

As another avenue of access, we enlisted research assistants familiar with the network's drug scene to identify and conduct interviews with other dealers and former dealers not revealed during the period of peripheral membership. To our surprise, nearly all of these interviews were granted with little resistance on the part of the subjects who typically spoke freely of their dealing exploits. Only once did a campus drug dealer identified by one of our research assistants prove difficult to pin down for an interview. On three separate occasions, he failed to show up as scheduled. Frustrated, we made it explicitly clear that he was entirely free not to sit for an interview with us, and under no circumstances would we ever reveal his identity. Ultimately, we were able to secure his interview by providing him with a signed letter reassuring him that his identity would be kept confidential. To protect the anonymity of all of our subjects, we crafted pseudonyms to identify dealers and other tangential people involved in the study.

We also conducted interviews with several university officials we felt would be able to offer insight into our hub campus's drug policy and enforcement, particularly with respect to the university's disciplinary procedures and how the punishments for known drug dealers are meted out. These interviewees held positions in various offices ranging from campus housing to university police. Most officials we contacted for interviews readily consented to our request. During the interviews, however, they tended to recite policy talking points. They often refrained from discussing the more subtle ways the policies were actually enforced and the extrajudicial considerations taken when deciding how to proceed in a campus drug-dealing matter. Some university officials were not as amenable to being interviewed. For example, the director of the campus police canceled interviews with one member of our research team twice. He then required that the research assistant submit questions to him beforehand. She complied with his request and submitted a series of questions revolving around basic university policy and known incidents of drug use and sales on campus. Nonetheless, after receiving the list of questions, the director ultimately declined our interview request and refused to respond to the particular questions in writing.

For the purposes of data analysis, we found Robert Merton's *post factum* sociological interpretation to be the analytical tool that best corresponded with the goals of the research. In outlining this research strategy, Merton suggested that the function of this approach is not to test a specific theory or hypothesis. Rather, the documentary evidence obtained is allowed to guide and illustrate the theory. Because it allows researchers to remain open to social dynamics and displays of power that might otherwise be obscured by more traditional research models, and because there is very little ethnographic and qualitative research on drug-dealing networks that operate at private universities, we found this method to have distinct advantages over other interpretive tools.

Throughout the course of the research, all efforts were made to triangulate our data; we attempted to verify individual accounts and events provided in interviews with participant observation and subsequent interviews with other dealers. Our intent was, as articulated by Daniel Miller, to "evaluate people in terms of what they actually do, i.e., as material agents working with a material world, and not merely [in terms] of what they say they do."[19] While we were able to verify the bulk of accounts that appear in this book, some of the narratives provided are solely the account of the individual dealer being interviewed. Our approach, as well as the absence of constrictions that can be imposed by past findings, allowed us to, as anthropologist Clifford Geertz suggested, enter the research as objectively as possible and allow the gestures, overtures, behaviors, and statements of the dealers in our network to serve as a story they tell themselves about themselves.

The Dealing Community

The approximately fifty subjects at the center of this study were all college students at various Southern California colleges and universities, but most attended one particular private university that served as the focal point of this research. With two exceptions, each of the dealers in our network was active (they had not yet walked away from drug dealing) when we were acquainted with them. During the primary period of interviews and observation, these subjects ranged in age from eighteen to twenty-four and all but three of the dealers we formally interviewed were men. We do not think that this reflects a selection bias; rather it reflects a gender imbalance among college students who choose to sell drugs. Regarding other demographic data, with the exception of two Hispanics, one African American, one Black/Caucasian person, one Persian/Caucasian-American, and one Asian/Caucasian person, all of the dealers in our network were Caucasian. Further, among the relative few minorities listed above, most either white-identified and/or their nonwhite ethnic attributes were imperceptible. As was the case with gender, we did not choose to interview principally white dealers. We simply did not encounter many who were nonwhite. As is the case with most of the private universities in Southern California, the vast majority of the student body at our study's hub university is white.

With the exception of the one African American dealer, all of the dealers in this network were from families that range from middle-upper class to affluent/upper class. In fact, some of our dealers had parents of considerable prestige, status, and economic standing. For example, at least one and possibly two subjects had parents who were current or former city mayors in other states. Other parents included international and domestic businesspeople, car-dealership owners, doctors, psychiatrists, and accountants and accounting executives for major firms.

In drug research literature, a distinction is often made between drug markets that are "open" and "closed."[20] The drug market that made up our network's home turf could be primarily described as closed. In open markets, dealers sell to any potential customers, only screening out those who they suspect of being police or posing some other threat to their operation. Dealers who operate in closed markets sell only to customers they personally know or customers who can be vouched for by other buyers. Indeed, on at least one occasion, a dealer interviewed for this study noted that he refused to sell marijuana to someone claiming to have a mutual friend because that friend in common was not present to vouch for him. Closed markets offer both dealers and customers more security and, because of the closer interpersonal ties and consistent supply streams, closed markets offer customers some degree of quality assurance over the drugs they buy.

While the dealers in this community sold and consumed various types of drugs, most of the activity revolved around soft drugs, particularly the sale and consumption of marijuana. Still, some of our dealers sold modest quantities of cocaine, and others dabbled in party drugs like ecstasy. The subjects range from those who sold drugs solely to support their own drug habit (sometimes unsuccessfully, as they are either bad businessmen who give away too much of their product to friends or, like the character Smokey in the 1990s cult film *Friday*, they simply keep more of their product for personal consumption than they put on the market for sale), to those who provided relatively large quantities of drugs that were then distributed to a significant number of drug consumers and smaller distributors at area colleges. While in many cases these categories are not mutually exclusive, of our fifty subjects approximately thirty focused overwhelmingly on marijuana and other traditional "street drugs." The remaining twenty subjects focused predominantly on prescription drugs and typified the classic "user-dealer" model; these twenty subjects provide a vivid window into the "secondary market" that is the focus of Chapter 4.

Like Brice and Dallas, the vast majority of our network's dealers graduated from drug sales before or at the same time they graduated from college; a few others elected to make a career of drug sales rather than enter the legitimate work force. Some of the dealers we interviewed were more articulate and candid than others; therefore, more of their comments are included in this book. These interviews, observations, and discussions stirred the reflections that follow on the drug activities of affluent youth, the ignorance of these activities by those in positions of formal authority, and the impact both have on shaping the perception of drug dealers in the United States.

Outline of the Book

In the chapters that follow, we offer a description and analysis of this affluent Southern California drug-distribution network. Chapter 2 explores the first illicit drug market that we came across during the course of this study. Chapter 3 uses observational and interview data to more deeply explore what we have identified as six primary motivations for the distribution of illicit drugs among the members of this college dealing network. This chapter also takes a look at the distinctly different motives and rationalizations that exist among dealers in the pharmaceutical market.

The focus of Chapter 4 is a relatively vigorous prescription-drug market that we came across almost by accident. We found that drugs like Adderall and OxyContin are traded relatively freely among college students, but for seemingly different reasons and significantly less money than the aforementioned illicit drugs. We discuss this secondary market in terms of what drugs are sold; the size and scale of the market; how drugs are obtained (as they all originate from a legitimate source); and dealer/user characteristics.

Chapter 5 discusses our dealers' perceptions of self. Specifically, we examine how members of our network view themselves in light of their ongoing participation in illegal activity. We also explore how they justify and neutralize their illicit behavior through what we have coined "mental gymnastics." Finally, in this chapter we briefly shed some light on how other people's opinions of our dealers are, in part, influenced by our dealers' views of themselves.

Chapter 6 examines what we refer to as the "un-risky business" of drug sales at and around a private college campus. We discuss actual versus perceived risks and our network's dealers' competence as criminal actors in light of these risks. We also look at how our dealers were treated by criminal justice system and university officials on the few occasions that they were implicated for engaging in illegal drug activity.

In the final chapter, we catch up with some of our dealers and see where they are now. We ask the question, were any of their dreams deferred by their foray into the world of illicit drug sales? The chapter ends with a brief discussion and reflective assessment of US drug policy as we enter the second decade of the new millennium.

As this manuscript neared completion, the national news media and prominent law enforcement officials momentarily engaged the issue of illicit drug markets on college campuses. Operation Sudden Fall, a joint yearlong undercover operation by the Drug Enforcement Administration and the San Diego State University Police Department yielded 125 arrests, predominantly of college student drug dealers and drug users. This event offered additional insights into the world of college drug dealers, provided additional fodder for this research, and constitutes the majority of this book's epilogue.

Notes

1. To protect the identity of the subjects in our study, we have created pseudonyms to identify all dealers and tangential persons.

2. The first phases of this research were published in Mohamed and Fritsvold, "Damn It Feels Good to Be a Gangsta."

3. Thanks to Peter Moskos for the term, "silent majority."

4. The state of California alone operates thirty-four adult prisons and contracts with six out-of-state facilities to alleviate overcrowding within existing in-state institutions. Municipal governments in the state operate hundreds of county, city, and other local jail facilities.

5. US Department of Justice, Bureau of Justice Statistics, Sourcebook of Criminal Justice Statistics, "Number and rate (per 100,000 US residents) of Persons in State and Federal Prisons and Local Jails."

6. According to Christopher Hartney in a November 2006 report from the National Council on Crime and Delinquency, the United States incarcerates at a rate 4 to 7 times higher than its Western peers in the UK (145), France (88), Germany (95), and Italy (102). More telling, US incarceration rates are still unrivaled by undemocratic nations such as Iran (206), Zimbabwe (139), China (118), Cuba (487), and Russia (607). China, with over 1.3 billion citizens, has an estimated incarcerated population of 1.5 million people, while Russia has fewer than 1 million. See Hartney, "US Rates of Incarceration."

7. Fellner, *Punishment and Prejudice: Racial Disparities in the War on Drugs.*

8. Currie, *Crime and Punishment in America,* p. 13.

9. Duke, "Drug Prohibition," p. 571.

10. www.pbs.org/kcet/tavissmiley/special/forums/transcript.html.

11. Kentucky Senate Judiciary Committee, Testimony of Secretary J. Michael Brown.

12. We will frequently refer to Southern California throughout this narrative. Geographically speaking, this region is roughly defined as that part of California south of Santa Barbara (approximately 100 miles north of Los Angeles) encompassing the major metropolitan areas of Los Angeles, San Diego, San Bernardino, and Riverside. Collectively, this region has a known population of approximately 25 million people and is home to well over sixty colleges and universities.

13. US Department of Justice, Drug Enforcement Administration, "Drug Trafficking in the United States."

14. *The Economist,* "Marijuana: Home-Grown."

15. Bailey, "Pot Is Called Biggest Cash Crop."

16. Goodhue, Green, Heien, and Martin, *Current Economic Trends in the California Wine Industry.*

17. Among persons aged twelve or older, the rate of current illicit drug use in 2006 was 9.5 percent in the West, 8.9 percent in the Northeast, 7.9 percent in the Midwest, and 7.4 percent in the South. See US Department of Health and Human Services, Substance Abuse and Mental Health Services Administration, Office of Applied Studies, *Results from the 2006 National Survey on Drug Use and Health: National Findings.*

18. Adler, *Wheeling and Dealing.*

19. Miller, *Capitalism,* p. 17.

20. Sampson, *Drug Dealing in Privately Owned Apartment Complexes.*

2

The Primary Market: Dealing Marijuana, Cocaine, and Party Drugs

In Steven Soderbergh's Oscar winning film *Traffic*, Robert Wakefield, a conservative Ohio Supreme Court judge played by Michael Douglas, is appointed by the president to take charge of the US drug war. As the primary wrinkle in the plot, while moving through the conventional paces of the street-drug war Wakefield discovers that his teenage daughter Caroline, a child of privilege, is a drug addict. In a classic Hollywood ending, Caroline is saved from her downward spiral of smoking cocaine, shooting heroin, and budding prostitution by a father who realizes he can no longer afford to put his work before his family. In one of the film's closing scenes, Caroline is shown in a hazy room participating in an Alcoholics Anonymous meeting. She says, "Hi, my name is Caroline. I'm not sure I'm an alcoholic. I mean, I don't really like to drink. For someone my age, it's a lot easier to get drugs than it is alcohol."

While the list of reasons for illicit street-drug use by college students runs the gamut from self-medication to a simple desire to get high, the fact of the matter remains that for many people who are too young to legally purchase alcohol, street drugs are indeed easier to come by. And, as we found, the entrepreneurial spirit possessed by many ambitious young college students, the need to "fit in" and feel a sense of belonging, the perceived invulnerability that often accompanies youth, and a readily available wholesale illicit drug supply converged to virtually guarantee that the demand for street drugs among the privileged college set would not go unmet. Moreover, we found that these drugs are supplied, quite logically, by those who have the easiest access to the customer base—fellow college students. The end result of all of these factors is a vibrant street-drug using subculture or, perhaps more accurately, a social and economic network that exists in plain sight but nonetheless manages to fly beneath the radar of both formal and informal agencies of social control.

Our research actually unearthed two parallel markets that served the drug-use demands of this relatively affluent college drug scene. The second market, that which revolved around the illegal use and trafficking in prescription drugs, will be discussed in Chapter 4. The present chapter focuses on what we have identified as our network's primary market, one that caters specifically to the street-drug using needs of largely affluent, predominantly white college students. We began this study as an exploration of marijuana dealing within this particular student population, and marijuana was indeed the drug of choice among our network's dealers and users. However, in the process of researching the business of selling pot to college kids by college kids, we also uncovered a related and robust cocaine and "party drug" trade.

As we began to identify dealers in this primary market and, more importantly, as we gained their trust, we discovered answers to questions about what specific drugs they trafficked in, to whom they sold their drugs, from what sources they obtained their supply of illicit drugs, and the amount of profit they made over the course of their transactions. We also gained valuable insights into how this market functioned differently from the well-researched traditional street markets trading in the same illicit substances. The remainder of this chapter will focus on these discoveries.

Dopeman, Dopeman, Wherefore Art Thou Dopeman?

Identifying the drug dealers who would ultimately serve as the backbone of our network was certainly far less complicated than settling the fabled Shakespearean feud in Verona. In fact, finding college drug dealers willing to share their trade secrets and let us drop in on their action proved considerably easier than we originally anticipated. Intuition, experience, and word of mouth all suggested there was an active university-based drug market we could academically explore in our corner of California. But going into the research we never imagined we would happen upon or be introduced to a handful of key and dozens of lesser dealers. Moreover, we never dreamed that, with the exception of one difficult dealer, all of these individuals would willingly and almost eagerly sit for interviews with us.[1] Indeed, some dealers would ultimately be open to our presence while they actually conducted their business.

In order to protect the anonymity of our informants as well as the integrity of our research, we will not delve too deeply into the specifics of dealer identification. Suffice it to say that going into the project, we were already on good terms with one of the network's key dealers and from this relationship we were able to employ a snowball sampling technique, relying upon his referrals and people we met in his social network to generate additional subjects. We also were able to identify dealers through a reverse snowball technique in which we first identified users, most of whom were not the least bit coy about their affinity for drug use, and had these users introduce us to their suppliers. Finally, in a bit of a humorous twist, some of the dealers that became an integral part of this study actually volunteered themselves as subjects when, through word of mouth, they caught wind that we were interested in learning more about the drug trade operating on and around the affluent college campus that our network primarily serviced.

The Millionaire Marijuana Club

Recent national drug use data show that young adults aged eighteen to twenty-five, the same age category that all of our dealers and their clients fell into, have substantially higher rates of current illicit drug use than any other segment of the US population. Nearly 20 percent of people in this survey group were current drug users compared to approximately 10 percent of twelve to seventeen year olds, the next highest illicit drug use group with respect to age. Marijuana was by far and away the illicit drug of choice among this high-use group with eight times the number of current users than cocaine, the next illicit drug most commonly abused by eighteen to twenty-five year olds.[2] Therefore, it comes as no surprise that the focal drug of our primary network was marijuana; the "devil weed" was what the majority of students demanded and correspondingly the drug that the majority of our network's dealers trafficked in.

The clientele that provided the foundation for this drug-dealing network were demographically indistinguishable from the dealers;

the customers were relatively affluent, primarily Caucasian current or former college students, and they were actively pursuing traditional success pathways. Characteristically, most of the customers entered college with some previous marijuana use experience and many current customers could be described as veteran marijuana users who were relatively experienced in the nuances of marijuana purchasing rituals and marijuana use. While a significant number of customers exclusively used marijuana, others occasionally dabbled in harder drugs like hallucinogenic mushrooms, peyote, ecstasy, and cocaine. The propensity for illicit drug use among this demographic was readily apparent in the seemingly unyielding demand for marijuana within this network. Throughout the course of the study, there was never a situation in which a drug dealer at any level was suffering from a customer shortage or had to actively seek out customers to support his or her illicit enterprise. Rather, on several occasions, we observed customers who were unable to locate an adequate supply of marijuana and were subsequently mired in the doldrums of the "weed wait."

Contrary to drug policy folklore, studies have shown that marijuana is neither intrinsically or socioculturally a gateway drug for the use of harsher drugs. Among members of our network, the same might be said for drug sales as there seemed to be some exclusivity among its various illicit drug markets. Most of our dealers were content to exclusively or almost exclusively distribute marijuana rather than branch out into selling other drugs. It is difficult to fully explain why this was the case, but our sense is that the pot dealers were loyal to marijuana for two reasons. First, they all smoked relatively substantial amounts of marijuana and were therefore comfortable with the nature and economics of pot transactions. Also, there was a sense among this group that, as far as illicit drugs are concerned, marijuana was less serious than drugs like cocaine or ecstasy and, ipso facto, so was trafficking in marijuana. The relatively few pot dealers who did sell harsher drugs like cocaine or ecstasy could best be described as "reluctant dabblers"—dealers who preferred to traffic exclusively in marijuana but dabbled in the sale of other drug for greater profits, to meet varying consumer demands, or for ego gratification. Still, for most of our dealers, their foray into drug sales was limited to marijuana.

For all of our dealers, their venture into drug sales began with marijuana and, for most, it ended there too. Striking us as strange was the yet unanswered question of supply. Specifically, while we had already identified an active drug market, we were still in the dark about where these men and women in their late teens and early twenties procured their wares. It struck us as strange that an eighteen-year-old freshman transplant to California, even one very interested in selling marijuana, could so quickly discover where to obtain large enough quantities of illegal drugs to sell.

What we found was that, as with Ashcan, hometown sources proved to be an effective initial source of bulk marijuana supply for several of our network's dealers. Ashcan was a twenty-one-year-old senior with one parent of Middle Eastern descent and the other a Caucasian American. For all intents and purposes, he looked white with light olive-colored skin, brown hair, and rosy cheeks. Relative to other dealers in this study, he sold modest amounts of marijuana and, according to him, only actively sold for a year or two. While living on campus in the residence halls during his sophomore year, Ashcan recalled that the dealer who served the needs of those particular dormitories was detected by campus housing officials and forced to shut down his operation.[3] Seeing an opening in the market and in true entrepreneurial fashion, Ashcan decided to step in and try his hand as a marijuana dealer. Having familiarity with those who supplied him with pot in high school, he reached out to these hometown friends to pre-weigh, package, and ship him bundles of marijuana to sell in the dorms.

ASHCAN: I [had it mailed] from Ohio, where I grew up, for really cheap. It was about $25 an eighth and I sold it for $50 an eighth out here . . . I didn't have any weighing equipment[4] so [my friends back home] weighed it all and put it in bags and everything . . . I'd send them a check for how much I wanted and then shipping. And they'd weigh it in eighths and send it to me in little packets of eighths.

For most of our dealers, their relatively recent arrival on the Southern California drug scene did not serve as a barrier to market entry because, like Ashcan, most of our network's dealers had more than a passing familiarity with marijuana sales organizations before ever enrolling in college. Indeed, while nearly all of the dealers we spoke with did not start selling pot until arriving in California, all but one were habitual marijuana users in high school; all had a functional understanding of how marijuana markets operated; and many of our dealers had a strong enough bond with their hometown supply sources to segue this relationship into personal proprietorship. Ultimately, if their stay in the pot-dealing game was longer term, dealers who relied on hometown sources for their initial marijuana supply often became acquainted with and more established in local marijuana networks and were then able to use these relationships to tap nearby supply chains. However, in times of local weed droughts typically brought on by law enforcement disruptions in supply chains, the non-native dealers could stay afloat by re-tapping old hometown sources.

Rasta, one of two African American dealers we encountered in our network, was the only dealer we came into contact with who actually acquired his marijuana through the legal marijuana loophole created by California's Proposition 215 and subsequent Senate Bill 420.[5] Intended as a medical marijuana law, Proposition 215 was passed in 1996 by 56 percent of California voters and effectively decriminalized the possession of marijuana by people who possessed a "written oral recommendation" from their physician stating he or she would receive benefits from the use of medical marijuana. This proposition was further clarified in 2003 by the passage of SB 420, which established an eight-ounce "personal use" limit on the amount of dried marijuana that a patient can possess at any given time, unless a physician deems larger quantities necessary. Rasta suffered a college football-related injury resulting in chronic pain. Rather than going the prescription pharmaceutical route, Rasta was able to successfully obtain a physician's prescription for medicinal marijuana. While SB 420 limits the amount of marijuana a patient can possess at any given time, and it and other state drug-trafficking laws certainly prohibit patients from giving away or selling their prescription marijuana, these laws are apparently rather flimsily enforced. Accordingly, Rasta was able to use his prescription card to secure reasonably large quantities of marijuana for personal use and retail sales. Rasta was certainly not among our network's drug-dealing heavyweights, and was rather peripheral in that he would only sell pot to a small subnetwork of close friends and teammates. However, his transactions did yield him plenty of pocket money, nice clothes, and 20-inch chrome rims on the late-model sports car his parents had purchased for him.

The path to becoming a pot dealer was a little less cumbersome for the would-be dopemen who were, by virtue of being raised in Southern California, already familiar with the local drug scene and therefore had access to more immediate sources of supply. A sampling of the larger private universities in Southern California shows that, typically, 50 percent or more of students enrolled at these institutions come from within the state of California. The primary California college around which our network revolved is no exception to this rule, typically recruiting slightly more than half of its incoming freshmen from secondary schools within the state.

This practice of local familiarity serving as a relatively smooth conduit into drug dealer status is certainly not exclusive to Southern California. As Gator, a former dealer from a college drug-dealing network outside of California to whom we were introduced by one of our research assistants, recalled:

GATOR: From the first week I got to campus, everyone who wanted to get high knew I was from [the area] and started calling me asking if I had any weed. People I'd never seen in my life would walk up to me in the dorms and ask if I could get them some pot. They seemed so desperate. So, I called some people I knew from high school and began hooking kids up. The next thing I knew, I was a pot dealer.

Profit Without Honor

Business and Business Administration are the most popular courses of study at most private Southern California universities, and the primary university at and around which our network operated was no exception; business majors accounted for nearly 40 percent of the undergraduate student population. Therefore, it made sense that a prominent drug-use culture and rudimentary laws of supply and demand, coupled with a user-based knowledge of marijuana sales protocol, seemed to spawn the initial foray into drug sales for many of our dealers, a disproportionate number of whom were majoring in business. One such person was LaCoste, a blonde-haired, blue-eyed, preppy gangsta-dressed freshman from the Midwest who, by his own declaration, was "untouchably wealthy." At the time we met him, he drove a $50,000 SUV that his parents gave him, and from his dormitory room sold a relatively large amount of marijuana and a smaller yet still considerable amount of cocaine because "Dude, that's the moneymaker . . . the yeyo . . . that's where the money's at."[6] He also was known to dabble in party drugs like ecstasy, and he exclusively sold to a student-user client base. When asked how he would describe the drug use climate at the university, he bluntly stated, "Everybody—literally every single person—everyone [here] does coke. Everybody, I swear to God I'm not lying. You bust it out at a party, put it on a glass table and just leave it there and everyone will be over there like [sniffs] . . . It is so easy, it's just you can make tons of money." Of course all students at our network's hub university were not using cocaine, but hyperbole aside, LaCoste's characterization of a sizable and active subculture of illicit drug use proved to be an accurate one.

Stopper, one of the few female dealers we interviewed or encountered, echoed LaCoste's assessment that an established campus subculture of drug use and a critical mass of incoming students that had preexisting familiarity with illicit drug use created fertile terrain for the growth and sustenance of an underground drug economy. At the time of our formal interview with her, Stopper was a graduating senior who spent the better part of her sophomore year selling dried marijuana and a crystallized form of it from her dormitory room. Like the majority of our dealers, she was upper-middle-class and white from a politically conservative family. After arriving in California from her home state of Colorado, Stopper recalled:

Stopper: Beginning with [orientation] week, it was pretty much split down the middle between those that attended every event and those that partied. I chose to hang out with the fun kids, those that drank and partied. From day one, you know who parties . . . you knew who smoked. You knew which ones of them knew how to get weed and who didn't.

Stopper's point was clear; if you came to the university and were interested in getting high, you could readily find a social niche as well as a pot hookup. And if you were someone who "knew how to get weed," it was just as easy to establish a foothold in the underground economy and become a dorm-room dealer.

More often than not, entertainment and news media present a rather myopic image of drug markets. In these depictions, the drug dealers are overwhelmingly minority and impoverished, selling dope in rundown urban neighborhoods to desperate junkies who will seemingly do anything for a fix. In contrast, the drug markets that we observed and gathered information on in our network, both those existing on our study's primary campus as well as the off-campus markets that catered to college students, were remarkably unlike those of television lore. There were no gun-toting dreadlocks asking for passwords through the peepholes of steel reinforced doors. Nor were there chained-up pit bulls foaming at the mouth outside of dorm rooms, poised to sink their teeth into robbers looking for drug loot or campus cops on a drug raid. Instead, the environments in which drugs were exchanged for money in our network tended to be significantly more casual and social, and as Brice, one of our primary dealers remarked, "friendly-like." Appropriately, unlike the rapid exchange of drugs for money characteristic of urban open-air drug markets, it was not uncommon for relatively standard marijuana transactions in our network to take an hour or more to complete.

Part of the reason for this long-sale approach was that the buyers were indeed frequently friends or at minimum fair acquaintances of the distributors. After all, they typically attended the same university, in many cases had known each other since freshman year, were apt to have a class or two together, and were very likely to travel in the same social circles. But more important than the familiarity dealers and clients had with one another and the absence of street corner tensions that often exist during open-market drug transactions was the web of informal but quite pronounced rules of etiquette that governed these closed-market money-for-drugs exchanges and more or less mandated a drawn out sales ceremony.

As part of this ritual, not unlike California's famous See's Candies or the deli counter at the local supermarket, our network's drug customers were generally permitted to sample the product before committing to a purchase. Afterward, the shopper would typically sit around, kibitz with the dealer and anyone else hanging around, and imbibe their newly purchased marijuana, generally offering the seller the first smoke. Superficially, this aspect of the ritual seems to serve as a "quality assurance program" of sorts, allowing the customer to see if he is buying what was advertised and if the price being asked is fair. However, almost never did these turn into negotiation sessions. Stopper describes the post-transaction rituals and their meanings like this:

STOPPER: You go over their house and you pick up a sack [of marijuana] from them and you feel like, "Oh, I should hang out with them," almost like you had to do them a favor in addition to paying them. There's the unspoken rule that you have to share your first bowl with whoever you are buying it from . . . It was always like, they ask you a couple of questions about how everything was going . . . It was almost like they wanted it to be a more personal relationship as opposed to more formal.

Another reason for this sampling and post-purchase practice is that it is simply part of the slower paced and more casual marijuana sales rite that has the luxury of occurring in closed markets, those dealing situations where the exchange takes place behind closed doors and dealers can afford to select customers rather than in open-air type settings in which any random passerby is a potential client; it is a learned and an expected part of the marijuana sales protocol in these more privileged sales environments. The pre- or post-purchase sharing of a smoke is also a display of mutual trust and good faith by both parties involved in the transaction. It is as if the dealer is saying, "I stand by my product and trust you in my home," and whether it is a genuine feeling or not the buyer is saying, "I'm not just here interacting with you because you are my weed hook up." These customs can only exist in these closed markets where the dealer has the privilege of being more discreet and discerning than his street corner counterparts to whom he or she chooses to sell drugs, particularly since most of the dealers we observed were not entirely dependent on drug trafficking for their livelihood.

While some buyers we observed and spoke with were uncomfortable or nervous spending so much time in the presence of their supplier and the requisite large quantities of weed, they still hung around, smoked, and chatted. What became clear in these more unnatural and less sincere social situations was, again, the ritual required a certain degree of lingering so as not to offend the dealer and potentially jeopardize a good source of marijuana; it was an essential part of establishing the "membership" necessary to ensure an open and fluid drug supply. As sociologist Howard Becker wrote in his classic "Marijuana Use and Social Control," "In becoming defined as a member, one is also defined as a person who can safely be trusted to buy drugs without endangering anyone else."[7] Supporting Becker's observations, Stopper said,

STOPPER: It's not like you're going to buy a pack of gum. If you alienate these people . . . there's an element of trust involved in something even as minor as buying weed. You don't want to piss them off. You don't want to insult them. You're going to come back the next week or the next day . . . You just don't want to burn that bridge. You eventually become connected to whoever sells to you. You can literally call them at two in the morning and say, "Can I drop by?" If you guys have a good relationship, they'll say "yeah."

Modern Day Lewis and Clark

While typically an advantage in both entering and sustaining activity in the illicit marijuana trade, familiarity and subsequent dependency on regional Southern Californian marijuana supplies occasionally proved a hindrance for some of our dealers. Mexican drug-trafficking organizations dominate the production of high-potency marijuana in the region and the bulk of the region's marijuana is believed to be imported from Mexico. Thus, the US-Mexico border is largely held to be the frontline in the drug war. In one December 2007 seizure alone, US Border Patrol agents found 7 tons of marijuana contained inside a 30-foot shipping container placed over the opening of a 1,300-foot-long tunnel going under the US-Mexico border.[8] Accordingly, our network's pot-supply chains experienced occasional interruptions because of local police activity, state and local drug law enforcement, statement interdiction efforts by the Mexican government, and immigration law enforcement efforts. These supply chains were also disturbed by legal run-ins experienced by larger local distributors, who were easier to scrutinize because of the concentration of law enforcement in the region and therefore were either arrested or had to temporarily quiet their drug activities until the heat cooled off. There were also a number of other intangibles beyond the control of the dealers and their regional distributors that negatively impacted local pot supplies from time to time. Therefore, even our hometown dealers who had the most immediate and steady sources of marijuana could suddenly find drugs in short supply.

In these times of relative drought, out-of-town dealers who maintained contacts in their hometowns, particularly in those regions where there was an unaffected local marijuana supply source, could call upon their old acquaintances to ride out the local shortage. For the local dealers, however, these lean times motivated some of them to increase their relatively low-risk private campus drug-dealing activities in order to continue to meet the demand for pot. During periods of marijuana drought, for example, Surfer Boy would drive from his home in northern San Diego County to Long Beach, California—

approximately 150 miles round trip—to buy several pounds of marijuana from a connection. Although he is actually a fair-skinned Latino, Surfer Boy's moniker was given him by us because of his physical, attitudinal, and cultural resemblance to a stereotypical surfer. He wore a somewhat shaggy and unkempt hairstyle and traditional surfer attire, including flip-flop sandals, board shorts, and surf logo t-shirts. Similar to Ashcan, without any statement of his ethnic background, one would assume he was white.

California freeways are heavily policed by California Highway Patrol (CHP) officers who have a history of performing drug-related pretext stops—the use of minor traffic violations as an excuse for stopping and searching a car for illegal drugs. In fact, this practice was so commonly exercised by CHP officers that a class action suit was filed against the department by the American Civil Liberties Union on behalf of racial and ethnic minorities alleging they were unfairly detained and subjected to searches. The lawsuit ultimately resulted in the CHP agreeing to discontinue the formal pretext-stop practice and also impose a ban on "consent searches," situations in which officers ask motorists for permission to search their cars even in cases where there is no probable cause for the request.[9] Studies on racial profiling have shown that African Americans and increasingly Latinos are most apt to be subjected to these pretext stops; however, hippie, surfer, stoner-types are oftentimes stopped and searched because they fit the profile of someone who may be transporting illegal drugs. While most of our dealers did not necessarily fit this latter profile, several, including Surfer Boy, did.

The northbound portion of Surfer Boy's trip to Long Beach not only exposed him to an interstate corridor heavily policed by CHP, it also exposed him to an artifact of a 1940s Border Patrol experiment—the San Onofre immigration checkpoint. Although located 75 miles north of the Mexico-US border crossing at San Isidro, and just a few miles from the Orange County–San Diego County border, the Border Patrol officers who staff this way station have full authority to detain and search any motorist they deem suspicious of smuggling undocumented aliens or narcotics away from the border area. Although designed as a "second line of defense" against illegal border crossings, through the power of broad-sweeping federal immigration law, the checkpoint in San Onofre is used as often for extra-immigration purposes as it is to determine someone's legal immigrant status. Most commonly, this includes the detention and search of suspected drug couriers, and in post-9/11 United States it also involves the screening of other "suspicious" motorists.

Despite the apparent law enforcement risks, Surfer Boy chose to pass through the Interstate 5 corridor and San Onofre checkpoint in his journey to remain in business during local marijuana droughts. The checkpoint is located at the northern end of Camp Pendleton, a massive Marine Corps base located at the northwestern tip of San Diego County, and there is no alternative coastal area land route that Surfer Boy could have used to make the trip to Long Beach. Still, given his dependency on local suppliers, Surfer Boy found it necessary to assume these risks in order not to disappoint his clients and preserve his reputation as a campus dopeman.

Even more brazen than Surfer Boy's jaunts to Long Beach was the journey by two mid-tier network dealers to ensure that they could meet their customers' demand during one of these marijuana supply ebbs. Like most of our network's dealers, C-Money and The Rat were young white men of privilege who exclusively sold marijuana to a primarily college student customer base. Unlike many of our network's dealers who came to college with past pot experience, this duo reported that they started smoking marijuana during their freshman year after joining a fraternity in which pot use was commonplace. While sophomores, other members of their fraternity began routinely approaching them, asking where they might "score some bud." C-Money and The Rat decided that they would effectively double the amount of pot they typically purchased for their own use and sell the remainder to their fraternity brothers and other friends. Ultimately, this translated into a base-level, three-ounce-per-week enterprise, although they sold much larger quantities from time to time.

During a regional pot shortage triggered by a law enforcement crackdown on local suppliers, student-dealer friends from the Pacific Northwest alerted C-Money and The Rat about "good product" for a low price up north. Even in times of supply drought, lower quality local marijuana derogatorily referred to as "Mex," shorthand for inferior grades of Mexican marijuana, typically remained accessible to the network's dealers. However, for many dealers whose status, identity, and reputation are constructed around having readily available high-quality marijuana on hand, dabbling in inferior pot is not something they enter into lightly. While selling "dirt weed" to regular customers could most certainly jeopardize a dealer's client base, selling inferior strains of marijuana in closed markets like the one in which our dealers operated could, more importantly, compromise the dealer's social status, a status that is largely constructed around the dopeman identity. Therefore, seemingly without much contemplation of the law enforcement risks, C-Money and The Rat road-tripped from California to Oregon in order to make a $6,400 stopgap purchase for two pounds of high quality marijuana.

Independent from C-Money and The Rat, Brice, also a white, upper-middle-class marijuana dealer who received a business degree from the university, recognized the economic and marketing advantages to restocking up north—very high quality pot at a relatively low price. Supply and market information of this type seemed common knowledge among a good number of our network's dealers, many of whom had close friends in Northern California, Washington, or Oregon with access to locally and regionally grown high-quality marijuana. The higher grades of marijuana could routinely be purchased in the Pacific Northwest for $100 less per ounce than in Southern California, because the domestic producers of marijuana did not have the additional cost of smuggling the drugs past the watchful eyes of federal agents on the US-Mexico border.[10] Thus the expense of the trip, but not the potential risk, would be offset by the relative cost of the product. Accordingly, Brice, too, embarked on several traversals of this modern-day Oregon Trail in order to maintain his foothold in this Southern California drug market.

Interestingly, and consistent with his and other network dealers' status as anti-targets in the war on drugs, during just one of these restocking missions Brice reported being stopped five times by various law enforcement agents, none of whom thought him suspicious enough to even request consent for a search of him or his vehicle. In yet another of his many encounters with law enforcement from which he emerged unscathed, Brice recounted an experience he had while making a roundtrip marijuana run from San Diego to Los Angeles, again riding out a regional supply shortage. As he passed through San Onofre, he was momentarily detained at the checkpoint and asked by a Border Patrol officer, "You don't have any marijuana in there, do you?" Of course, as was usually the case with Brice, he did have pot in the car. However, almost amusingly and consistent with the notion that members of this affluent, primarily white drug network were anti-targets relatively immune from law enforcement scrutiny even when off of their home turf, Brice boldly replied, "I'm not that type of person." The officer seemingly agreed with Brice's self-assessment and allowed him to pass without a search of his car or any further fetter. When we asked Brice what measures he routinely took to avoid the police, he responded,

BRICE: I don't know. I just wasn't worried about it. I mean, it is always in the back of your mind . . . but I just wasn't worried so much. I think we're a very low priority. We buy a pound or two and split it up and sell it. The guy we are buying from, ya know, buys five to ten [pounds] and the guy he's buying it from fuckin' should be nervous because he's buying like one hundred [pounds].

Consistent with our dealers' statuses as anti-targets, Brice's sense of unimportance (in the eyes of the law) and immunity was not only bolstered by the lack of police scrutiny into his college drug dealing, but also continued to be reinforced after he completed his business degree and graduated from college. At this time, Brice decided to downsize his dealing enterprise while attempting to enter the legitimate workforce. Nonetheless, a downsized Brice still rendered him a significant player in the network's marijuana trade and meant that he was often driving around town with substantial quantities of marijuana in his car. On numerous occasions since his graduation, police stopped Brice for speeding. During each of these stops, he was in possession of several pounds of marijuana and also, as was more typical than not for him, under the influence of the drug at the time. Nonetheless, and characteristic of the experiences of most of our dealers, during these stops, his vehicle was never searched, he was never asked to consent to a search, and he was never arrested.

Overall we found transportation and distribution strategies within this network to be haphazard in ways that an average street-drug dealer would find unconscionable. Often, members of this college network did not actively employ even basic risk-minimization strategies. In brazen disregard for one of the ten commandments of the street-drug trade,[11] the basic codes of drug dealing understood by the majority of street-drug dealers as popularized by slain rapper Notorious B.I.G., these dealers stored and sold their drugs directly from their homes—residences where high customer traffic was common. Signs of an active drug trade were easily visible through open front doors to their homes, through unobstructed windows, and occasionally directly from streets busy with motor vehicle and foot traffic: triple-beam scales[12] like those used to weigh materials in eighth grade chemistry class but, beyond that stage of primary education, typically only found in the homes of drug dealers because of the scale's ability to weigh-out drugs to a very precise one-tenth of a gram; two- to three-foot-tall colorful glass bongs; hand-carved wooden marijuana pipes; sums of cash not typical of the starving college student strewn about table tops; and a mound of marijuana resting in an overturned Frisbee waiting to be crushed up into "bong-load" amounts. Indeed, the field notes of one of our researchers offered the following description of a typical visit to C-Money and The Rat's apartment:

I was greeted at the door by The Rat because C-Money was in the process of taking a bong load. Their house looks as if they had a party recently; there are about twenty-five to thirty beer bottles standing sporadically throughout the living room and kitchen. They are lacking a lot of furniture, so their bong looks like it takes up more room as they have it sitting in the middle of their coffee table . . . C-Money rolled a blunt and started to pass it around [even though] they had just finished smoking about forty minutes prior . . . They had numerous other smoking paraphernalia lying around the house. There was an ashtray visible, as well as their personal sack and a bubbler (a pipe that holds just a small amount of water in it to give the marijuana a smoother taste). They couldn't stop telling me how excited they were about the little garden that they were growing and about how they would be making all profit and really be smoking for free. When they showed their gardening project, The Rat was saying how they had to get four air fresheners to hang around the door to try and combat the smell. It was not really working, as you could still easily smell the marijuana growing in the air. As I was leaving, the two were talking about ordering pizza because they "didn't feel like going to get some-thing, and it always tastes better delivered."

C-Money, The Rat, and the rest of our network's dealers did not operate in the open-air conditions of street corner drug markets, but their haughty demeanor and risky behavior should have negated most of the visibility advantages typically offered by operating in closed markets and within private residences. Even when they left the safety of their homes to deliver drugs to customers, a courtesy extended by some of our network's dealers, their demeanor and behavior was equally brash. For example, LaCoste, admittedly one of our more arrogant dealers and one whose activities we discuss at length later, was well known for and took great pride in smoking "blunts"—cigars split open, the tobacco poured out and replaced with marijuana—while driving around our network's primary campus and throughout the city with drugs in his car. Occasionally, while making drug drop-offs to customers who lived in on-campus housing, he would nonchalantly approach their doors with a lit blunt in his mouth, a practice corroborated by several individuals who knew him.

Quite unlike typical urban drug dealers who go to great lengths to minimize visibility in their efforts to turn a profit, none of the dealers in our network seemed to have fear of arrest as a paramount concern as they went about their daily drug-dealing activities. In fact, most did not employ even perfunctory safeguards against law enforcement detection, displayed rather cavalier attitudes toward the police, and seemed indifferent at best to the possibility of apprehension. Indicative of these feelings, Surfer Boy told us he would occasionally consume several beers before taking the road on his San Diego to Long Beach drug purchase runs. Brice also described similarly high-risk deviant motoring habits while making his restocking trips to Oregon, saying that he would typically get high in the car while driving back to California with several pounds of marijuana on board.

These were just a couple of examples of what proved to be a pattern of *rational* recklessness among the dealers in our college drug network. Indeed it seems as though our dealers did not have much to fear; over the entire time we studied this network, only one of the dealers with whom we came in contact encountered any serious legal repercussions related to his drug-dealing activity. These attitudes and the near nonexistent formal consequences for their illegal actions support the fundamental conclusion that there exists a persistent and active bias in the eyes of the public and in the criminal justice system when it comes to the US drug trade and the contemporary war on drugs. Essentially, as our dealers' experiences demonstrate, if a person does not fit the stereotypical drug courier or drug dealer profile of young urban minority male, regardless of whether levels of actual drug dealing and drug use are on par with or exceed that of the stereotypical dealer's, trafficking in illegal drugs becomes a significantly less risky enterprise.

No Foul, No Harm

The primary drug market we uncovered proved to be one in which illicit street drugs were often easier to obtain than alcohol by underage college students. And for anyone interested in marijuana, cocaine, ecstasy, or other typical street drugs used among college students, irrespective of age, there was generally someone much like them who was ready, willing, and able to supply their needs. Most of the primary market dealers we interviewed and observed were selling large enough quantities of marijuana and other drugs to warrant serious stretches of incarceration under current drug-sentencing schemes. However, none of them incurred this fate, even when people in positions of formal authority were clearly aware or otherwise suspected them of illegal drug trafficking. As we discuss in greater detail in later chapters, only one of the thirty or so street-drug dealers we encountered as a part of this network ever saw the inside of a courthouse as a repercussion for his drug dealing activities. And, suffice it to say that today he remains a free man.

This underscores a conclusion reached thirty-five years ago by William J. Chambliss, whose work is revisited later in the book, in his classic piece "The Saints and the Roughnecks," a study of two deviant groups of high-school-aged boys and their interactions with their community and law enforcement personnel. As Chambliss wrote, "Selective perception and labeling—finding, processing and punishing some kinds of criminality and not others—means that visible, poor, non-mobile, outspoken, undiplomatic 'tough' kids will be noticed, whether their actions are seriously delinquent or not."[13] To take Chambliss's analysis to its next logical step, invisible, well-off kids who possess substantial amounts of social and symbolic capital, even when their actions are seriously delinquent, stand a reasonably good chance of walking away scot-free. And even when they are identified as rule breakers, as we saw time and time again with our network's dealers, their status allows them to escape deviant labels.

In the final scene of *Traffic,* a flustered, frustrated, and emotionally torn Judge Wakefield is set to deliver his introductory address as the nation's new drug czar. He begins, "There is a war on drugs and many of our family members are the enemy. And I don't know how you wage war on your own family." As we found through our examination of this primary drug market, the short answer to the judge's rhetorical question is "you don't."

Dealer Bio: Brice

Brice earned his moniker by virtue of being the quintessential capitalist; "Brice" in the Latin tradition loosely translates to "an entrepreneur."[a] He is the older of two children, born to affluent parents in the Pacific Northwest. While he began his drug-dealing endeavors midway through his college career, he seemed well-versed in marijuana use and the corresponding rituals from his high school years. Through the bulk of the study, Brice was pursuing a business degree and was also an active member of the professional business fraternal organization on campus. In many ways, Brice served as a key gatekeeper for this study and proved to be an invaluable resource throughout the course of the project.

Before Brice immersed himself in the Southern California illicit drug game, this market of customers was almost exclusively supplied by one person, affectionately referred to as "The Monopoly" within the network. While Brice was in effect competing with The Monopoly, there was more than enough demand to minimize, if not completely eliminate, any visible friction between the two dealers. However, many in the network joked that Brice was a classic trust-buster who "broke-up The Monopoly." While never formally interviewed for this project, The Monopoly told one of the researchers that he was once questioned by his neighbors about all the foot traffic at his off-campus apartment. He joked at the obvious absurdity of his hastily constructed cover story, that he was running an adult soccer league that somehow demanded regular meetings at his apartment.

In addition to his prowess as a marijuana dealer and cultivator, Brice was a well honed marijuana aficionado and could detail the horticultural history of many of the more well-known strains of particularly potent marijuana. Like Saul Silver, James Franco's drug dealing character in the 2008 film *Pineapple Express,* it seemed that one of the joys Brice derived from being a large-scale drug dealer was the ability to acquire personal supplies of many "name brand" marijuana strains like

(continues)

Dealer Bio: continued

"purple kush" (because of its purple hairs and coloring), "orange crush" (after its orange coloring and the famous R.E.M. song), and "Afghani" (supposedly grown in Afghanistan).[b] Brice kept a special canning jar that archived personal amounts of these name brand specimens. He claimed to be saving most of them for his eventual "retirement" from drug dealing, but would occasionally smoke some on birthdays and other celebratory events.

In contrast to the majority of accounts of drug dealers in the criminological literature, Brice's operation had a self-service component. At the beginning of the day he would put individual eighths of marijuana and small amounts of cash in a large Ziploc bag. For many customers, he would simply toss them the bag and they would essentially serve themselves, picking the eighth of their choice and making change from the existing cash if necessary. Somewhat surprisingly, Brice once explained that he never had a single problem with the "self serve" bag being light on cash or marijuana.

Brice's drug-dealing endeavors and his social life were indistinguishable. He would routinely spend all day in his house, playing darts, hackysack, selling and indulging in marijuana with the constant stream of friends and acquaintances who would visit. Of particular note was a party he and Cecilia threw on April 20, the infamous "420 day" of marijuana cultural lore.[c] For this event, Dallas crafted three intricate and fully functional marijuana bongs out of watermelons that he subsequently filled with ice and water and ceremoniously dubbed "the Nina, the Pinta, and the Santa Maria." In addition to two kegs of high-end beer and a series of marijuana-infused cakes and cookies, they executed an Easter-egg hunt with a twist. Over several city blocks, hundreds of Easter eggs were hidden that contained candy and small of amounts of money. Of particular appeal to the attendees, they let it be known that the green Easter eggs contained small nuggets of marijuana. Each of the twenty green eggs had assigned spotters so no one other than

(continues)

Dealer Bio: continued

the college students in attendance would find them. This type of event was indicative of the tolerance for personal freedoms within the community, but also of a total disregard of the potential consequences from law enforcement.

Noticeably, Brice's marijuana business facilitated a sedentary lifestyle, and a poor diet. After nights out at local bars, Brice was notorious for making sandwiches that reflected his indulgent tendencies; Brice would use toast to contain about a half-inch thick layer of cream cheese and a half-dozen slices of bacon straight from the pan, no grease-straining necessary.

Notes: a. Online baby-name guides were used to facilitate moniker choices. Several of these guides linked the Latin name "Brice" with entrepreneurialism.

b. In one of several similar scenes describing the different strains of pot he had at his disposal, Franco's *Pineapple Express* character Saul says, "This is like if that Blue Oyster shit met that African Kush I had—and they had a baby. And then, meanwhile, that crazy Northern Light stuff I had and the Super Red Espresso Snowflake met and had a baby. And by some miracle, those two babies met and fucked—this would be the shit they birthed."

c. See Halnon, "The Power of 420," for a complete discussion.

Notes

1. It seems the enthusiasm exhibited by many of our dealers to participate in the study was not an anomaly in social science. J. T., the primary informant in S. Venkatesh's *Gang Leader for a Day* was also noticeably enthusiastic about the prospect of his life story and his own criminality contributing to scholarly work and went to significant lengths to facilitate Venkatesh's research.

2. US Department of Health and Human Services, Substance Abuse and Mental Health Services Administration, *Results from the 2006 National Survey on Drug Use and Health: National Findings.*

3. Again according to Ashcan, this dealer was not arrested by city police. Instead, the matter was handled internally by campus police and university disciplinary officers. However, as a consequence of his drug dealing activities, he was barred from living in on-campus housing. We were not able

to corroborate this outcome with university officials because too much time had passed. But outcomes like this were entirely consistent with those seen in other confirmed on-campus drug cases.

4. See endnote 12 for more on the equipment used to weigh drugs.

5. Interestingly and perhaps not coincidentally, "4-20" (four-twenty) is also a colloquialism used by stoner youth to refer to the smoking of pot and to self-identify oneself as a member of a pot-smoking subculture.

6. "Yeyo" is a slang term for cocaine that was popularized by the classic film *Scarface*. It is also used in contemporary urban hip hop music. For example, in "So What You Saying," drug dealer turned rapper Beanie Siegel rhymes about his prowess as a cocaine (yeyo) dealer, "Yo, I'm the coke copper plus the rock chopper . . . I don't play when it come to yae [yeyo], I cop cook and collect my dough in one day."

7. Becker, "Marijuana Use and Social Control," p. 215.

8. California Border Alliance Group, *Drug Market Analysis,* May 2008.

9. Broder, "California Ending Use of Minor Traffic Stops as Search Pretext."

10. Within this particular network, marijuana prices were relatively standardized. One-eighth ounce (a common retail quantity) of good quality marijuana retailed for $50. "Name brand" strains of pot like those featured in *High Times* magazine would routinely retail for $55 to $60. Conversely, inferior quality weed would sell for $40 per one-eighth ounce. Full ounces of marijuana were typically available in the low-to-mid $300 range, quarter-pounds in the $1,200 range, and pounds could be purchased for around $4,000, again depending on quality.

11. Like any other business and social network, the street-drug trade is governed by a set of maxims or "commandments" that all street hustlers live by, or at least should live by, in order to minimize risk in an inherently dangerous industry. Perhaps no one captured these basic principles better than slain rapper Notorious B.I.G. in his song "The Ten Crack Commandments" in which he lists basic rules of the drug trade. In order of appearance, these rules include: (1) never let anyone know how much money you have or how much money you make—money breeds jealousy; (2) never let people know your next move or your specific plans—stealth is essential to survival in the drug trade; (3) never trust anyone—even family members will turn on you given the proper incentive; (4) never get high off your own supply; (5) never sell drugs out of your home—you are too easy to find, neighbors might notify authorities, and asset forfeiture is that much easier; (6) never give drugs to anyone on credit—junkies are not good for paying you back; (7) keep family and business completely separated—money and blood do not mix; (8) never keep large quantities of drugs or cash on your person—it is too easy to be robbed (even by those you trust) or popped by the police; (9) unless you are in the process of getting arrested, keep your distance from the police lest you be labeled a snitch, a fate that is bad for business and your health; and (10) consignment (getting drugs from a larger dealer on credit) is not for small-time dealers and you should not buy a quantity of drugs from a supplier that you cannot reasonably sell in a short period of time—if you do not have the

cash to pay the supplier back, you will likely pay in other ways including with your own life.

12. Because of their precision and perhaps because of what they convey—"drugs available here"—triple-beam scales were standard fare among all of our network's dealers who purchased marijuana in quantities greater than an ounce at a time. An average drug-dealer grade triple beam could cost anywhere from $150 to $250 and were accurate to 0.1 grams. Oddly, marijuana is usually sold in pounds, ounces, and fractions of ounces, yet, for the sake of precision, dealers measure the pot in grams and then convert it to ounces. For example, if a customer wishes to purchase an ounce of marijuana, the dealer will produce the triple beam and weigh out 28.35 grams of weed.

13. Chambliss, "The Saints and the Roughnecks," p. 31.

3

Why Rich Kids Sell Street Drugs: Wankstaz, Wannabes, and Capitalists in Training

Criminology, as a social science, was built around attempts to explain the origins of criminal and deviant behavior. Based upon historic suppositions within the discipline, the discourse of US drug policy has been guided by the overwhelming assumption that drug dealers are motivated predominantly by profit. Most theorists adopt a Mertonian approach toward the subject, arguing that this motivation to sell drugs is particularly acute when social-structural marginality blocks the socially prescribed means to attain the socially prescribed goals in a given society.[1] One of the most obvious, yet provocative, questions that guided this research was *why*—specifically, why do affluent college students, poised to embrace a series of legitimate avenues for upward mobility and success, choose to become drug dealers? With seemingly so much to lose, haphazardly delving into criminality appears at the very least counterintuitive. Ultimately, what we found was that these affluent drug dealers contradict some longstanding criminological assumptions about crime, the public policy dialogue concerning the war on drugs, and the archetypical portrayal of drug dealers and users.

After several years of observation and interviews with the dealers who formed this affluent college drug network, we were able to identify six primary motivations that we feel in many ways explain why affluent college students make the seemingly irrational choice to participate in drug crime. These material and nonmaterial motivations proved valuable enough to entice these dealers to risk the status, comfort, and privilege they already enjoyed and could count on enjoying in the future provided they followed the socially proscribed pathway to success that accompanied their socioeconomic status. Indeed, our dealers and their motivations proved similar to those discussed by Lise-Marie Van Nostrand and Richard Tewksbury who wrote, "Included among the reasons dealers sell drugs is not only for financial gain, but also as an alternative to low-paying jobs, from a desire for status and power, out of hedonism, and out of the need to support a drug habit."[2] As a final caveat before moving into the particular motivations revealed in our study, we think it important to note that these motives are not mutually exclusive. Rather, our dealers were apparently motivated by a combination of tangible and identity-based rewards and, at different times and in response to varying social circumstances, their reasons for selling drugs often drifted among the various motives.

Motive #1: Underwrite Costs of Personal Drug Use

While the affluent drug dealers in this study did not constitute an entirely homogeneous group, the vast majority of them consumed a considerable amount of marijuana, a finding that was as anticipatable as it was devastatingly obvious from an even cursory glance around their respective dwellings. As LaCoste unanomalistically said, "I smoke tons of pot, that's the problem, tons of it." The majority of these dealers not only consumed large quantities of marijuana, but pot use was a routinized part of their daily existence and often coexisted with social, professional, and scholastic commitments. Indeed, marijuana was not reserved for weekend bingeing or celebratory occasions; rather, a regimen of marijuana use was seemingly a staple of daily life.

At the time of his first interview with us, Beefy was a twenty-year-old, white, middle-class college student with a 3.1 grade point average, and a campus drug dealer of several years. His statements exemplify the omnipresent role of marijuana in the everyday lives of many of these affluent drug dealers.

Do you smoke everyday?
BEEFY: Yeah. I smoke before work. If I work all day I will come home on my lunch break and smoke. I smoke before most classes. Not usually tests, but sometimes. Yeah [laughs].

What was your job?
BEEFY: I worked at Bank of America as a teller, still do.

Throughout this study, we found that many of these avid pot smokers were initially motivated to venture into drug dealing, in significant part, as a mechanism to underwrite the costs of their personal drug use. In fact, this was by far the most common explanation offered by dealers to explain why they initially became involved with drug dealing and the underground economy. Even the smaller-scale dealers that we spoke with were able to avoid paying "retail prices" for their own marijuana or made enough of a profit to offset the costs of their personal drug habit, a trade practice commonly dubbed "selling for head smoke." In fact, per their calculations, by cutting away three-eighths of an ounce for their personal use and putting the remaining five-eighths up for sale, heavy smokers turned roommate-dealers C-Money and The Rat only spent about $30 of their own money for every ounce of marijuana they purchased.

In all, these affluent drug dealers seem to exemplify the "user-dealer" model that pervades the criminological literature. Moreover, this research provides support for Richard Tewksbury and Elizabeth Ehrhardt Mustaine's findings that college drug dealers often sold drugs in conjunction with their own drug use.[3] For many of the dealers in the sample, their illegal businesses not only offset the costs of their personal drug use, but also facilitated an unchecked indulgence in marijuana use that was readily apparent throughout this study. When asked why he chose to become a drug dealer, LaCoste tersely explained,

LACOSTE: I don't know, I really just do it to smoke, that's the only reason I sell pot. Then you just start selling tons of pot. Then, like now, I get to smoke tons of pot.

The sentiments offered by LaCoste were mirrored by the experiences of Raoul D., another dealer in our sample. Raoul D.'s trajectory into the underground economy was relatively unique because he did not begin using or selling drugs until midway through his collegiate career, unlike most other dealers who were using marijuana and sometimes other drugs in high school. A white, upper-middle-class male, Raoul D. had previously abstained from drug use because he was a successful athlete and had been recruited to play football in college. His future athletic and academic aspirations prevented him from experimenting with drugs and generally facilitated a healthy lifestyle. However, reminiscent of a Hollywood cliché, he dislocated his shoulder during a football game his freshman year. This injury ended his football career and devastated Raoul D. because athletics had been his "life for the past seven years." He was prescribed Vicodin to manage the pain after having shoulder surgery and "really enjoyed the feeling it gave him." He "started smoking pot with friends" because "he did not care about doing drugs and harming his athletic ability anymore." Soon thereafter, Raoul D. had developed what he estimated to be an $800 per month drug habit, a habit that ultimately prompted his foray into drug dealing. While he initially bought larger amounts of marijuana for the purposes of reselling it to friends for his own "head smoke," his dabbling in the underground economy snowballed into a substantial commitment to criminality. Eventually, Raoul D. oversaw a drug dealing enterprise that moved roughly five pounds of marijuana and four to eight ounces of cocaine per month—all sparked by a life and mindset-altering injury and the desire to offset the costs of personal drug use.

Cecilia, a biology student and native to our network's California hub city, eventually became the largest female dealer in our sample. Evidently, her initial foray into drug sales was a somewhat organic evolution and not a distinct, conscious decision. As an area native and veteran marijuana user, her experience and connections in the underground economy were an asset within the college community; an asset that helped her offset the costs of her personal drug use.

What motivated you to get involved in the first place?

CECILIA: Um, what motivated me? Not having to buy it [pot] myself ultimately . . . I had enough people calling and troubling me anyway when I was in college because they knew I smoked so they were certain I must know where to get some. And it ended up starting out as an "everybody pitch in altogether" movement. You know, it changed from that because it is not always convenient, so I will just front it for them. And so then you have your four or five friends that you are always sort of servicing, and then before you know it you are getting larger and larger sums to service more and more of your friends. It's not something that you sit . . . or at least not something where I sat down and said "hmmm, I think I'll do this." You know, it just sort of started out and it was you know . . . you were sort of rewarded by again not having to pay for it yourself. And that allowed you to be more generous with your friends.

In addition, Cecilia expressed that the expansion of her business was further facilitated by the increasingly large demands of her friends. These friends were not only looking to Cecilia to acquire quality marijuana, but to acquire quality marijuana within the familiarity and relative safety of the closed market "college umbrella."

CECILIA: I know for me personally that many of my friends expressed almost like a sense of gratitude because they got to stop going to this weird sketchy place where they felt kind of anxious and not really safe and not really you know in the protected . . . again in that umbrella feeling that you have when you are in college because it is all of your friends. So a lot of people, especially my girlfriends, expressed those sentiments to me so I think that might have been part of what perpetuated it on some level.

Motive #2: Underwrite Other Incidental and Entertainment Expenses

The criminological literature archives a plethora of accounts of individuals reluctantly venturing into drug sales and other criminal behaviors out of necessity, social-structural marginality, and the scarcity of legitimate means for upward mobility. In stark contrast to this body of literature and most studies of drug dealing, the bulk of the dealers in this study had their living and scholastic expenses covered by their parents, and their college-related expenses were also sometimes supplemented by academic scholarships and other financial aid. In addition, many dealers had disposable income from sporadic part-time jobs and allowances and credit cards provided by their parents. Therefore, in all cases, our network's dealers were not strapped for cash or otherwise pushed into drug sales out of any kind of economic hardship or necessity.

For many dealers in the sample, beyond covering the costs of their personal drug use, drug sales became a mechanism to underwrite the other incidental and entertainment expenses typically associated with the college lifestyle. The following exchange with Ashcan provided a good encapsulation of this particular motivation. As an aside, this conversation also reveals that Ashcan's relatively moderate and occasional marijuana use cast him as a bit of an anomaly among most of our network's drug dealers, a population that tended to engage in rather exorbitant pot smoking.

What would you sell marijuana for?
ASHCAN: Mostly beer money. And I had some parking tickets to pay and my parents don't really want me to get parking tickets, so it helps out—the extra money—so I didn't have to tell them or anything like that.
You said parking tickets, what else?
ASHCAN: Well, when I was a freshman, I drank a lot, so you know the alcohol budget was extensive. And just other stuff; you know, shoes, clothes, whatever. I just had money around, so why not?
Did you smoke a lot of pot yourself?
ASHCAN: Actually, I stopped smoking that much when I started selling it. But, in high school I smoked a lot; and before I was selling I smoked a lot but I kind of didn't really [sell drugs then] for some reason. I never really thought about that.
So, you weren't really dealing drugs to support your own habit?
ASHCAN: No, I didn't need to. I never really thought marijuana was addictive. So I didn't have a problem quitting.

Similarly, Cecilia explained that her profits, while relatively modest, helped to underwrite her incidental and entertainment expenses and those of her roommates.

What did you spend your profits on?
CECILIA: Profit? There wasn't a lot of profit for me because I was keeping up with the habits of my roommates at the time mostly. So I think that was the profit, was that everyone in the house got to not pay and enjoy you know that extra spending money for whatever that was worth. Um, any amount of extra money that I did make if there was any . . . which wouldn't be a lot . . . certainly was spent on holidays and small trips . . . just generally like spending money . . . oh I need twenty bucks to go out to have a happy hour drink and skim off the top kinda thing you didn't typically notice. I never really felt

like I had a large sum of money and went and spent a large sum of money on anything.

Finally, true to his form and in support of the idea that many of our network's dealers chose to sell drugs as a means to underwrite entertainment and other incidental expenses, an interview with LaCoste offered the following explanation (of many that he either gave or displayed) for his choice to become a student drug dealer.

Do you ever save any of the money [that you make selling drugs]?
LaCoste: Hell no! Hell no, I blow that shit! Strip clubs and fucking gambling, throwing money around [laughs] . . . I just get shit-faced and then I get all competitive and what not, and lose all my money.

LaCoste went on to explain that, as an eighteen year old, he also thought it necessary to spend a considerable sum of his ill-gotten profits to acquire top-of-the-line fake IDs to better facilitate his partying lifestyle. He even went so far as to spend top-dollar for a Mexican counterfeiter who specialized in making US identifications for undocumented Mexican immigrants.

LaCoste: I've got a couple of good ass [fake IDs]. I had one made in Mexico. That's like the best one, but I lost it when I was drunk. Ah man, it was so bomb, like police scanning, black light, hologram . . . it was like a real ID! I was like a citizen. I was a person in the DMV's shit! It was great. I'm such a drunk though. And I got this California one right here. [He shows us the ID.] And then I got this Texas one in the car . . . Those are essential for going gambling and stuff.

Motive #3: The Spirit of Capitalism

Ashcan's earlier statements provide evidence that for some, the principal motivation to plunge into criminality was quite straightforward—disposable income. Typically, these initial profits were relatively modest, but the taste of the lifestyle they facilitated often ballooned into a gluttonous arbitrage opportunity. At the time of the study, these affluent drug dealers were disproportionately current or former business majors and some already owned and operated their own legitimate small businesses. They embodied the entrepreneurial spirit of capitalism and the corresponding centrality of the profit motive, a spirit that further motivated their venture into criminality. These well-heeled, well-trained, and rather pragmatic capitalists often recognized the economic opportunity becoming a drug dealer provided based on their initial sampling of the market. Early dabbling in the college drug market very quickly revealed ubiquitous demand and minimal market risks; a return on their investment was a virtual lock, and the perceptible risks of adverse social or criminal justice consequences were negligible.

In *Why Our Drug Laws Have Failed and What We Can Do About It,* conservative Orange County, California, Judge James P. Gray makes a compelling case for reevaluating US punitive drug control strategies. A cornerstone of his analysis, which also was central to his eventual unsuccessful candidacy for the US Senate, is the need for a dramatic drug policy shift emphasizing demand-side strategies to control drug crime. Gray conveyed this message during his 2002 testimony to the Little Hoover Commission, a self-described bipartisan, independent state body that promotes efficiency and effectiveness in state programs.

> But no matter what we do, we cannot repeal the law of supply and demand: As long as there is a demand in our country for illicit drugs, the demand will be met. Otherwise stated, there is no way in a free society that we can effectively prohibit the sale of small amounts of drugs for large amounts of money.[4]

While certainly not the dealers about whom Gray was primarily speaking, the affluent drug dealers that made up our network further support Judge Gray's conclusions. Ashcan and LaCoste both reveal how a base-level market analysis motivated their initial drug-dealing ventures, although the eventual trajectory of their respective businesses differed substantially.

ASHCAN: It was an easy way to make money. Because, in the [dorms] . . . my spring semester, a bunch of people got busted and there was nobody dealing and there was a demand. So I thought, what the hell. I wasn't cash strapped or anything like that. I mean, there were a few weeks when I didn't really eat that much 'cause I didn't have that much money left, so it kind of helped to have an extra forty or fifty bucks lying around.

Relative sensibility, tact, and a healthy dose of caution perhaps spawned by campus authorities forcing a few of his would-be peers to close up shop (again without formal law enforcement intervention) seemingly restrained the scope and financial yield of Ashcan's modest drug-dealing operation. However, many of the other dealers we encountered readily expanded their businesses upon realizing the potential for profit created by the ubiquitous demand for drugs on college campuses. Despite some substantial and profitable criminal enterprises, not a single subject in this study abandoned their legitimate pursuits entirely. However, fueled by the spirit of capitalism, many dealers nurtured their fledgling drug dealing operations into more diverse drug-dealing enterprises. For example, LaCoste sold marijuana exclusively for only a few weeks. He quickly realized that product diversification and larger quantities of drugs would allow him to do far more than merely underwrite the costs of his own drug use and incidental social expenses. As for most of the dealers we interviewed, marijuana remained the staple of LaCoste's illegal business. However, he eventually offered a product line that also included ecstasy, hallucinogenic mushrooms, an assortment of prescription drugs,[5] and cocaine, the real "moneymaker." According to LaCoste, aside from its markup, cocaine was so profitable because of its widespread popularity with "everybody" at the network's hub university.

LaCoste: Dude . . . [cocaine is] fifty dollars a gram. A hundred and fifty an eight ball [a quantity equivalent to an eighth of an ounce or 3.5 grams]. Ah, yeah, that's where the money's at. Pick up like a six hundred or seven hundred ounce of yey [cocaine]. Yeah, you make tons of money just 'cause it's so expensive.

According to LaCoste and the few other dealers who routinely sold both cocaine and marijuana, market dynamics artificially inflated the price—and thus profit potential—of the "white lady." Generally, in this market there were an insufficient number of drug dealers attempting to meet the massive drug-use demands of the student-user population. Beyond that, in its powder form, as LaCoste's aforementioned accounting breakdown shows, cocaine can prove cost prohibitive for many. However, given the relative affluence of the network's consumer base, powder cocaine was in relatively high demand and, perhaps because of perceived risk or distributor access factors, cocaine had even fewer suppliers than marijuana. For some, pragmatically choosing to take advantage of this market opportunity was nothing more than a simple economic calculation, a calculation that would further sharpen the teeth and claws of these emerging cubs of capitalism as they eventually graduated from the illicit college drug-dealing market to hopefully become lions in the larger world of legitimate capitalism.

Motive #4: Ego Gratification and the Pursuit of Status

When asked explicitly about their motivation to begin selling drugs, dealers almost universally offered pragmatic answers focused on financial benefits. It seemed that framing their own criminality as a rational business decision was, in part, an attempt to absolve them from self-identifying as criminals or at least to mitigate some of their seemingly irrational decisionmaking. The narratives offered by LaCoste, Ashcan, and Raoul D. typified the initial and explicit responses posed by many dealers that their goal in selling drugs was to offset personal drug, entertainment, and other incidental expenses. However, as the interviews progressed, elements of other implicit, less palatable justifications became apparent. We found that for many dealers ego gratification, the pursuit of status, peer recognition, and unadorned greed contributed significantly to their choice to enter and continue in the drug game.

While elements of this fourth motive were evident in interviews with nearly all of our dealers, many seemed to deliberately talk around issues of gained status and none reveled in the social status afforded by their position as a drug dealer more than LaCoste. By self-declaration, LaCoste was "very popular" at his Midwest high school, where his wealth and family identity facilitated some degree of status. However, as an eighteen-year-old freshman in Southern California, his fashion-forward designer clothes and $50,000 SUV failed to distinguish him on a campus and in a region with a reputation for overt materialism. Consequently for LaCoste, heavy pot smoking and drug sales became a variable that he was able to manipulate in order to differentiate himself from his equally wealthy peers on campus and to quickly enhance his reputation and status. LaCoste boastfully described the status benefits of being a drug dealer and heavyweight drug user,

LACOSTE: You can give pot to whoever you want, do whatever you want, buy a ton of shit! . . . I'm like a fierce pothead and I just really just won't ever stop smoking . . . you can ask like any of my friends, all I do is smoke weed. That's all I do. Nobody can out smoke me.

With his characteristic swagger, LaCoste revealed the sense of importance and status that he derived from his reputation as a drug dealer,

LACOSTE: If you said, where'd you get pot, where can I get pot? I'm sure my name would be mentioned at least 50 percent of the time. Just 'cause, from the minute I got here, I was like "does anybody need weed?" I was like, "Who needs weed? I got that shit . . . come and get it!"

In trying to explore LaCoste's motives for selling drugs, at least those beyond the bravado-laden airs he projected, of paramount interest to us were the multiple layers and sometimes disingenuous nature of his comments related to the topics of status and ego gratification. For example, when asked directly if being a drug dealer made him feel powerful, he responded, "Not really." However, he then added,

LACOSTE: I could be powerful. I could tell somebody to whoop your ass [laughs] and your ass would get whooped. [But] that's not really powerful. Plus, I gave up fighting for Lent.

Despite his brief overt denial of feeling empowered by his position as a campus drug dealer, the vast majority of LaCoste's boastful commentary did lead us to determine that ego gratification and the pursuit of status were instrumental in his choice to become, and continue on as, a drug dealer. At least to us, it was clear that he did derive an inflated sense of self-importance and positional significance as a direct result of being a relatively well-known drug dealer.

Indeed, for many of our dealers, including LaCoste, ego gratification, popularity, and the pursuit of status proved to be robust motivating forces within this affluent drug-distribution network. Certainly, the pursuit of status through the seductive world of upper-class drug hustling is not limited to the college set. For example, Patricia Adler also found that the self-perception of upper-level drug dealers and smugglers were fueled by the power and ego produced by their instrumental role in the underground economy: "Dealers built commitment through the ego gratification they derived from drug trafficking. Their self-images were lodged in the power they wielded over others by withholding or supplying them with drugs (for both business use and personal consumption). Dealers reveled in their social status."[6]

We deemed deeper exploration into the specific question as to why criminality and drug dealing seems to equate to status among affluent college students as tangential and beyond the immediate scope of this research. However, some recent scholarship suggests a connection between consumerism, illicit drug use, and marketing strategies that may inform the present inquiry. In *Chilling Out: The Cultural Politics of Substance Consumption, Youth and Drug Policy,* Shane Blackman argues that illicit drug use has become a regular and accepted form of commodity consumption in modern US society. In a culture that values consumerism, materialism, and even hypermaterialism,[7] drugs apparently become another accepted form of indulgence and consumption. Blackman also highlights the deliberate and strategic implantation of drug images into advertising and marketing campaigns. Many of these campaigns explicitly target young people and evoke images of luxury and leisure. He notes, "Drugs routinely appear in Hollywood films and are the subject of popular songs in the charts. At the same time drug imagery and drug symbolism is used to sell ordinary products from soft drinks . . . to cars."[8]

Since popular culture and advertising campaigns apparently teach young people to connect their lifestyle with illicit drug use, it seems commonsensical that young, affluent college students would derive status from immersing themselves in drug crime and otherwise flirting with the perceived dangers associated with being a drug dealer. Again, pursuing status through deviance seems particularly practical in social situations where the traditional trappings of material success are commonplace and an additional edge is needed to really stand out among one's peers.

Motive #5: Sneaky Thrills and Being a Gangsta

RAOUL D.: I am almost as addicted to selling as I am to
getting faded.

In addition to the previous tangible, material, and identity-based
motivations, a critical mass of the dealers in our sample seemed motivated by the simple thrill of deviant behavior, the ecstasy of getting
away with activities they knew to be criminal, and otherwise display-
ing the ornaments of pseudo gangstaism. In his book *Seductions of
Crime,* Jack Katz reasoned, "It is not the taste for the pizza that leads
to the crime; the crime makes the pizza tasty."[9] Katz's argument, we
think, well explains some of our network's drug dealing activities.
Specifically, the affluent, predominantly white drug dealers we interviewed and observed were, by virtue of their socioeconomic status
alone, not motivated or driven into drug crime by economic necessity.
Rather, the "sneaky thrills"[10] of anti-authoritarianism and attempting
to outwit formal agents of social control seemed to serve as an additional enticement into criminality. As we explore later in our discussion of "unrisky business," on the rare occasions when these dealers'
illegal activities are detected by campus authorities or other formal
agents of social control, they can rather easily mobilize the necessary
symbolic and actual capital to avoid the full ire of the drug war
hawks. Additionally, when it seemed socially or personally beneficial, some of these dealers would openly revel in their ability to vol-
untarily take risks and challenge traditional expectations.
  LaCoste personifies the pseudo-gangstaism and sneaky thrills
that apparently further motivated some of our dealers to immerse
themselves in the drug game. He somewhat brazenly utilized both his
dormitory room and SUV as the homebases for his illicit drug-
dealing operation. In fact, LaCoste openly arranged a drug sale from
his dorm room during one of our interviews with him. In the middle
of answering a question about the quantities of marijuana he typically
purchased, his cell phone rang.

LACOSTE: Hold on. Yeah, what do you want? . . . Yeah, there's herb
[marijuana] above the fucking refrigerator . . . Yeah there is . . . No
there's not, it's in my car. I'm sorry, I was really drunk. Remember,
we went out there and put it in there? . . . But where's my car at? It's

up at what? . . . Do you need some? . . . Send him here, I'll give him one . . . What? Ah, I'll come down there . . . I'll come down there in fucking twenty-five minutes, alright? Is that straight? . . . Peace . . . [He hangs up the phone] What else now were we talking about?

Among his many other flagrant statements of disregard for authority, LaCoste would also routinely illegally park his SUV in the loading or fire zones directly in front of his residence hall. And, per his statements, both locations would typically have stashes of contraband sufficient to warrant his arrest. These actions seemed to suggest that he was not tremendously concerned with the campus police detecting his illegal activity, a suspicion he confirmed when asked about the danger posed by campus authorities.

LaCoste: They can kiss my ass. They can't touch me. They can't do anything to me . . . I'd rather get caught by [the campus police] than the [real] police.

We concluded that LaCoste's renegade attitude was nurtured by a belief that the status and resources of his family would ultimately mitigate any possible university or criminal justice consequences, a conclusion supported by several other off-the-cuff and flippant remarks made by LaCoste in regard to formal authority figures. Apparently, his pomposity was not totally unfounded. Indeed, discussions with several university officials revealed that the campus authorities were very much aware of LaCoste's drug dealing endeavors. In addition, they suspected that he had perpetrated other crimes on campus, including a series of recent thefts from dormitory rooms. In the typical fashion of our hub university, however, officials tended to watch LaCoste and other prominent suspected dealers from afar, reluctant to formally confront him for fear that he would bring his parents' wrath down upon the university or that a major drug bust would bring unwanted attention to the campus. There were a couple of "meetings" with residence-life officials in which LaCoste was made aware that they felt some of his activities were suspicious. But beyond that, there was never any formal intervention on the part of university police or administrators. And, as we have already discussed, this negated any external authorities' investigation into his illegal activities as campus authorities served as the gatekeeper for outside law enforcement interests.

Dealer Bio: LaCoste

LaCoste was not our network's biggest dealer by any stretch of the imagination, but he might have very well been our network's most interesting character. He earned his moniker specifically because of his fashion-trendy preppy appearance. A conventionally handsome nineteen-year-old freshman with dishwater blonde salon-shaggy hair and blue eyes, LaCoste looked every bit the part of an Abercrombie model and not at all the stereotype of a drug dealer. He tooled around campus and the nearby beach communities in his parent-provided $50,000 SUV with a booming sound system and mounted atop gangsta-requisite 20-inch chrome rims, a vehicle that also served as his drug-dealing office on wheels. A self-described "criminal," gangsta rap was his music of choice and LaCoste reveled in the fact that he was a relatively large supplier of marijuana, cocaine, and an array of party drugs to the college network that served as the focus of this study. He was also the only dealer we encountered who had serious pre-college criminal charges, specifically for illegal possession of firearms and possession of marijuana with intent to distribute.

His father's position as a high-level accounting executive in the Midwest provided LaCoste with a seemingly limitless supply of cash and other symbols of material wealth, yet he still felt compelled to sell drugs and was able to make a good bit of money as a college drug dealer. Indeed, it could be argued that his passion was his drug dealing and other nefarious activities such as burglarizing neighboring apartments in his dormitory, looting unattended vehicles in the university's parking structures, and stealing random items like propane tanks and satellite dishes from homes in the nearby beach neighborhoods. In fact, over the course of our interviews with him, LaCoste would frequently comment on the rush that he received from brazenly breaking the law. Interestingly, in an interview with a university housing official conducted a few weeks after our first interview with LaCoste, it was revealed to us that LaCoste was the primary suspect in a number of com-

(continues)

Dealer Bio: continued

puter and other electronics thefts in his dormitory, the same types of thefts he bragged about during his exchanges with us. However, the housing official informed us that university higher-ups were reluctant to move forward with any formal allegations against LaCoste until they had concrete proof of his direct involvement in the burglaries and thefts. In no uncertain terms, it was conveyed to us that senior administrators at the university would rather let LaCoste flame out in other ways than face the potential ire of his father and "the dream team," his father's crew of lawyers. Further, the hope was that while LaCoste was still enrolled at the university his father's rather deep pockets could be tapped for financial contributions.

Perhaps, for these precise reasons, he was not one of our network's most enduring dealers and his Southern California escapade as a drug dealer lasted for less than a year. It seems that he spent too much time honing his skills as a hustler in the relatively insulated, affluent, private college world and not as a student. After his freshman year, LaCoste was academically disqualified from our network's hub university and returned to the Midwest. Associates of LaCoste's later informed us that he had, once again, run afoul of the law and was facing another set of felony criminal charges.

The specter of symbolic capital is once again raised as apparently LaCoste's socioeconomic status and family prestige afforded him a higher level of protection from formal scrutiny than the already-high threshold afforded all of the university's students. In fact, during an interview about campus drug activities, one university administrator cited LaCoste as an example of the tenuousness of policing students suspected of being involved in drug crime. Saying, "He must have some very influential parents," this particular official noted that university higher-ups were "proceeding with caution" in the investigation of LaCoste's suspected criminal activities. While momentarily breaking from arranging drug deals via telephone from his dorm room, LaCoste's sense of unassailability was strikingly evident.

LaCoste: I won't get caught though. There's nowhere to get caught. [And even if he did get caught], I got really good lawyers . . . See, I got these lawyers that are really good. Like real good, like the "dream team" and shit [laughs]. And, I don't know, catch me . . . if you can.

Are you afraid of the campus police?

LaCoste: What [are the campus police] going to do, take my weed away? Ah shit, then take my weed. Take all of it . . . First of all, I'm probably not going to get caught, but what, you get kicked out of school or go to jail for like ten years? I mean, either way, neither one's gonna happen.

While, on the one hand, LaCoste's bravado and the kid gloves with which his drug and other illegal activities were handled might seem difficult to comprehend, it is important to understand them in the context of a tuition-dependent university located in a major US city that markets itself to its potential student-clients and their families as a place of safety in the broadest terms. In this light, a major drug bust is bad for business in two significant ways. First, in a competitive climate where reputation is everything, drug arrests and publicly acknowledging the existence of an on-campus flourishing drug market clearly would not do much for short-term new student recruitment. Further, if students like LaCoste who come from well-to-do families were treated by university officials like garden variety corner boys, any endowment growth or other capital development plans specific to their families would most certainly be dashed. Therefore, the prudent approach, as dictated from on-high, is to handle cases like LaCoste's as cautiously as possible. Interestingly, this waiting game on the part of the administration paid dividends when LaCoste was academically disqualified from the university and forced to move back home to the Midwest. While the university was unable to mine his father for donations, at least university officials no longer had to concern themselves with any damage to the school's reputation by being forced to act on LaCoste's criminality.

Returning briefly to the notion expressed by LaCoste that the thrill of the hunt is perhaps more satisfying than the spoils themselves, Katz reinforced the centrality of nonmaterial motivations for criminal and deviant behavior like that we observed when he noted, "getting away with something in celebratory style is more important than keeping anything . . . in particular."[11] Clearly, LaCoste's flamboyant arrogance and seemingly calculated disregard for negative consequences speaks to these sneaky thrills derived from drug dealing.

While this air of invincibility was not universally embraced by all dealers in our sample, many were motivated by the sneaky thrill of the game; apparently mimicking the renegade, thuggish images that are commonplace in popular culture, politics, and mainstream media's depictions of drug dealers. For our dealers, it apparently was desirable and socially beneficial to appear tough and for them to be able to, at least intermittently, embrace the trappings of gangstaism.

As is often the case nationwide, many Southern California college campuses are located in or adjacent to neighborhoods where bona fide "thug life" is quite pervasive. Merely blocks away from LaCoste's dorm room, visible posturing and posing as a gangsta would likely result in adverse consequences and bring an uncharacteristic element of violence to the network's dealing activities. Reminiscent of Susan Faludi's notion of "ornamental culture,"[12] several of our network's dealers seemed to be driven by the relative fame drug dealing bestowed upon them as the tall Pygmy, or the proverbial big fish in a small pond. It seemed that this subset of affluent drug dealers was rather content to embrace the image and notoriety derived from their status as pseudo-gangstas, a status that proved situationally convenient, likely to generate peer approval and respect, and at times could be exhilarating. Even if limited in scope, the "thug life" aspect of this motivating factor was perhaps best captured by Houston-based rapper Scarface's lyrical proclamation, "Damn, it feels good to be a gangsta."

Motive #6: Warding off the Emasculating Force of Privilege

In "A New Vision of Masculinity," Cooper Thompson writes, "Traditional definitions of masculinity include attributes such as independence, pride, resiliency, self-control, and physical strength. This is precisely the image of the Marlboro man and, to some extent, these are desirable attributes for boys and girls."[13]

The expectations posed by the iconic US cowboy, an image conveying the ultimate rugged individualist, resonate in US culture. Not surprisingly, we also found that this image served as a motivating force within the network's group of affluent drug dealers. Dovetailing with sneaky thrills, embracing pseudo gangstaism and the pursuit of status, our network's dealers are also apparently motivated by a desire for independence. Like most college students, these affluent drug dealers were in a transitional phase in their lives. While they are not under the immediate supervision of their parents, most are still directly dependent on their parents for tuition, room, board, and other expenses. On elite college campuses, with the necessities of life readily provided, they are far from the anti-authoritarian, independent US cowboy of cultural lore. Thus, drug dealing also becomes a mechanism to embrace traditional expectations of masculinity and to ward off the emasculating force of privilege.

By flamboyantly embracing the trappings of gangstaism and the often-displayed hyper-masculinity accompanying the role, our network's upper-middle-class male hustlers could use their drug-dealing activity as a means to publicly reject the perception of them as spoiled or coddled kids. Further, risk-taking behavior (although the risks were somewhat artificial) and bucking against the status quo and behavioral expectations imposed upon them helped these dealers carve out some degree of autonomy despite their lifestyle of dependence. In describing this connection between voluntary risk-taking behavior, resistance, and identity construction, Stephen Lyng wrote "Criminal edgework represents a form of escape and resistance to the prevailing structures of political and economic power."[14] These affluent drug dealers may be "crowding the edge" precisely because it helps create a sense of individual identity that is distinct from the status of their parents. This criminal edgework may also allow these dealers to construct an identity of masculinity or ruggedness in what otherwise might be perceived as a pampered or emasculating existence. Indeed, visible and voluntary risk taking may serve the function of resisting the emasculating forces that stem from the wealth, privilege, and ascribed upper-class status that trickle down from their families. Economic self-sufficiency, or at least the demonstrated ability to make your own money, especially via the underground economy, is alluring to our network's male dealers precisely because it evokes the masculine, independent, anti-authoritarian, rugged individualism of the Marlboro Man. Recall Ashcan's statements regarding his motivation to become a drug dealer—for beer money and to avoid having to ask his parents to underwrite the cost of his parking tickets. Later in the interview, he speculates about his future as a drug dealer. Quite obviously, drug dealing facilitated his independence from his parents.

AsHCAN: Well, once I get into law school [which he ultimately did], then I might do it [sell drugs] if I need some money or something. 'Cause they do not let you work your first year of law school. So I might have to, even though my parents will probably give me money. I just don't like asking my parents for a lot of money.

While less explicit than some of the other motivations that we uncovered and outlined, we inferred that the ornamental and financial independence, or feelings thereof, produced by dealing drugs helped these dealers ward off the emasculating force of privilege.

Combinations and Permutations

As we noted at the beginning of this chapter, we do not believe that these six motivations that propelled "good kids" into drugs are mutually exclusive. On the contrary, while one or a handful of motivations might be prominent, we conclude there is no magic bullet or single dynamic that comprehensively captured why our network's dealers entered the illicit drug game. An afternoon conversation with Brice exemplified the ways these motivations intertwined in different combinations and permutations, enticing and then subsequently rewarding the dealers for their criminal behavior. Conspicuously absent in Brice's comments was any allusion to the ego gratification and pursuit of status that seemed to be powerful driving forces for some of our other dealers. Rather, it seems that he largely was motivated to become a drug dealer to underwrite the costs of his own indulgence in marijuana use, to underwrite other entertainment expenses, and by the spirit of capitalism.

Brice: I don't know if anyone chose it as a career path you know. I mean, I mean it was something to do when you are young and allowed for a . . . for a . . . fun lifestyle. It allowed for . . . I would just say the lifestyle more or less ya' know . . . Um . . . And ya know, we were all in school or just out of school and primarily I mean I don't think anyone did that as their career path. I just think it was something that they were doing at that time.

Got it. Looking back on it, why do you think most people, including yourself, started selling drugs?

BRICE: The original reason I did is simply because of the economics of it. Buy more at a [wholesale] price. And so I never could justify myself buying that much for myself, so I probably wouldn't have like the willpower or whatever . . . to make whatever last however long it was supposed to last until I would buy more. So what I would try to do is . . . when I was originally starting was try to sell ya know enough to either pay for it . . . or get my stuff at a . . . price.

What did you spend most of your profits on, looking back?

BRICE: Well I would say the vast majority went right back in the pot. Ya know that vast majority. At a time it was profitable enough to make income off of it. Where I could say . . . umm . . . pay credit card bills, stuff like that. Monthly house bills, rent check, stuff like that. Well I would say ultimately, like life long term, because of everything that happened. Everything I ever made went right back into it.

These six interconnected motivations enticing affluent college students into the underground economy effectively debunk some prevailing popular culture and academic assumptions about deviant behavior. While financial motivations were significant within this population, it was not necessity that pushed these affluent young men and women into drug dealing. If fact, these dealers seemingly had the skill sets, social positioning, networking advantages, education, and desire to thrive in the larger legitimate economy. Their financial motivation was more about indulgence than necessity, more about convenience than desperation. This is a striking finding given one of the prevailing assumptions about the origins of criminal behavior and the policing of drug crime, specifically, that acquisitive crimes are the byproduct of social-structural disadvantage and exclusion from the mainstream, legitimate economy. Moreover, the combination of material and identity-based motivations within this population further complicate rational-choice theories of crime and the accompanying deterrence-based models for criminal justice policy. Within this group, material rewards were seemingly no more important than the ability to appear as masculine, tough gangstas, at least when these appearances were deemed socially desirable and beneficial. Of course, when these traits were not advantageous, our network's dealers could conveniently morph back into their "good kid" personas without consequence. It seems that in certain circumstances privilege and luxury do not dissuade criminality, but rather encourage it. The interconnectedness of these six motivations suggests that for some the Katzian "seductions of crime" are too tasty to resist.

Notes

1. Merton, "Social Structure and Anomie."

2. Van Nostrand and Tewksbury, "The Motives and Mechanics of Operating an Illegal Drug Enterprise," p. 58.

3. Tewksbury and Mustaine, "Lifestyles of the Wheelers and Dealers."

4. Little Hoover Commission, p. 1.

5. LaCoste was prescribed pharmaceutical drugs after being diagnosed with ADHD. He routinely sold these prescription drugs for profit, along with the other drugs within the purview of his drug-dealing business. He represents a crossover between the market for traditional illicit drugs and the emerging market for pharmaceutically derived drugs described in other chapters.

6. Adler, "Wheeling and Dealing," p. 151.

7. Blackman, *Chilling Out.* See also Currie, "Crime and Punishment in America."

8. Ibid., p. 52.

9. Katz, *Seductions of Crime,* p. 52.

10. Katz, *Seductions of Crime.*

11. Ibid., p. 52.

12. Faludi, *Stiffed.*

13. Thompson, "A New Vision of Masculinity," p. 631.

14. Lyng, "Crime, Edgework and Corporeal Transaction," p. 359.

4

The Emerging Market:
Peddling Prescription Drugs

KYLE (NINETEEN-YEAR-OLD COMMUNICATION MAJOR): Prescriptions
allow you to take pills legally to get wasted, which is kinda unique.
And it's easier getting prescriptions because all you need to do is
see the doctor you wanna see. And it also works being so close to
Tijuana. You don't gotta see the doctor for that.

Academic research literature often reads like a classic detective story
in the sense that, in the end and in most cases, the hero gets his or her
man or woman. In this particular metaphor, the hero is the researcher
and more often than not and with only minor surprises the research
literature suggests that scholars find what they set out to look for. To
be sure, much of the literature indicates some relatively insignificant
unexpected turns along the way. But, at the end of the day, the hero
prevails as the research narrative tends to validate the speculation that
initially launched the project.

Over the more than five years that we spent exploring our particular
affluent college drug-dealing market, specializing in the trafficking of
marijuana and cocaine, our past experiences and preliminary information on college drug dealers certainly did lead to many anticipated outcomes, particularly with respect to trafficking in marijuana. However, as
we delved deeper into the world of collegiate drug hustlers, we inadvertently stumbled onto some rather important discoveries that rendered
our investigations more like the bumblings of Inspector Jacques
Clouseau than the precision-like plodding of Columbo. Perhaps the
clearest example of this came when we unintentionally happened upon a

robust market centered on legally manufactured but illicitly used and distributed prescription drugs.

While we were certainly no strangers to the unauthorized (and therefore illegal) use of pharmaceuticals, particularly among the college student set, the extent to which these students were abusing these drugs and how they obtained them caught us a bit off guard. As an informant from the primary campus on which this research was set said rather nonchalantly of one of the many heavily abused prescription drugs among members in our network, "Oh yeah. Everyone uses it." As another informant said of the same drug, "Everyone in my surrounding [on campus], it seems like everyone has something to do or is doing something with [it]." Once we began to get a sense of the rather broad scope of prescription-drug abuse in our network, we went on to make several preliminary assumptions about the nature of the pharmaceutical trade and the functioning of the underground prescription-drug market. Unlike the seemingly prophetic discoveries of many of our scholarly brethren, several of these initial suppositions proved incorrect.

Two of the more significant erroneous assumptions we made about the prescription-drug market were related to the method of trafficking and distribution in illegal medications and the means by which the drugs were originally procured by our student users and dealers after these drugs left their legitimate pharmaceutical production plants. As far as trafficking and distribution were concerned, we initially assumed that the market that facilitated trafficking in these particular drugs would be roughly parallel to the marijuana and cocaine markets we had already uncovered. Specifically, we thought that the bulk of the drugs would be purchased on the black market; the supply would be controlled by a few key primary dealers; the motivation for sales would mainly revolve around some material- or ego-gratifying purpose; the rationales used to neutralize both the use and distribution of illegal pharmaceuticals would be somewhat consistent with those we found among our street user and dealer populations; and risk management strategies would be minimal. While we were not entirely off the mark on all counts, only this final assumption about pathetic risk minimization strategies proved nearly identical to the characteristics of the primary market centered on marijuana and cocaine.

With regard to the secondary sources of the illegal pharmaceuticals (understanding that virtually all prescription drugs on both the licit and illicit markets have in common pharmaceutical companies as their primary or original source), we presumed that the bulk of these drugs would be purchased in large quantities from sources in Mexico and illegally brought back into California for resale. As we discuss later in this chapter, while not entirely incorrect, we overestimated the extent to which our users and dealers were obtaining their drugs from south of the border. More importantly, we similarly underestimated the role that "legitimate" sources played in supplying drugs for illegitimate distribution and personal use.

What follows is an overview of what we identify as our networks' secondary drug market, a robust market characterized by the illicit sales and use of prescription drugs and marked by an accompanying culture accepting illicit prescription-drug abuse by relatively affluent college students. In describing this secondary market, we examine the nationwide phenomenon of pharmaceutical abuse. Additionally, we draw attention to the scope of the illicit prescription-drug market among the students in our network, what drugs they commonly used, and how they used them. We also explore the channels through which our users and dealers initially obtained pharmaceuticals ultimately headed for illicit distribution, the rationales they provided for abusing and dealing in prescription drugs, and finally the perception of risk associated with behaviors they knew to be unlawful. We conclude this chapter by offering some brief speculations as to why, in spite of the very clear public health implications presented by increasing prescription-drug use among college-aged people, the lenses of law enforcement and public policy seem stubbornly trained on traditional illicit drug distribution and use.

Pill-A-Palooza: What's Popping Among the Affluent College Set

According to the US Department of Health and Human Services, an estimated 20 million Americans aged twelve or older were current illicit drug users in 2007.[1] This translates into roughly 8 percent of the US population aged twelve or older who used marijuana, cocaine, crack, heroin, hallucinogens, inhalants, or prescription-type psychotherapeutics nonmedically within one month prior to the survey interview. Of these 20 million drug users, more than one-third

(34.7 percent) were prescription-drug abusers, making nonmedical prescription-drug abuse second only to marijuana as the most significant category of illicit drug use in the United States. By way of comparison, during the same year, there were only 2.1 million current cocaine users and 1 million users of hallucinogens. Perhaps most compelling is the fact that since 2004 the illicit drug-use category with the largest number of "recent initiates," the government's way of saying first-time users, was the nonmedical use of prescription pain relievers. In contrast to the focus of virtually every antidrug campaign since the war on drugs began, it seems that in the new millennium the nonmedical use of pharmaceuticals has become the true "gateway" to US illicit drug use.

Over the course of more than twenty-five interviews with both prescription-drug users and dealers who carried on their illicit activity in the same physical setting as the marijuana and cocaine dealers operating in our principal drug market, we discovered several primary categories of prescription drugs in high demand among the members of our college drug network. Interestingly, unlike our network's street-drug users who tended to exclusively deal and use one primary illicit drug, there did not appear to be pronounced drug exclusivity among our prescription-drug users. Among this user group, we found that some tended to illicitly use a primary drug, but more tended to use a variety of prescription drugs for particular social or practical reasons. For example, the "normal" prescription-drug abuser in our sample might illegally use an amphetamine-type drug like Adderall as a study aid or pre-party energizer and later on that same day use a central nervous system (CNS) depressant like Valium to "come down" and induce sleep.

The specific prescription-type drugs most commonly abused and trafficked in among the people we observed and interviewed fell into three general pharmaceutical categories. The most popular drugs of all were stimulants prescribed to treat attention-deficit hyperactivity disorder (ADHD) and included one of two brand-name drugs in particular: Ritalin and Adderall. Opioids made up the second prescription-drug category with substantial abuse potential among our subjects and informants. These individuals frequently reported the illicit use and sale of prescription opioids like OxyContin, Percocet, and Vicodin, drugs ostensibly manufactured and prescribed to treat moderate to severe pain but highly prone to abuse for the euphoria and sense of calm they induce. The final category of regularly abused and distributed drugs among our network was CNS depressants and tranquilizers like Valium, Xanax, and Librium. Medical uses of these drugs include the treatment of anxiety, sleep disorders, and stress.

Of all drugs across these three categories, by far and away, Adderall was king; it was the drug most commonly abused by our users and the pharmaceutical most frequently sold by our dealers. As Chase, a twenty-year-old communication major, bluntly replied when asked his "expert" opinion on what the most popular prescription drugs were among the student drug-using population in our network, "Adderall, for sure." In its rate of abuse and abundant black market availability, Adderall was our network's prescription-drug equivalent to marijuana. And, as we discuss later in this chapter, Adderall also proved to be the easiest drug to obtain fraudulently from legal distribution sources. While nearly 75 percent of all illicit prescription-drug users primarily abuse pain-relieving opioids, stimulant abuse among our dealers and users was not surprising given the particular reasons many college students abuse prescription-drugs, including the "need" to cram for exams, an extra boost to get pumped up for a night of partying, or for good old fashioned drug-induced fun. Brad, a twenty-two-year-old business major, minor pharmaceutical dealer, and heavy prescription-drug abuser captured this last aspect of stimulant and other prescription-drug abuse well.

BRAD: Well, I never really thought when I was younger that I'd ever be into popping pills, but everyone was into it. And obviously I've tried them and I've enjoyed it and I still enjoy it. It's just a really relaxing experience and it enhances your time when you're drinking too so . . . it's just a good time. [I definitely don't take the drugs] to get rid of pain, although yes with this sore back every once in awhile I'll use that as an excuse to take them, but it's for the entertainment.

These high levels of stimulant abuse among college students also reflect the increased medicalization of ADHD, a disorder that for most of its recognized existence was understood to be specific to youthful populations. In the early 1990s, for a variety of social, proprietary, and clinical reasons, the medical boundaries of ADHD were expanded to include adults. The obvious drug-use consequences of this extended medical jurisdiction were summarized well by researchers P. Conrad and D. Potter who contend, "By redefining ADHD as a lifelong disorder, the potential exists for keeping children and adults on medication indefinitely."[2] Not to be overlooked, the further medicalization of ADHD stood to provide a substantial profits boost to the pharmaceutical companies who manufactured ADHD drugs; at least one of these companies reportedly reaped at least 15 percent of its annual gross revenues from the existing juvenile ADHD drug market.[3] Not coincidentally, these same companies were also actively involved in carrying the diagnosis of ADHD over into adult populations.

A related yet far less frequently discussed variable in the prevalence rates of adult ADHD and the subsequent availability of Adderall on college campuses is the nexus between socioeconomic status, race, and access to mental health care. Indeed, a good bit of evidence suggests that a diagnosis of either juvenile or adult ADHD depends largely on these variables. For example, recent national data indicate that nearly 75 percent of adults diagnosed with ADHD were white. Moreover, as Ronald Kessler, a professor of healthcare policy at Harvard Medical School said, "ADHD is now a boutique diagnosis for middle-class people."[4] Further, it is safe to say that ADHD has become somewhat a luxury disease for many people who merely lack organization in their lives but can afford to have their underperformance medicalized without the stigma attached to many other disabilities. Again, in the words of Conrad and Potter, "Clearly a diagnosis of adult ADHD carries with it a certain currency in the public sphere . . . Not only are individuals with ADHD the potential beneficiaries of a 'medical excuse' for their life problems, but they may be eligible for specific benefits under the Americans with Disabilities Act."[5] But, more central to drug use and distribution patterns among the members of our college prescription-drug network, a diagnosis of ADHD, even a spurious one, grants the individual legal access to powerful pharmaceuticals.

None of this discussion of overmedicalization is meant to suggest that ADHD is not a legitimate disorder; the medical community has recognized the validity of attention deficit and its antecedents for decades, clinically defining it as a disorder in the mid-twentieth century. However, due to the fact that the diagnosis of ADHD remains in large part a doctor's subjective interpretation, the standards for diagnosis are clearly looser than those for other ailments and disorders. In the end, the pharmaceutical gatekeeper can somewhat easily be gamed and access to prescription strength stimulants can be gained with relative ease.

To Snort or Not to Snort:
The Question of Ingestion

While most illicit users of prescription drugs in our study ingested their wares in a more conventional physician-recommended oral fashion, the heavier more hardcore users would crush the prescription pills into powder form and snort the drug in a fashion similar to that preferred by traditional cocaine users. In seems that snorting the drugs offered a quicker and more intense high than taking the drug in pill form. For example, Giovanni, a small-time dealer and heavy user of OxyContin with a more than one-hundred-dollar-per-week habit, stated that he no longer bothered swallowing his illegally obtained pills because the effects were not as intense as when he first began taking the prescription opioid. Instead, in a near-classic case of chasing the dragon,[6] he exclusively crushed up the pills and snorted them in an attempt to obtain a more immediate, higher high. Fortunately, if such a thing could be said of illicit pharmaceutical use by college students, none of the people we spoke with had graduated to intravenously injecting their drugs.

Another common drug-use tactic reported by members in our network was the poly-drug "cocktail" method in which two prescription-drugs with competing physiological effects would be taken simultaneously in order to create a unique interaction effect and stronger rush than that obtained by taking one of the drugs on their own. Pursuing this sort of rush is similar to the cocaine and heroin "speedball"[7] that dates back in the United States to at least 1900 but more contemporarily popularized by addicted US soldiers returning from Vietnam. Several of our network's prescription-drug abusers would, for example, combine an amphetamine-type of drug with a CNS depressant in order to trigger an intense new high or, alternatively, a mild hallucinogenic effect. More commonly, however, they would use one prescription drug to counter the effects of the other. For example, quite a few of our heavy Adderall users reported taking doses of Xanax to "come down" from the effects of the amphetamines.

Another variation of the cocktail that we came across involved combining a prescription drug with another nonprescription drug like alcohol or marijuana in order to intensify the "buzz" typically felt by ingesting either substance on its own. Similar to the "luding out" phenomenon of the 1970s, our student users would commonly mix drugs like prescription sleeping pills with alcohol to achieve an intense drunken, sleepy high. Perhaps the most frequently reported example of this alternative cocktail phenomenon involved the deliberate mixture of an opioid, such as Vicodin, with a nonprescription CNS depressant like alcohol. The combination of these two multiplies the effects of the Vicodin, intensifying the sense of euphoria without needing to increase the dose of the drug. Oftentimes, if our users did not have ready access to an opioid, they would seek a similar sensation in the form of a "poor man's cocktail" with the most popular combination being vodka and the stimulant-beverage Red Bull.

Naturally, any variety of this cocktail approach comes with potentially grim health risks. Because of the stress it places on the liver, mixing alcohol with Vicodin, for example, can have serious life-threatening complications. The severe negative effects of mixing non-complimentary prescription drugs can be even more instantaneous. In 2007, celebrity Anna Nicole Smith died from a lethal combination of prescription drugs, the same fate suffered by her son Daniel only six months prior. In early 2008, Heath Ledger, an actor poised for super-stardom and most famous for his roles in the Oscar-winning film *Brokeback Mountain* and the posthumously released blockbuster *The Dark Knight,* was found dead in his New York City apartment. An autopsy performed by the medical examiner of New York identified the cause of death as "acute intoxication by the combined effects" of prescription medications including OxyContin, Vicodin, Valium, Restoril (a prescription sleep aid), and Xanax. The Smiths' and Ledger's cases are not anomalistic and are certainly not limited to celebrity hospital blotters. In 2006 alone, over 740,000 people visited US emergency rooms for the treatment of negative effects attributable to the nonmedical use of prescription or over-the-counter drugs. While unintentional drug poisonings have been increasing steadily since the 1970s, this 2006 figure represented an increase of more than 140,000 from the year prior.[8] And the majority of these visits (54 percent) were brought on by the nonmedical use of multiple drugs.

In 2004, for the first time in US history, unintentional deaths attributable to prescription opioids like OxyContin numbered more than the total deaths involving both heroin and cocaine. During congressional 2007 testimony on unintentional drug poisoning deaths, epidemiologist Leonard Paulozzi elaborated on these dramatic increases in prescription-drug fatalities and pinpointed the root cause of the phenomenon:

> The mortality rates from [unintentional] drug poisoning (not including alcohol) have risen steadily since the early 1970s. Over the past ten years they have reached historic highs. Rates are currently more than twice what they were during the peak years of crack cocaine mortality in the early 1990s, and 4 to 5 times higher than the rates during the year of heroin mortality peak in 1975 . . . Mortality statistics suggest that these deaths are largely due to the misuse and abuse of prescription drugs.[9]

Awareness of health risks as they relate to the young adult members of our network and their choice to continue with prescription-drug abuse and sales is more comprehensively discussed later in this chapter. However, suffice it to say that several of the people we spoke with were personally aware of the dangers associated with illicit prescription-drug use, drug mixing in particular. Herman, a nineteen-year-old business major who only admitted to using prescription stimulant drugs "for studying," but who we learned through an informant was much more experienced in illicit pharmaceutical use than he let on, discussed a scary moment that he had with a drug cocktail. "One time I took Ritalin and I smoked some weed a couple of hours later and my heart started beating really quickly and I got nervous. I blacked out on the floor. It was one of the most scariest experiences I've had."

Herman, like all of our other users and dealers, was well aware of the dangers associated with prescription-drug use and drug cocktails. In his case, he was personally aware. However, like everyone else that we spoke with who was involved in the network's prescription-drug trade, this awareness did not deter Herman from continuing his nonmedical use of pharmaceuticals, begging the question: what draws relatively affluent college students, young adults with much to lose and little to gain, to put their futures and lives at risk by illegally using prescription drugs?

Why College Kids Use Prescription Drugs

While a few of the prescription-drug users with whom we came into contact had legitimate medical reasons for which they were prescribed their drug of choice, the vast majority of the student users in our network illicitly used pharmaceuticals for reasons entirely unrelated to any medical condition. Further, we found that those who legally possessed prescription drugs for therapeutic purposes tended to either use their prescriptions in ways that were inconsistent with the ailment for which they were prescribed or were more inclined to distribute them to their friends and associates, either gratis or for small profits. In talking with and observing the students who operated within our study's drug-trafficking ring, we came across several plausible reasons for the high levels of overall drug abuse among the affluent college set. The most obvious of these was, as the quote that opens this chapter suggests, feeding the desire to get "wasted." But other often heard rationales included abusing prescription drugs as a mechanism to cope with stress, to regulate otherwise normal physiology and emotions, to fit in with "desirable" peer networks, as part of a larger agenda of post-adolescent rebellion, and addiction. We also encountered explanations for the high rates of drug abuse and risk-taking behaviors that were more specific but not entirely exclusive to prescription drugs. The most significant of this subset of rationales was the perceived need to use prescription drugs as a study aid. What follows in this section is a discussion of some of the more prominent explanations for pharmaceutical abuse among our collegiate network's users and dealers.

Because I Got High

In simple terms, college students use prescription and street drugs because they are people, and people, particularly those in younger age groups, seem to be in perpetual search for different ways to get high and enhance or alter their day-to-day lives. As twenty-year-old Dirk explained his affinity for prescription drugs, "It's more relaxing or it's more fun to go to the movies and take a hydrocodone than it is to just go to the movies with a friend. It adds to the particular act." Or, in the oddly rational words of Chase, a twenty-year-old student-athlete majoring in communication and a relatively hearty user of illicit pharmaceuticals, taking Adderall and other prescription drugs allows you to get "pretty buzzed without having to drink as much."

While nearly cliché in drug literature, the known history of recreational mind- and mood-altering drug use extends at least as far back as 5000 BC when the Sumerians ingested opium to induce "joy." Records of the production of alcohol date back to 3500 BC, and, shortly thereafter, people began using marijuana for ritualistic and medicinal purposes. Cocaine can perhaps be viewed as the baby of the bunch; it was not until 1860 that German chemist Albert Nieman set the stage for recreational cocaine use by successfully isolating the essential alkaloids in dried coca that make possible the transformation of a common South American plant into a popular and abuse-prone white powder.[10] Ironically, in spite of its then unknown potential for abuse and dependency, one of the originally touted uses of cocaine was as a treatment for morphine addiction. While cocaine is relatively new, for thousands of years prior to Nieman's discovery, indigenous South American Indians used the raw coca leaf as a stimulant and appetite suppressant, as well as for other spiritual and medicinal purposes. Coca was so central to many pre-Columbian Indian civilizations that groups like the Incas even regarded coca as "the divine plant."

Many of the constituent components of prescription drugs are identical to commonly used street drugs. In fact, as was seen with the early "medicinal" uses of cocaine, many contemporary illicit street and prescription drugs were truly one and the same with pharmaceutical stalwarts like Merck and Parke-Davis legally producing hundreds of thousands of pounds of refined cocaine bound for the legitimate US pharmaceutical market by the late nineteenth century.[11] It was not until 1914, in what was effectively a legislative end run, that the legal production and distribution of cocaine was brought to a halt by the Harrison Act.[12] The close relationship between street and prescription drugs is also commonly recognized within illicit drug-using subcultures, as evidenced by pharmaceutical nicknames that reference their street-drug counterparts. For example, as homage to the drug whose sensation it most closely mimics and its widespread abuse in rural Appalachia, OxyContin has become well known by its moniker "hillbilly heroin." Other examples of this naming process include "poor man's coke" or, more simply, "speed" for Adderall. And for Ketamine, an animal tranquilizer turned popular club drug that separates perception from sensation, "special la coke" is a commonly used street name referring to the common white powder's snort-able form it takes after being cooked down from a liquid. Beyond these similarities, as we discussed in the previous section, prescription drugs are also often ingested in ways that mimic their street-drug counterparts.

While drug distribution of all sorts of drugs has been a mainstay of the medical and quasi-medical communities for centuries, the use and abuse of what we know today as prescription drugs has a much briefer history that really only took form in the middle decades of the twentieth century. It was during this period that the lines between pharmaceuticals and the practice of medicine began blurring as an active research pipeline led to the consolidation of the pharmaceutical industry and the literal cranking out of new and efficacious prescription drugs. Over a period of just twenty years, between 1939 and 1959, annual sales of pharmaceuticals increased from $300 million to $2.3 billion.[13] By the late 1960s, it was clear that Americans had developed an insatiable hunger for prescription drugs and "big pharma" was gearing up for famine relief. Accordingly, in 2007 alone, the world's top five pharmaceutical companies hauled in approximately $235 billion in total revenues and, in that same year, three of the fifty most profitable companies in the world were pharmaceutical giants.[14]

It is abundantly clear, then, that misuse of prescription drugs is already a key contributor to the overall problem of drug abuse in the United States. It is also quite clear that the pharmaceutical industry, the primary producer of both licit and illicitly consumed prescription drugs, plays no small role in fueling the crisis. As has been the case with drugs for thousands of years, many young people abuse prescription drugs, quite simply, to just get high. As Jimmy summarized, "If you want to feel more energetic, you can take Adderall to feel more energetic. If you want to relax a little more, you can take a Valium and you can relax if you feel uptight. It fixes whatever feeling you don't like at that particular time."

Cramming and the Pressures of College

Beyond just getting high, the "need" to take stimulants to complete academic assignments or to aid in eleventh-hour exam preparation was the most often given reason for abusing prescription drugs. As one of our network's prescription-drug dealers said when asked what the most popular pharmaceuticals were among the affluent college set, "You have to throw in Adderall because kids are really keen on it for studying and they actually rely on it for cramming." As another said, "Adderall has a really high effect for kids who are trying to focus and do well especially around finals time."

Indeed, the nonmedical use of prescription drugs among today's students, particularly those that report illegally using these drugs either to relax from the stresses of school or as a study aid, is consistent with the cultural cues they are receiving from multiple sources. Among the most powerful of these sources are the medical industry, which tells them that there is a cure for what ails them; the pharmaceutical industry, which tells them through massive advertising that they *have the cure* for what ails them; and the academic industry, which defines what ails them by consistently telling students that they are busier and under more pressure to succeed than any previous generation's college students.

In fact, there is no credible evidence to support the notion that today's college students have any more responsibility on their plate than their predecessors. Nonetheless, many of the students we interviewed used these cultural signals as a justification for their prescription-drug abuse. Take, for example, the quite typical and rote justification for pharmaceutical abuse offered by Emilio, a twenty-year-old international relations major attempting to wean himself from a self-described dependency on prescription drugs. "I had two Adderall last night, but that was only because I had to stay up all night to write three and a half papers and study for this huge test that I had to memorize like something like fifty note cards that were filled." In contemporary college culture, longstanding student tendencies like procrastination and poor preparation brought on by partying and lack of organization have been overshadowed by the myth of increased pressure placed upon today's students. Not only has this myth become a primary justification offered by students in support of prescription-drug abuse, the demand for these drugs has directly led to a mammoth black market economy dealing in legally manufactured but illegally distributed pharmaceuticals.

Addiction

Regardless of the volume of prescription drugs they took or how often they illicitly used pharmaceuticals, most members of our network did not view themselves as having drug-dependency issues. Similarly, they also tended not to view the quantities of prescription drugs that they ingested on a daily basis as substantial, even if their levels of use were toward the high end of the prescription-drug consumption spectrum. Twenty-one-year-old Ilene's characterization of her drug use was typical of this tendency to downplay the significance of pharmaceutical abuse by members of our network, "I don't take massive quantities, no more than probably taking five or six Vicodins a day or like ten Valiums probably a day."

Some of our users, like Freddie, admitted to a physical or psychological dependency on prescription drugs. When asked about his use of Vicodin, prescribed him to treat chronic back pain, the twenty-two-year-old business major said, "Sometimes you know I just go a little overboard, so my girlfriend holds on to them for me and she'll give it to me when my back hurts. She knows for sure." Still, most of our users were less willing to acknowledge or even consider the possibility that they had developed an addiction to prescription drugs, and many described textbook signs of dependency. For example, we asked Chase, the twenty-year-old communication major, if he had experienced any physical or psychological effects as a result of his illicit prescription-drug use. He somewhat defensively replied, "The Adderall affects me in positive ways."

Dirk, a twenty-year-old sociology major, when asked the same question as Chase similarly responded in a way indicating, at minimum, a psychological dependency on prescription drugs. He said, "Yes definitely. Adderall has definitely helped me to focus more and I feel actually like it's more of a confidence boost when I do my work." In his very next statement, Dirk suggested what could be a physiological addiction to hydrocodone, a drug that "brings you down and messes with your emotions" but one that he nevertheless continued to take illicitly on a regular basis.

Perhaps Emilio's self-deceiving thoughts on his drug use best capture the dependency and denial expressed by many of our network's prescription-drug abusers:

EMILIO: Well, with the harder ones you feel bad and that's why you keep doing them again. I wasn't really addicted. It was one of those things that was me just feeling like shit and, uh, I just needed something to make myself feel better and like numb the pain and, uh,

I guess like weed and stuff like that just didn't do it for me anymore so, uh, I didn't really get addicted to any of 'em per se you know like I just tried a whole bunch different stuff.

Failure to See the Harm in Prescription-Drug Abuse

The health and law enforcement risks associated with prescription-drug abuse by college students are explored later in this chapter. However, in the context of explaining why affluent college students choose to illegally use prescription drugs, it is important to note that many of them simply do not view pharmaceutical abuse in the same light that they do traditional street-drug use. We speculate that this denial of harm is related to growing up in a culture and society that has normalized prescription-drug use in spite of the potency, addictiveness, and dangerousness associated with these drugs. Our students were reared in the tradition of "just say no," but this popular antidrug slogan was only meant to encompass those drugs that came from the dark man in the hoodie, not the gentleman in the white lab coat. We further theorize that, in the affluent homes in which most of our network's users and dealers were raised, unfettered access to physicians was normal, as was the physical presence of prescriptions sitting in the medicine cabinet. Finally, today's college students, regardless of affluence, have grown up in a media world in which the top ten drug companies alone spend over $15 billion per year convincing consumers that their product is right for them.[15]

Regardless of the reason for their prescription-drug use, none of the students we spoke with in our network saw much wrong with the illicit and nonmedical use or abuse of pharmaceuticals. The fact that a legitimate manufacturing source produces the prescription drugs they elect to abuse seemingly distracts these people from the reality that they are actively engaged in law-violating behavior and, more significantly, may be placing themselves in life-threatening situations by misusing prescription drugs. As DEA Deputy Assistant Administrator Joseph T. Rannazzisi testified before Congress in 2008, "Many feel that if a doctor can prescribe it, the drug can not be as harmful to your health when compared to what some might consider more conventional 'street' drugs such as heroin or cocaine.[16] Indeed, this misunderstanding and neutralization of prescription-drug abuse seemed customary among our pharmaceutical dealers and users. Most of the people with whom we spoke gave comments similar to these offered by Jimmy when asked how he felt about his counternormative behavior: "I don't feel particularly guilty about taking prescription drugs. I mean they're prescribed to a lot of people that take it everyday, for you know symptoms that I'm mildly feeling at the time, you know."

The Dormitory Drug Rep: A Brief Taxonomy of College Prescription-Drug Dealers

Prescription-drug dealers in our network were a much more diverse lot than the street-drug dealers we encountered over our years of study. By diverse, we are not referring to racial and ethnic diversity; with the exception of one person of Iranian descent, all of the prescription-drug dealers and users we interviewed were white and all came from relatively privileged backgrounds. But we did find that virtually anyone who had pharmaceuticals they did not intend to use, anyone willing to take the trip to nearby Mexico to illegally stock up on prescription drugs, or, as it turned out, those entrusted with keeping prescription drugs out of the wrong hands could potentially serve as de facto dope dealers. At the end of the day, anyone with access to a supply of in-demand prescription drugs might potentially share or sell their drugs for a relatively low price to friends and acquaintances. Interestingly, while these individuals regularly and routinely exchange drugs for money, in all cases and in direct contrast to our network's street-drug dealers, the peddlers of prescription drugs tended not to view themselves as dealers. Instead, for reasons explored a little later in this chapter, they tended to downplay the central role they occupied in a truly illicit drug economy.

We have identified four general categories of prescription-drug dealers supplying drugs in and around our college network. While we would have liked to rank them in terms of their relative contributions to the illicit prescription-drug trade, no single category of dealer seemed more prominent than another. Additionally, as summarized by twenty-one-year-old Ilene, we found that many of our network's users of illegal pharmaceuticals were not terribly discriminating or loyal to any particular supply source, so long as they got their drugs.

Dealer Bio: Diamond

Despite his position of importance within the network, Diamond did not exhibit the flair and egoism characteristic of some of the other drug dealers in this study. He was typically subdued and occasionally downright nice, even when in the midst of relatively significant transactions. Drug dealing seemed to be intertwined with his daily existence; friends would continually come by his house before or after going surfing, being out at local bars, or to place online bets on his computer. In fact, Diamond and several of his customers regularly combined a drug deal with placing online bets on sporting events. For Diamond, marijuana dealing was not sexy, it was routine. Immersed in the surrounding beach culture, personal freedom and drug experimentation seemed like cultural staples. On one occasion, Diamond's triple beam scale broke. As a testament to the ubiquitousness of drug dealing in the area, Diamond exited his apartment only to return moments later with a scale borrowed from a neighbor several doors down.

Diamond earned his moniker by virtue of being the highest-volume dealer in our study. He was selling between five and ten pounds of high-quality marijuana per week, at roughly $4,000 per pound and for slightly more if it was of particularly good quality. At the height of his operation, Diamond grossed between $80,000 and $160,000 per month in ill-gotten revenue with anywhere from $10,000 to $20,000 of these proceeds entering the ledger as profits. Brice and eventually Cecilia were among his regular clientele, routinely purchasing a pound or two of marijuana from Diamond every week. Diamond was in the business of selling to other dealers, who were typically purchasing a minimum of a quarter-pound of marijuana per visit, and he seemingly did not sell to individual marijuana users. Surprisingly, despite the magnitude of his illegal business, his foray in the drug-dealing game was as sloppy and haphazard as any dealer in our study.

The vibe between Diamond and Brice spoke more of a marijuana cooperative than an archetypical, hypermasculine

(continues)

80

Dealer Bio: continued

business transaction between drug dealers. On one occasion, Brice forgot to pay for two pounds of marijuana and hours of imbibing passed before he exclaimed "Hey . . . how much did you want for this?" to which Diamond responded with an unbusinesslike and absentminded "oh yeah." While their friendship likely facilitated some degree of nonchalance, Diamond exhibited the lack of risk minimization and bungling that was characteristic of the entire network. On one occasion, Diamond was observed collecting money from Brice and apparently adding it to monies already collected from other large customers. Indicative of his casual manner, Diamond had large sums of money stuffed hastily into three pockets of his cargo pants; some stacks of bills were in rolls, others struggling to stay contained in various plastic bags, others in paper clips; large sums of money were routine and apparently did not warrant any more attention than a receipt for a six-pack of beer. When we approached Diamond's apartment one evening, all elements of his business including marijuana, a triple beam scale, cash, drug paraphernalia, and customers making a buy, were visible through his street-front windows from across a busy street. Drug dealing was routinized and risk minimization was near nonexistent.

Diamond's roommate was an avid surfer and a marijuana dealer of similar scope. Both Diamond and his roommate had exclusive clientele, but likely made bulk marijuana purchases in cooperation. One evening, Diamond and his roommate disclosed their secret to being successful college-student drug dealers, maximizing their academic results while minimizing effort. They carefully explained that their strategy was to study very hard at the beginning of the semester and do very well on the first exam or assignment in a particular class. Subsequently, they could slack off because the professor would have already determined they were good students and be predisposed to give them good grades—despite their minimal effort for the rest of the semester.

ILENE: I would find individuals that know other individuals that have them and do not mind to sell them, and I would buy them off other people who have prescriptions, and I have also contacted people that have gone to Mexico and purchased them, and I've actually purchased them from Mexico too . . . I've purchased Valiums from this bald guy off the street, took me into a strip club in the bathroom and gave me 180 Valiums.

One final caveat is worth noting before getting into specific dealer categories; with the exception of the fourth category of dealers, all of the dealers we encountered were also prescription-drug abusers engaged in a social network framed around a pharmaceutical exchange, a sort of Craig's List for the drug dependent. And even those users in our network who had aboveboard prescriptions for particular pharmaceuticals tended to abuse other drugs that were not prescribed them by a medical doctor.

A Friend Indeed

The first grouping of dealers in our pharmaceutical taxonomy included people who possessed surplus prescription drugs that also happened to be in high demand among the college user set. Most of these dealers were either prescribed a larger quantity or dose of drugs than they were interested in using, or they decided to cycle off of their prescriptions altogether. In spite of their decision not to personally consume the drugs prescribed them, these dealers continued to refill their prescriptions either explicitly for the purposes of "hooking up" their friends and acquaintances, as a means of barter for other pharmaceuticals not prescribed them, or, in some cases, to appease their parents who insisted they remain on their drugs as a condition of their education. The most common drug sold or otherwise distributed by this category of dealer was the attention-deficit hyperactivity disorder drug, Adderall.

Naturally we wondered why a college student diagnosed with ADHD would choose not to use his or her prescription when doing so would quite assuredly negatively affect focus and concentration and therefore jeopardize their academic standing. In a rather heartbreaking testimonial, Emilio offered an answer to this question. The twenty-year-old international relations major had been prescribed Adderall when he was eight years old as part of a treatment regimen for his then juvenile ADHD. After twelve years of taking the powerful amphetamine, Emilio described what proved to be a classic case of Adderall burnout:

> EMILIO: I do kind of feel stupid because it kind of . . . my brain . . . I still get tweaks from it a little bit and especially with Adderall. I really wish I hadn't been on that since third grade because I just . . . I kind of have little shakes all the time, just kind of cracky. And I think my . . . I'm pretty sure I have a bad heart because of it; because they put you on so much Adderall when you're younger that it just can't be possibly good for you. Just for your developing heart and such, but . . . umm . . . and I think it's done a lot to my personality also. It kind of makes me a little bit jumpy. Other than that, I don't know. And that's kind of like why I think I did a lot of these depressants just to make up for the jumpiness from the Adderall. I'm pretty much against putting kids on Adderall these days, even though it does help them get their work done. I never really got a dependency on it because I never really enjoyed taking it. I just had to because otherwise I would just not pay attention or I would just kind of space off all the time. I'm learning how to deal with it myself now which is . . . I don't know . . . it makes me feel better but it does make my life a little harder.

Emilio and several others in his situation—those who had been required to take amphetamine or other mood-altering drugs for a good part of their lives—opted to use college as a time to see what it was like to be "normal" and to experience life without being dependent on those particular medications. However, for many reasons, not the least of which being the insistence of parents paying a hefty fare for their kids to receive a private-college education, these students continued to have their prescriptions filled. Rather than let the drugs go to waste, they would frequently opt to either give away, trade, or sell their monthly allotments to students without ADHD who wanted to get high.

The Mexican Backdoor

The second category of prescription-drug dealer we encountered was the bulk retailer who obtained drugs through what we call the "Mexican backdoor." As the moniker suggests, these student-dealers would schedule trips to the reasonably close Mexican border town of

Tijuana solely for the purpose of illegally procuring bulk quantities of drugs from Mexican pharmacies whose staff proved less diligent in upholding prescription requirements than their north-of-the-border counterparts.

For the more ambitious dealers, another common source for illegal bulk pharmaceutical purchases through this backdoor was black market dealers who sold larger quantities of prescription drugs primarily to US customers than what could usually be obtained at the Mexican pharmacies. Our network's prescription-drug dealers would meet these suppliers in Tijuana bars, strip clubs, and other nightlife establishments picking up several hundred pills at a time. They would then take a taxi to the US-Mexico border, walk through the border crossing with the hundreds of illegal pills stashed on their person, and be on their way. Once back on their home turf, these dealers would resell most of the drugs to friends and acquaintances; use them as currency in exchange for other drugs; or distribute the drugs among their peers in trade for free drugs the next time someone else made the trip through the Mexican backdoor. As one of our dealers nonchalantly described it, "Freshman year . . . I just met the kids that made it common practice to go down [to Mexico] to make a little bit of money, you know." While this backdoor approach was used to gain access to all of the commonly abused prescription drugs in our network, we found that opioids like OxyContin and Vicodin, the most difficult pharmaceuticals to obtain through licit and illicit stateside means, were most often the objects of drug runs to Mexico.

The Pharmaceutical Fraudster

The third category of prescription-drug dealer in our network was the medical *fraudster,* a person who used guile to obtain prescription drugs through otherwise legitimate channels. The fraudster's road to pharmaceutical procurement involved several steps that began with a personal interest in or peer demand for a particular prescription drug. After establishing the drug of choice—Adderall proved to be the most commonly targeted drug in these cases—the fraudsters would identify the specific medical condition for which the drug was commonly prescribed and the symptoms associated with the condition. Identification of appropriate symptoms proved to be only a mouse click away as all of the major prescription drugs coveted by members of our network have web pages that provide marvelously detailed listings of the symptoms and condition the drug was approved to treat.[17] Once these symptoms were committed to memory, rehearsed, and the presentation of symptoms vetted by peers familiar with the particular medical condition, the fraudster would locate a medical doctor, usually through a friend's recommendation, get into character, put on a display, and more often than not walk away with the desired prescription. As one of our network's users and small-time dealers described:

> I have a prescription to Adderall, which I got from the doctor, mostly at my urging. I basically suggested to him that I had problems studying and focusing, which was not really true. But I wanted to get Adderall and experiment with it I guess, and my doctor pretty much believed or did anything I told him. He was so desperate to do anything that might help me and please my parents. In fact, I was so good at lying about it that he gave me a huge prescription.

Even those users and dealers in our network who did not become fraudsters seemed very much aware of the ease with which they might obtain a legitimate prescription for some of the most widely abused prescription drugs. As Kyle, a nineteen-year-old freshman and one of our heavier pharmaceutical users, rather plainly commented when asked whether he had a prescription for Adderall, his pharmaceutical of choice, "No. I can if I want to, but I don't." Our network's users and dealers also seemed quite skilled in the art of "doctor shopping," the practice of seeking out physicians with loose prescription pads or the visiting of multiple doctors for purposes of obtaining multiple prescriptions.

Hypocritical Oath

While technically not a part of the college campus drug-dealing scene, it is important not to understate the key role the legitimate medical community plays in supplying heavily abused prescription drugs to college students. Therefore, we have chosen to collectively identify healthcare providers, specifically less than meticulous medical doctors, as the fourth organism in our taxonomy of collegiate prescription-drug dealers. In spite of the fact that they are entrusted as the primary gatekeepers for prescription-drug access, it seems that many members of the physician community have little or no incentive to more closely regulate their personal distribution of pharmaceuticals or to pursue drug-free therapies as a means of dealing with the physiological and psychological symptoms that many of their patients appear to present. In fact, the US Department of Health and Human Services reports that of all people aged twelve or older who used pain relievers nonmedically in the past twelve months, over 19 percent reported getting the drug from just one doctor. Over 55 percent reported obtaining their illicitly used prescription drugs from a friend or relative, over 80 percent of whom said they originally obtained the drugs from just one doctor.[18] So while the DEA and FBI have been spending millions of dollars to crack down on the Internet pharmacies,[19] a supply source responsible for supplying about one-tenth of 1 percent of illegal prescription drugs in the United States, it seems their resources would be better spent on more closely scrutinizing medical doctors. As California Attorney General Jerry Brown said in 2009 when announcing the rare criminal indictments of two doctors involved in the Anna Nicole Smith overdose case, "Doctors do not have a license to pump innocent people full of dangerous chemicals . . . People in white smocks in pharmacies with their medical degrees are a growing threat." Brown went on to say that medical doctors who facilitate prescription-drug abuse among Hollywood's elite pose a threat just as troubling as that posed by drug pushers in poor neighborhoods.[20]

This is not, by any means, meant to be a blanket condemnation of medical doctors. Many people legitimately need the prescription drugs most prone to abuse in order to manage pain, successfully navigate through day-to-day life, and to treat a host of other serious ailments. Further, much of what we see as a lack of medical oversight can be directly attributed to the corporatization of medical care and the increasing demands placed upon medical doctors to see more patients in less time. The end result is quick-fix treatments and potentially unnecessary and heavy-handed prescription-drug therapies. However, the fact still remains that the doctors, not the shareholders in their HMO, are the keepers of the key to the domestic medicine cabinet. And ultimately, they are the ones entrusted by oath and by law to responsibly and carefully monitor the distribution of prescription drugs. As we found in this study, this trust was routinely breached.

Little Pharma: The Why and How of
the Junior Elite 'Scrips Dealing Game

Our network's pharmaceutical peddlers were remarkably different from the street-drug dealers we observed and interviewed in several significant ways. Perhaps the most compelling contrasts were found in the roles that material gain and social status played, or did not play, in the decision to become a drug dealer. While making money was certainly not the exclusive driving force behind most of our network's street-drug dealers' entrée into drug trafficking, the desire not to "pay retail" for personal drug use, the yearning for "extra beer money," and other material influences were still significant motivating factors for our traditional drug dealers. In contrast, the profit motive was an almost nonexistent motivating force in our prescription-drug dealers' choice to sell drugs. In fact, most of the dealers we spoke with were not even sure how much money they made on prescription-drug sales because they were not doing it for the purpose of profit. Instead, many were merely selling their surplus pharmaceuticals at cost. For those who did incorporate a small markup, they still were not aware of their net profits and only saw the inflated price as a means to occasionally "off a couple of parking tickets" and pay other small expenses.

Our best calculations suggest that our network's prescription-drug dealers averaged between $50 and $100 per month in illegal drug proceeds. And while occasionally a dealer would come back from Tijuana with a "big score" and make a reasonable profit, only one of the pharmaceutical traffickers in our network earned any significant money on a consistent basis. While still meager in relation to our higher-end street-drug dealers, this particular prescription trafficker could take in about $1,000 in ill-gotten profits if he sold his doctor-prescribed monthly supply of Adderall for its maximum campus "street value" of $5 per pill. This price represented a 500 percent markup from the $1 per pill retail pharmacy cost, but these were costs he did not personally assume as they were covered by his parents and his medical insurance.

These relatively low earnings are not meant to suggest that larger profits cannot be made in illicit pharmaceutical sales; they absolutely can, particularly if you consider that the going rate for some of the more difficult to get pharmaceuticals like OxyContin can be as high as $1 per milligram with a typical 80 milligrams per pill.[21] However, we did not see costs anywhere near this high among our network's traders and we speculate that proximity to Mexico played a key role in keeping in check the price of opioids and other harder to obtain drugs. Further, we had the opportunity to speak with one full-time illegal pharmaceutical dealer outside of our network who, by conservative estimates, easily cleared five times per month what our biggest campus prescription dealer brought in. Ironically, he in part illegally traded in pharmaceuticals as a means to put himself through pharmacy school. The fundamental point, however, is that for our network's prescription-drug dealers profit was not high among their reasons for entering the prescription-drug trade.

Nor did a boost in status seem to serve as a primary motivating factor among the pharmaceutical-dealing set. While it may seem strange to associate status elevation with illicit drug sales, as we found with our street-drug dealers, assuming a deviant role can bring recognition in a social setting where drug use is common and the traditional trappings of material success are the norm rather than what makes one distinctive. Nonetheless, most of the prescription dealers shied away from their label as a drug dealer, and this timidity in accepting the label was not for fear of criminal justice scrutiny. Indeed, dealers like Emilio were the norm, expressing a reluctant acceptance of their role in drug dealing, but always with a degree of deprecation in saying things like "I sold a couple Adderall, but I don't like to do it too much." Giovanni, a twenty-two-year-old economics major, shared similar thoughts in downplaying his status as a dealer saying, "If I had a little extra . . . if I wanted to do [prescription drugs] with my friends, I would make them pitch in for what it costs, but never really bulk selling . . . nothing major."

So the question remains, if profits, status, and *sneaky thrills* were not the primary impetuses behind the decision to illegally sell pharmaceuticals, what would compel these rather privileged young adults to engage in what they knew to be illegal activity? While not at all intended to diminish the fact that they were actively breaking the law, many of our pharmaceutical dealers indicated that they never actively sought to become drug dealers. Instead, they somewhat incidentally happened upon the trade either because they had surplus drugs prescribed them that they had no intention of using or because they had an ill-gotten supply of drugs that exceeded what they could reasonably consume themselves. Toward this last point, we found that many of our dealers did not view themselves as drug dealers because they only interstitially occupied drug-dealing roles. In defiance of a street-drug trade maxim, our prescription dealers routinely got high on their own supply and principally got involved in pharmaceutical dealing to ensure a source of supply for themselves.

This selling of drugs on the side is not completely out of step with traditional drug dealers, many of whom maintain full-time jobs. But unlike our prescription dealers, most of our street-drug dealers still primarily sell drugs as a source of supplemental or secondary income. These prescription part-timers were also different in that they were involved in broader prescription-drug-using collectives in which, at varying times, one person would give away or, more commonly, sell off their surplus drugs only to be on the receiving end of the drug exchange a few weeks later.

Neutralization theory and what Mills described as "vocabulary of motive" provide another interesting explanation for why these relatively privileged college students would potentially jeopardize their futures by illegally dealing in pharmaceuticals. In short, many of our dealers did an end run around the negotiation of illegality by simply denying the fact that they were involved in criminal behavior. This practice stood in stark contrast to their college peers dealing in street drugs, most of whom seemed to revel in the idea that they were actively engaged in law-breaking behavior. Indeed, Freddie's comment was characteristic of this schizophrenia in his denial of illegal activity in one statement and seemingly unconscious admission of criminal behavior in the very next breath. "I don't sell drugs. But if a friend is hurt or something like that you know that I can hook them up with a few." As part of this internal negotiation process, other dealers we interviewed attempted to downplay the extent to which their trafficking behaviors were actually illegal. For example, Brad, a twenty-two-year-old business major, offered the following response when asked about his prescription-drug dealing activities.

BRAD: I've never been directly involved with sales although . . . I've even contributed some funds here and there for some [drugs] . . . I guess you could say I've been indirectly involved in the sales side of it . . . It's pretty much a network that I formed my freshmen year through meeting everyone at the dorms . . . I just met the kids that have made it common practice to go down [to Mexico] to make a little bit of money you know.

Reminiscent of D. Scully and J. Marolla's paradigm-shifting study of convicted rapists,[22] it seems that Brad and other dealers we spoke with had already committed themselves to culturally derived vocabularies of motive that served to lessen accountability and allowed them to negotiate a nondeviant identity, at least in their minds. Not unlike a fusion between the denial of responsibility and injury theorized by G. Sykes and D. Matza in their classic "Techniques of Neutralization,"[23] we also routinely found our prescription-drug dealers simultaneously negating personal culpability for their law-violating activities while suggesting that their behavior did not cause any real harm in spite of the fact that it was illegal.

Risk vs. Reward

While generally immune from the scrutiny of domestic law enforcement agencies, over the course of our interviews, members of the drug network we examined nevertheless reported some rather substantial risks associated with their prescription-drug abuse and dealing activities. The risks our subjects described fell somewhat neatly into two categories: those risks that compromise the health and physical well-being of the user, and those risks involving unwanted attention from formal social control agencies including foreign and domestic criminal justice officials and campus police.

For some members, these risks caused them to temper their activities, but not to any great extent. For example, after experiencing a two-week-long drug-induced blackout, one heavy user admitted to cutting back on his pharmaceutical consumption, but had not come close to discontinuing his illegal prescription-drug use. This proved to be the rule rather than the exception in every instance where our subjects admitted to encountering risks associated with their illegal pharmaceutical use or sales; the risks never drove our network's members entirely away from their illicit prescription-drug activities. Instead, the desire to get high and, in some cases, the relatively modest material gains that stemmed from the profits associated with dealing in pharmaceuticals always prevailed over avoiding peril altogether.

Of all, the most effective risk-minimization tool at the disposal of our pharmaceutical dealers and users proved to be their social and economic status. At the policy level, similar to the saints and roughnecks described in William Chambliss's classic criminological piece on the systemic biases linked to status,[24] it is relatively clear that prescription-drug abuse and trafficking such as what we uncovered is not viewed as a high priority by those who shape criminal justice policy, regardless of how rampant these activities may be. This is particularly true when the rule breakers are well-off college kids and not disenfranchised corner boys. It seems that every gatekeeper, from the doctor whose job it is to screen out fraudulent attempts to obtain prescriptions for controlled substances to the Tijuana police officer whose city has been overrun by narco-traffickers, is either asleep at the wheel or has ulterior motives when it comes to preventing the illegal use and distribution of prescription drugs by relatively well-off white college kids.

Law-Enforcement Risks

The vast majority of the users and dealers in our study were never confronted for their illegal use or transportation of pharmaceuticals. Nor did most of them know anyone first hand who had faced any significant repercussion for similar illegal behaviors. There were a few third-party stories of friends-of-friends having their newly obtained prescription drugs taken from them by Mexican city police, and a few first-hand accounts of small bribes being paid to local Mexican cops during shakedowns. But none of the dealers or users of prescription drugs that we spoke with had any meaningful encounters with US authorities related to their prescription-drug activity, and only two had what might be described as a serious run-in with Mexican authorities.

Lowe, one of these two dealers, was a twenty-three-year-old business major who generally purchased his illegal pharmaceuticals in small quantities from a friend but who also occasionally took trips to Mexico to make larger purchases of anywhere from one hundred to two hundred pills. Of his trips south of the border, he said, "I've run into the Mexican police a bunch of times. It was terrible. I got arrested, [but] didn't have to go to jail though." The other instance involved Ilene, a twenty-one-year-old international relations major, and three of her friends who journeyed to Tijuana to buy large quantities of Valium for their personal use as well as for the purpose of distribution back in the states. As she described it:

ILENE: We went to a bunch of pharmacies and basically one person drove us to a strip club so they could get [the drugs] for us. My friend got 270 Valiums. As we were sitting in the restroom waiting for them to come back, this one guy [a strip-club patron whom they did not know] decides to rip up our pictures and then the cops come and then take him and tell my friends they have to give an interview about the guy downtown. They were like "no we don't wanna do that." So then they're like "why don't you wanna do that?" And then, like, we have this thing that two guys are carrying knives around in Mexico so "can we search you," throw 'em against the cars, like take 270 Valiums out of his pocket and arrest both of them, take 'em in the cop car, and me and my other friend were just sitting there, didn't know what to do, had no money in our pockets, because they had the money and car keys in his pockets. We go downtown to the station, and they had my friend in there for like three hours. The police officers were talking on [my friends'] cell phones, took like six hundred dollars from one of my friends that were [sic] in the car, and then let him out and then they told us to leave the country immediately.

In spite of being shaken up by this encounter, Ilene did not discontinue her heavy (up to ten pills per day) Vicodin, Valium, or Percocet habit, nor did she refrain from future illegal drug sales. Most remarkable, she also did not cease taking frequent trips to Mexico "to make purchases in larger quantities." Perhaps most importantly and consistent with the *anti-targets* theme, Ilene and all of the other prescription-drug abusers in our group were consistently able to maintain the public perception of *good kids* who attended a relatively prestigious university. They did not see themselves as being significantly harmed by prescription-drug use, nor did others in positions to scrutinize their behavior see their deviance as significant. Apparently the public perception and criminal justice risks associated with the illegal use, sales, and feigning of symptoms to acquire these drugs are negligible at best.

This public perception of our college drug offenders jibes well with how policymakers and law enforcers tend to differentially view those who deal in street drugs as compared to those who illegally use and deal in pharmaceuticals. While Brett Favre, Cindy McCain, Rush Limbaugh, Noelle Bush and countless other public figures have faced mild public humiliation for their prescription-drug abuses, none of these people have been subjected to the type of criminal justice scrutiny or public scorn faced by street-drug abusers. Instead, their addictions have been treated medically, blame for their drug abuse has been cast upon unscrupulous medical practices, and their addictions were ultimately used to elicit sympathy. Indeed, in the case of Rush Limbaugh's prescription fraud and "doctor shopping," which illegally yielded him approximately two thousand painkillers, charges filed against him in 2006 were dropped without a guilty plea so long as he continued his drug treatment and repaid the state of Florida nearly $30,000 in investigative costs. Most importantly, it is not their celebrity that affords them these privileges. Rather, it is primarily policy and the neutralization of harm ushered in through aggressive pharmaceutical marketing that gets them and their anonymous counterparts off the hook, relatively speaking.

In spite of the fact that in many states accidental prescription-drug overdoses result in more deaths than accidental overdoses from all illicit drugs, there seems to be a clear bias that favors those who traffic in and abuse prescription drugs. A snapshot from the state of Nevada provides a good example of this phenomenon. In 2007, 258 people died of prescription-drug overdoses in Clark County, Nevada, alone. With an estimated population of about two million residents, Clark County is perhaps most well known for Las Vegas, its county seat. The county's overdose fatalities amounted to more than the number of people who died in motor vehicle crashes that year, including those attributable to drunken driving, and sixty-one more deaths than the number of people who died from street-drug overdoses in 2007. During that same year, pharmacy technician Cambra Nye confessed to stealing nearly sixty thousand prescription-drug pills including Vicodin, Xanax, Viagra, and others, from the Clark County CVS pharmacy at which she worked. In spite of the obvious illegality of her actions, the fact that she stole these drugs for the purpose of illegally distributing the heavily abused and highly addictive narcotics (Nevada has the highest per capita rates of prescribed hydrocodone in the nation), and in spite of the obvious public health ramifications of her actions, Nye's punishment for her crimes did not involve any prison or jail time. Instead, she was ordered to pay restitution to CVS and sentenced to probation.

In a similar 2007 Nevada case, Roger Ly was charged in federal court with fifty-five counts of healthcare fraud and one count of conspiracy to distribute hydrocodone (Vicodin) and OxyContin, both controlled substances under federal law. Ly's scheme involved creating straw patients at the three separate Nevada pharmacies at which he worked, where he would submit prescriptions on behalf of the fictive patients. He would then fill and buy for himself the prescriptions, paying the co-pay and billing the patients' insurance for the balance. Once he had possession of the drugs, Ly would illegally distribute the ill-gotten pharmaceuticals to friends and acquaintances. After reaching an agreement with the US attorney's office, in 2008 Ly pleaded guilty to one single count of healthcare fraud and was sentenced to thirty-six months probation, ordered to pay $24,299 in restitution to his former employer, and was fined $2,000. As part of the plea agreement, all other charges against him were dropped and, in a separate action by the state licensing board, Ly was stripped of his pharmacist's license.

In both of these cases, the fact that Nye and Ly even faced criminal prosecution is anomalistic. Rather than treat cases like these as serious drug distribution matters and prosecute them with the same vigor that would accompany, for example, someone trafficking in $25,000 worth of heroin, the vast majority of these pharmaceutical fraud and trafficking cases are handled by the Nevada State Pharmacy Board and the drug traffickers are never criminally prosecuted.[25] In Ly's case, the sentence he received was not based on the threat to public safety that his actions created or the number of charges he faced. Instead, consistent with federal statute, his three years of probation was based on the amount of material loss involved in his fraud. Both of these cases clearly demonstrate that, when it comes to drug trafficking, there is substantial bias in the justice system based on, among other things, whether the offender is dealing in pharmaceuticals or street drugs. And, as the case of Nevada shows, this disparity is not based on any objective assessment of social harm or threats to public well being. Rather, it is more likely that the types of people who are apt to be abusing and trafficking in pharmaceuticals do not fit the stereotypical drug dealer profile that has come from the war on drugs and are, therefore, regarded quite differently by lawmakers and the criminal justice system.

Nineteen-year-old Herman's description of comparative encounters with Mexican and US authorities well summarizes the reality of criminal justice risk: "A couple times when I was in Mexico, I've been harassed by the police. One time one of my buddies had some pills on him, but we just paid them some dollars and got out. I've never had any problems over here in America because I don't really see too many police." As most of our Mexican backdoor users and dealers suggested, Mexican border-town police see the surging prescription-drug craze as an opportunity to shake down white kids from the states for small amounts of cash. Their US counterparts policing the border, on the other hand, seemed so preoccupied with terrorism, undocumented aliens, and street drugs that they could not care less about a rich college kid coming through customs with a few hundred OxyContin pills in his pockets.

Health Risks

Most of the pharmaceutical users and dealers with whom we spoke did not seem to have any direct major health issues or significant health scares attributable to their illegal prescription-drug activities, at least none they were aware of. Nearly all of them made mention of effects reminiscent of an alcohol hangover when they would ingest too many prescription drugs, take an ill-advised pharmaceutical cocktail, or combine certain prescription drugs with alcohol. Still, based on those who did report serious health consequences triggered by their illicit prescription-drug use, it is unlikely that awareness of serious physiological or mental health risks would have made much of a difference in the general prescription-drug abusing population's choice to continue on with illegal pharmaceutical activities.

As noted at the top of this discussion on risk versus reward, those who experienced serious health episodes while on prescription drugs and even those who experienced personal tragedy associated with prescription-drug abuse only scaled back their drug use rather than cut it out altogether. Emilio, the twenty-year-old small-time dealer and heavy user of prescription drugs we mentioned earlier, provided a solid example of this phenomenon.

EMILIO: Well . . . I guess like with uh Lamictal [a commonly prescribed drug for the treatment of bipolar disorder], if I drink on that I found out that I end up having seizures so I don't drink anymore on that. I've only done it twice and it's been a terrible, terrible situation. That's why I especially don't drink anymore and then . . . umm . . . Adderall, I've taken way too many of those before. That was bad news. I couldn't go to sleep for five days, that's not good for you.

Jimmy, a senior business major prescribed Adderall and Effexor (an antidepressant), but also fond of illicitly using "pretty much any sort of pain killer and muscle relaxant or anti-anxiety that comes along," described another account of a serious health scare brought on by his heavy prescription-drug use. "One time, I had like ninety-nine [pills] in three days and I lost track of two weeks. Basically, I had no idea what was going on . . . lost track of reality. You know I don't remember dick for two weeks." While erasing two weeks of your life on a drug binge is substantial, Jimmy described an even more dramatic example of the health risks associated with prescription-drug abuse when we asked him the same closing question we asked all of our prescription users and dealers, if he had ever experienced any event that made him rethink his prescription-drug activities. In a compelling, startling, and emotional response, Jimmy said,

> Jimmy: Yeah, my brother. One of my half brothers had back pain issues, was hooked on painkillers, ended up taking OxyContin, got hooked on it, tried to come off it himself because it wasn't, it didn't look right, and ended up committing suicide. Uh, so that's uh . . . that was about two years ago.

More surprising to us was the fact that his brother's death, which Jimmy directly attributed to prescription-drug use and addiction, did not dissuade him from illegally using Adderall or large quantities of an impressive laundry list of opioids and CNS depressants. Certainly, as has been shown with studies on male drinking patterns, this heavy prescription-drug habit could have in part been a way for Jimmy to self-medicate and deal with the grief brought on by the loss of his brother. However, one might still reasonably think that his brother's addiction and death would cause him to reconsider potentially contributing to a similar fate in one of the people to whom he routinely sold illegal prescription drugs. It did not.

Final Thoughts on College Students and Prescription Drugs

Ultimately, Mexican police shakedowns, drug dependency, seizures, prolonged blackouts, and even the death of family members had little or no deterrent effect on any of our network's members either in their pharmaceutical abuse or drug dealing. Some of this steadfastness can likely and quite simply be explained physiologically by addiction and the immemorial human thirst to get high. However, we feel the most compelling explanations for this phenomenon have deep social roots in class and racial bias, and relatively shallow yet strong roots in pharmaceutical politics on Capitol Hill.

On the one hand, from its very beginnings, US drug policy has operated as a furtive attack against the poor and people of color, not coincidentally groups largely underrepresented among prescription-drug abusers and dealers. As arrest and incarceration data loudly testify, from the outset of the contemporary war on drugs, policymakers made very clear who was to be targeted by the punitive anti-drug agenda that characterized the last two decades of the twentieth century. In spite of drug-use data consistently indicating a drug problem that knows no racial or class boundaries, medical data that clearly identifies nonmedical pharmaceutical use as a greater public health concern than street-drug abuse, and nonpartisan recommendations for drug-law reform, this myopic practice of training the eyes of US drug policy on the illicit activities of minorities and the poor is a trend that has quietly and sadly carried over into the new millennium.

On the other hand, a very pronounced pro-drug agenda has been quite successfully promoted by pharmaceutical manufacturing giants, the lobbyists they employ to spread their gospel to US policymakers, and the billions of advertising dollars they funnel into US media outlets every year. Rather than devoting resources to finding cures for serious illnesses, it could reasonably be argued that the primary mission of these companies has shifted to convincing lawmakers that flooding the market with highly abused drugs makes good public health sense and to convincing the US and international public that there is "a disease for every pill." In fact, recent research has indicated that nearly one-half of all pharmaceutical advertisements are geared toward encouraging consumers to consider medical causes for their everyday human experiences, and that these medical causes require drug therapies.[26]

Similar to James M. Graham's early 1970s observations of illegal amphetamine users and the sources that fed their addictions,[27] in spite of the array of prescription drugs being illicitly used and sold by the college students in our study, all of the drugs shared one important thing in common—the multibillion dollar, largely US, pharmaceutical industry as the initial source of supply. And interestingly, in direct contrast to the much merited demonization of Colombian cocaine suppliers from Cali and Medellín made infamous in the 1980s, no one in the public eye or mainstream media ever referred to Merck or Pfizer as a cartel.

At the end of the day, the message that this collection of biases, preferential treatments, and benign indifferences toward prescription-drug abuse and trafficking sends to the illicit pharmaceutical community is that their behavior is less deviant, less harmful, and subsequently more acceptable than street-drug activity. As we so clearly found within our affluent college drug-dealing network, it also suggests to them that they can go about their illegal pharmaceutical activities without any real risks of life-altering consequences or threats to their life goals.

Notes

1. US Department of Health and Human Services, Substance Abuse and Mental Health Services Administration, "Results from the 2007 National Survey on Drug Use and Health."

2. Conrad and Potter, "From Hyperactive Children to ADHD Adults," p. 568.

3. Ibid., pp. 559–582.

4. Lawson, "ADHD: Diagnosis Dilemma."

5. Conrad and Potter, "From Hyperactive Children to ADHD Adults," p. 574.

6. "Chasing the dragon" is an expression linked traditionally to the inhaling of smoke from heated opium, morphine, or heroin. The wispy cloud was often said to resemble the dragon's tail from Chinese folklore. In contemporary drug cultures, the meaning has also come to include typically vain attempts to recapture the sensation of the first high experienced on a particular drug or the elusive pursuit of an ultimate high.

7. The simultaneous use of heroin or morphine and cocaine, typically injected in the same needle. The cocaine acts as a stimulant, elevating the heart rate, while the heroin or morphine has the opposite effect, slowing the heart down.

8. Drug Abuse Warning Network, "National Estimates of Drug-Related Emergency Department Visits."

9. US House of Representatives, Testimony of Leonard J. Paulozzi.

10. Joralemon, "Coca in History and Political Economy."

11. Karch, *A Brief History of Cocaine.*

12. The Harrison Act of 1914 was the first significant piece of federal antidrug legislation and, in its original form, was primarily intended to outlaw the use of opium in the United States. At the time, Southern legislators were openly leery of expanding the police powers of the federal government and therefore the Harrison Act seemed destined to die. However, supporters of the bill race-baited the Southern resisters into signing onto the act by

adding cocaine to the list of effectively outlawed drugs, playing on preexisting yet baseless white fears of cocaine-crazed Negroes.

13. Greene, "Attention to 'Details.'"

14. *Fortune* magazine, "Global 500."

15. *AdvertisingAge,* "Marketer Trees 2008."

16. US Department of Justice, Drug Enforcement Administration, Joseph T. Rannazzisi, "Online Pharmacies and the Problem of Internet Drug Abuse."

17. The brand website for Adderall provides a good example of the ease with which someone can obtain a full list of, for example, common ADHD symptoms. Available at www.adderallxr.com/pdf/AXR_FPI.pdf.

18. US Department of Health and Human Services, Substance Abuse and Mental Health Services Administration, "Results from the 2006 National Survey on Drug Use and Health."

19. US Department of Justice, Drug Enforcement Administration, Joseph T. Rannazzisi, "Online Pharmacies and the Problem of Internet Drug Abuse."

20. Harriet Ryan, "Attorney general calls Anna Nicole Smith's boyfriend her "principal enabler," *Los Angeles Times,* Saturday, March 14, 2009, A8.

21. Lambert, "OxyContin Rushes into State's Drug Lexicon."

22. Scully and Marolla, "Convicted Rapists' Vocabulary of Motive."

23. Sykes and Matza, "Techniques of Neutralization."

24. Chambliss, "The Saints and the Roughnecks."

25. Allen, "Pharamacies a Popular Source of Illegal Drugs in Nevada." Also see US Attorney, "Las Vegas Pharmacist Charged with Health Care Fraud and Unlawful Distribution."

26. Moynihan and Cassels, "A Disease for Every Pill."

27. Graham, "Amphetamine Politics on Capitol Hill."

5

How Student Dealers
Rationalize Crime:
Mental Gymnastics

Would you consider yourself a drug-dealer?
BEEFY: Yeah, but I don't really like the label.
What would you rather be called?
BEEFY: I don't know. Just I don't know. I can't really think
of a . . . label that I prefer at the time . . . I don't really know. Call
me a supplier, or just a middleman or whatever, I don't know.

As captured in the above exchange, Beefy's reluctance to embrace or
acknowledge, even in confidence, that he was a drug dealer exempli-
fies a hallmark characteristic among members of the affluent
California collegiate drug-dealing network at the heart of this project.
Indeed, with only a few notable exceptions (LaCoste's earlier documented braggadocio and brazenness immediately comes to mind), we
found a general failure on the part of those who knowingly supplied
rather large quantities of illegal drugs to universally self-identify as
"drug-dealers." As Gresham Sykes and David Matza wrote in their
now classic 1950s piece examining the denial of criminal culpability
among deviant subcultures, "Much delinquency is based on what is
essentially an unrecognized extension of defenses to crimes, in the
form of justifications for deviance that are seen as valid by the delinquent but not by the legal system or society at large."[1]

Perhaps because, for all of our study's dealers, their drug-dealing
careers began as a recreational enterprise rather than one birthed from
necessity or the desperation that often comes with urban poverty, our
dealers did not feel comfortable claiming this deviant status. Perhaps

because university officials, local police, and other persons charged with enforcing the rules generally failed to apply the label of drug dealer to these young men and women or otherwise treat them as the city police and society in general would an urban street dealer, our study's dealers were reluctant to assign a deviant label to themselves. Perhaps, in spite of many of our dealers' emulation of and affection toward urban street culture as evidenced by some of the music they listened to, the cars they drove and how they chose to accessorize these vehicles, and some particularly "street" aspects of their drug-dealing vocabulary, our dealers were still a product of a US society that, for decades, has sold the public a monolithic drug-dealer stereotype that did not coincide with how our dealers were raised or who they saw when they looked in the mirror.

Whatever the reason, employing a series of semantic twists and other neutralization strategies, most of our network's dealers did all that they could, at least outwardly, to downplay their involvement in what was an unambiguously illicit enterprise. For example, a good number of the dealers we observed and interviewed would not refer to marijuana, the primary product sold by the network's dealers, as "drugs." Rather, that word was used exclusively to refer to drugs other than marijuana, illegal substances like cocaine, heroin, and methamphetamine. Through a combination of denial and neutralization and in spite of the tens of thousands of people doing time in US prisons for selling marijuana,[2] our network's dealers had collectively convinced themselves that selling these "hard" drugs signified real dealing, and the type of transactions in which they were involved were not significant enough to classify as criminally peddling drugs.

By way of example, one evening at Brice's home he received a phone call that, from hearing only Brice's end of the conversation, quite clearly had to do with an illegal drug transaction of some kind. As he hung up the phone, Brice said in disgust, "She wanted to know if I could hook her up with some *drugs*." Brice was well known in local pot circles as a go-to person for high quality marijuana, therefore his somewhat incredulous tone and apparent affront by the caller's request was remarkable. Indeed, as it turned out, the woman on the other end of the line was not looking for pot. Rather, she was in search of ecstasy, a popular synthetic drug with hallucinogenic and amphetamine-like properties. And although she obviously knew Brice and his pot exclusivity, at least when it came to the drugs he sold, she was calling him on the off chance that he either had a supply of ecstasy or knew someone else that did.

Brice's reaction to the call was typical of the attitude expressed by many of the dealers we interviewed and observed within our network. Somehow, from the perspective of this dealing population, marijuana was excused from being classified as a drug and therefore also immune to the negative connotations associated with other street drugs frequently consumed by the privileged college set. Interestingly, even in cases where our network's dealers dabbled in the sale and abuse of these harder drugs, their comments suggested that they still resisted classifying themselves or being labeled by others as drug dealers because they viewed their primary product, marijuana, as relatively innocuous. In near-textbook *denial of injury,*[3] our network's operatives saw their drug dealing activities as largely subject to interpretation when it came to the question of deviance. Consistent with Sykes and Matza's neutralization theory, for our dealers, determining wrongfulness and the conferring of a deviant status or criminal identity upon themselves hinged on their assessment of harm. Specifically, they commonly rationalized that, since no one was directly hurt by their drug activity and, more broadly, no one was harmed by marijuana consumption, while their behavior may clearly run afoul of the law, it ultimately was not deviant behavior because their drug dealing did not cause any great harm. After all, it was just weed and they were not forcing anyone to smoke it.

In Ron Howard's 1982 film, *Night Shift,* Henry Winkler and Michael Keaton played Chuck Lumley and Bill Blazejowski, two graveyard-shift city morgue workers about to enter the equally nocturnal yet much more lucrative and exciting life of pimping. In an early scene, a local pimp is murdered and a morally outraged Lumley rebuffs Blazejowski's suggestion that the two serve as stand-in pimps in order to protect the interests of his stable of women. In a classic semantic twist and an effort to neutralize the felonious ride that he and Lumley were about to embark upon, Blazejowski responds, "Pimps is an ugly word. We could call ourselves *love brokers!*"

Oddly reminiscent of this scene from a film he likely never heard of, Mikey, a twenty-two-year-old upper-level dealer in our network, provided a near-identical semantic feat and a classic example of self-deception in denying his criminal culpability as a drug dealer. As one of the more sophisticated and firmly entrenched dealers we were in contact with, Mikey had a crew of younger—in both age and experience—dealers working for him. Whenever specifically asked about how he perceived himself given that he was a young white child of privilege from an extremely wealthy family who chose to become a drug dealer, Mikey would immediately offer a correction and refer to himself as a "drug broker." He was also routinely overheard making this self-reference in casual conversation with friends, clients, and fellow smokers. To him, this "broker" versus "dealer" distinction was quite important. For one, in popular usages the term broker is typically reserved for those involved in legitimate business transactions and allowed Mikey to de-stigmatize himself in the midst of his continuous criminal activity. Further, at least in his mind, this playing with words elevated his status above that of stereotypical street-drug dealers; as he was quick to point out, he was responsible for all of the planning and organization that made it possible for those employed by him to sell their wares.

These mental gymnastics, the means used by our network's dealers to neutralize their criminality, were consistently evident in interview narratives, as well as in the observed everyday language of the network's dealers. Perhaps more interestingly, for those dealers we were able to remain in contact with as they transitioned out of the collegiate drug-dealing lifestyle, mental gymnastics remained a hallmark characteristic of how they discussed their past drug-dealing activities. For example, during a 2008 follow-up interview several years after the cessation of her dealing career, Cecilia offered a two-pronged explanation as to why she continued not to identify herself as a criminal, even when reflecting back on the peak of her drug-dealing enterprise. Similar to many of the other dealers with whom we spoke, Cecilia relied upon the fact that the bulk of her clientele consisted of college friends and associates, as well as the fact that she dealt only in what she perceived as a relatively innocuous drug, marijuana, to avoid ascribing a criminal label to herself and to shield herself from the stigma associated with carrying that label.

CECILIA: You were dealing with people who . . . again who were all in college and who were all your friends. And it depends on what kind of things we are talking about dealing. But, if we are talking strictly about pot, or marijuana, yeah I think sort of a culture goes along with . . . there is like a decriminalization . . . uhh . . . mantra. People are generally pushing for it not to be as criminalized as it is. So, I think it is twofold . . . people are you know surrounded by their friends and the people they care about, so it makes it hard to feel like you are a criminal in that sense. And then there is probably an attitude about it not really feeling really like it should be [illegal]. It is like when you are sixteen and you are drinking alcohol at a high-school party. You know that that is not like quote-unquote legal, but it certainly doesn't stop you.

Along the same vein, Brice engaged in similar mental gymnastics to reaffirm to us and, more importantly, himself that the dealers in this network were somehow immune from being self-labeled or labeled by others as drug dealers. Over the years that we spent with him, one of Brice's more commonly employed neutralization tactics revolved around profits and clientele. In his view, real drug dealers made more significant profits than did he or other members of the network. And similar to Cecilia's rationale, Brice rationalized that real drug dealers did not primarily deal dope to their friends, rather they had a client base comprised of mostly people they knew exclusively because of their status as drug customers.

BRICE: Because I view . . . they might be splitting hairs . . . but I view a drug dealer as someone who is making money. I was generally . . . sometimes, yes, I could make money . . . but the vast majority of the time it went right back into it. Or ya know . . . we all would go out and have a fun time and I would make sure to try to pick up the bill or something. Or just having a good time. I don't think . . . we were primarily dealing with friends. You did have people that you would never see on a regular basis . . . outside of that situation. But the majority were people that you would see. Ya know, they might not be coming over to your house, you might have to find them [laughs]. Ya know, but certainly I would agree with that statement that I may never sell like . . . I certainly wouldn't call myself a drug dealer. It definitely didn't feel like that at the time.

It seems that these affluent drug dealers simultaneously espoused two fundamental contradictions. First, there was a substantial disconnectedness between the behaviors in which they were actually engaged and how they chose to perceive themselves. The second contradiction routinely seen among our network's drug dealers revolved around their self-perception and adaptable self-identities that were themselves contradictory. With regard to the disconnect between behaviors and actions, as we already noted, most of the dealers we observed, particularly the more successful of our network's dealers, were overt and often brash chronic law breakers (rather than interstitial dabblers in the drug trade), criminals who chose not to universally identify themselves as drug-law breakers. Again, as Sykes and Matza noted in their classic study and as countless studies and documentaries on urban drug dealers and other groups of people willfully engaged in ongoing law-violating behavior have shown, these mental gymnastics are certainly not the exclusive province of our affluent California college drug-dealing set. Rather, the neutralization strategies employed by our network's dealers are seemingly common among people whom outsiders might readily identify as deviants.

Interestingly, their tendency to absolve themselves of any criminal culpability for their drug-dealing activities did not prevent many of the dealers we interviewed, observed, or were otherwise aware of, from frequently and often flamboyantly reveling in the status and celebrity accorded them for their immersion in pseudo gangsterism. LaCoste's blunt-smoking bravado and Brice's nights on the town were just a couple of examples of this celebratory lifestyle. Yet at other times, these same drug dealers viewed themselves as destined for lives of conventional success and conformity; they projected an internalized image as otherwise good kids who were simply flirting with nominal deviance while en route to becoming traditional and legitimate capitalists or otherwise filling acceptable social roles.

Reciprocal Labeling and the Absence of Criminal Justice Consequences

To paraphrase iconic sociologist and labeling theory pioneer Howard Becker,[4] with a few exceptions, involvement in particular illegal acts is not especially significant in identifying deviance. Rather, how influential members of society respond to the act and, subsequently, how the transgressors react to this social response are central in how social deviance gets defined. Fundamentally, labeling theorists are not focused on objective assessments of wrongdoing. Instead, what interests them is public perception of potential wrongdoing, and they frame their analyses around how an individual and his actions are perceived by society and also how individuals perceive themselves. This perspective assumes that society's most powerful members preside over the labeling process through their disproportionate influence in creation and enforcement of social and legal rules.

Since its introduction in the early 1960s, labeling theory has been favorably received by many criminologists and public figures who feel that the creation and application of US laws frequently places an undue burden on the poor and people of color. This key labeling assertion suggests that socially powerful groups do not simply define deviance in a way that diminishes their culpability in criminal activity and in ways that favor their political and economic interests, but these socially powerful groups also effectively manufacture deviance by picking and choosing winners and losers in the criminal justice system. As Becker himself wrote, "Social groups create deviance by making the rules whose infraction constitutes deviance, and by applying those rules to particular people."[5] Because powerful individuals in society oversee both the content and process of lawmaking, and these same people have disproportionate control over mechanisms of law enforcement, the least powerful members of society are unequally targeted and officially labeled deviant. Consequently, as a direct result of this dynamic, the formal mechanisms of social control actually cause deviance.[6]

Again, at labeling theory's core is the contention that the criminal justice system is not an autonomous, objective entity. Rather, the system is manipulated and gamed by society's wealthiest, most powerful, and most prestigious members in both conscious and inadvertent attempts to protect their own interests at the expense of the interests of the less powerful. Without question, any accusation toward social elites of racial and class bias or, more broadly, any assertion of unfairness embedded in the US system of justice is certain to generate disparagement and criticism, and labeling theory is no exception. Detractors and critics of the perspective assert that the approach is too radical and fails to take into account laws that clearly protect the interests of the majority over those of elites. However, even a cursory review of criminal justice statistics, particularly arrest and incarceration data related to the war on drugs, rather objectively supports labeling theorists' premise that a subjective bias favoring the privileged classes is acted out through lawmaking and law enforcement. It is no great secret that the vast majority of prison inmates were poor well before they were ever sent upstate. And, as we noted in the introduction to this book, nearly one-half of the US jail and prison population is black and more than 35 percent of all persons arrested for drug abuse violations and approximately 45 percent of state prison inmates serving time for drug offenses are black. Not only is this grossly out of step with African-American representation in the United States, but it is also grossly inconsistent with drug-user data that suggests racial and ethnic groups in the United States have drug-use rates that closely approximate their representation in the US population. As noted criminologist Ron Akers writes, "The probability that one will be arrested, convicted, and imprisoned is determined by one's race, sex, age, social class, and other social characteristics that define one's status in society."[7]

Ultimately, labeling theorists conclude that the deviant labels assigned by the more powerful members in society can have a profound impact on those individuals or classes of individuals who have received the label. It is also important to note one additional presupposition of the labeling perspective, that virtually every person in society is guilty of engaging in rule-breaking behavior at some point in their lives. And oftentimes, irrespective of who prison population demographics might suggest to be the most crime-prone members of society, both minor and major deviance are not bound by the class barriers that segregate US society in other ways. That said, both formal and informal agencies of social control tend to respond differently to these deviant behaviors based on who is committing the act, and this response can ultimately shape future acts of deviance or conformity.

This process is best captured through a discussion of two key labeling concepts, primary and secondary deviation. Primary deviation is used to define the nominal rule-breaking or original acts of transgression that most individuals engage in at some point in their lives. Those who are punished for their primary deviation likely internalize a stigmatizing, deviant self-image, a self-image that then contributes to future acts of deviance or, in sociological terms, secondary deviance.[8] In the criminal justice system, perhaps the most significant form of labeling in this context comes during the trial and sentencing of an offender. The literal drama inherent in this process, magnified by all the trappings of power and legitimacy afforded the state, weighs heavily on the self-perception of the individual. In other words, for many individuals caught up in the criminal justice system, particularly those who have already been told in other ways by society that they have no particular social value or contribution to make, being formally labeled as a deviant can have significant life-altering consequences. As Frank Tannenbaum writes, "He has been tagged . . . The person becomes the thing he is described as being."[9] Thus, the future criminality of an individual is largely determined through the process of punishment and the self-perception that stems from this process.

With regard to the present study on college drug dealers, one of our fundamental findings was that this population of affluent drug-dealers exemplified a *reciprocal* labeling effect; despite their obvious criminality, most of our dealers were reared in a culture that conveyed to them that conventional success was their birthright while simultaneously ignoring or downplaying their transgressions. Consequently, in spite of their often flagrant criminality, these anti-targets were able to maintain a regular commitment to a legitimate self-identity. We suspect this positive appraisal of self, one quite clearly out of step with their activities and how society tends to respond to their street-drug dealing counterparts, existed in significant part precisely because of the lack of intervention and consequent negative sanctions from formal agents of social control. Despite their unabashed and highly visible (if anyone bothered to look) criminality, actors in the justice system seemingly shared in our dealers' assessment of their drug dealing activity, that it was less severe and less worthy of formal condemnation than similar behaviors carried out in other social contexts.

Again consistent with the labeling perspective, the differential treatment this population received from the criminal justice system may have contributed significantly to the ways dealers evaluated and rationalized their own criminal behaviors. Across the board we found that, on the rare occasion that our network's dealers had formal interaction with law enforcement, their material wealth and status minimized the negative consequences of these interactions. Subsequently, these minimal official repercussions had the added effect of reinforcing the dealers' perceptions that their own behavior is somehow exempt from strict criminal classification. Also, as discussed in the previous chapter, these affluent drug dealers tended not to associate with larger criminal organizations; they were an autonomous group whose members usually had their drugs supplied by individual, larger-scale, primarily regional marijuana cultivators. A lack of diverse criminal associations might have also impacted the way these affluent dealers perceived their own identity and contributed to the reciprocal labeling process. It is likely that a drug dealer that is associated with a street gang, *La Cosa Nostra,* or has served time in prison for other crimes would construct a deviant self-identity. We reason that the persistent lack of deviant labels applied to these otherwise deviant actors allowed the dealers in our network to downplay their own criminal behavior and to avoid internalizing a universal deviant self-identity.

Dealers within this population also frequently minimized the perception of their own criminality by subscribing to some pervasive society-wide assumptions about crime and caricatures of stereotypical criminals. For example and in spite of statistics indicating relatively equal involvement in illegal drug activity, studies suggest that Americans typically associate drug crime with members of minority groups.[10] If society's crime mirror consistently reflected drug dealer and other criminal images that were wholly different from them, it stands to reason that the dealers we came across in this college drug network may have logically perceived their own demographic as largely nondeviant or at least less criminal than their urban counterparts. After all, they were not likely to see people like themselves doing a perp-walk on the evening news, as the objects of police scrutiny for drug and other crimes in televised cop shows and other forms of crime-based infotainment, or otherwise reflected back in society's crime mirror. Ann, one of our network's few female street-drug dealers, captured some of the ways these biases likely contributed to the largely nondeviant self-perception that characterized most of the dealers with whom we came into contact.

ANN: I mean if someone really wanted to bust us they could, all they would have to do was get someone to sit on our house to get some evidence against us to be able to go in there. No one cares that much. I think a lot of it has to do with the people we are, we don't live in the ghetto. We don't make noise, we don't have parties, we don't bring attention to ourselves, we are quiet, we pay everything on time. In the beach environment you can get away with a lot more.

Ultimately, Ann and most of our other dealers' assumptions about their demographic attributes as well as their collective belief that their drug crimes were trivial relative to "real" drug crimes led to a minimized perception of their own criminality. This willingness to label or identify others as truly criminal proved central to the mental gymnastics necessary to mitigate their own overt criminality and to avert any of the consequences associated with being labeled as deviants.

No One's Really Getting Hurt:
Neutralization and the Veil of Legitimate Pursuits

Neutralization theory, which falls under the broad paradigmatic umbrella of criminological "learning theories," originally proposed that adolescents do not make a steadfast commitment to either conformist or deviant behavior. Rather, they "drift" between obedience to established norms and violation of these norms. A commitment to escalated levels of deviance is facilitated by learning rationalizations for these behaviors from others. In other words, people engaged in sustained deviant behavior often learn excuses, justifications, or neutralizations of these behaviors that help them negotiate or downplay to themselves their violations of social norms. Sykes and Matza's original neutralization model placed these learned rationalizations for deviant and criminal behavior into five broad "techniques of neutralization" categories: (1) denial of responsibility; (2) denial of injury; (3) denial of the victim; (4) appeals to higher loyalty; and (5) condemnation of the condemners.[11]

In quick summary of these techniques, Sykes and Matza argued that, when employing "denial of responsibility," individuals believe they are not accountable for their deviant behavior because of environmental or circumstantial factors, ultimately convincing themselves that conditions beyond their control pushed or pulled them into the acts of deviance. For example, a drug dealer might argue that a lack of legitimate means for upward mobility essentially forced him or her into the drug game. "Denial of injury" argues that deviance is ultimately determined by whether or not there was a clear victim who experienced actual harm. If the act involved willing participants, such as drug users or groups engaged in mutual combat, there is no reluctant victim. "Denial of the victim" claims that the injured party deserved the resulting harm from the deviant act. Through an "appeal to higher loyalties" the perpetrator concedes that an act may violate codified law or society's general norms and values, but, claims the action adhered to or promoted some eminently important, alternative value system. For example, a drug dealer may argue that drug prohibition violates our individual rights as Americans, echoing the entrenched liberalism perspective on victimless crime—that we all "have the right to go to hell in our own way."[12] Lastly, "condemning the condemners" minimizes the significance of deviant acts by highlighting the wrongdoings of the victims, or those that criticize their actions.[13]

Since its original conception, Sykes and Matza's "techniques of neutralization" have been applied and tested in a variety of different contexts. In 1970, Thomas P. Priest and John H. McGrath examined how juvenile marijuana users implemented techniques of neutralization to cope with their deviant behavior.[14] Henry Mannle applied the model to juvenile sexual behavior, examining the gender and racial differences in sexual deviance.[15] The five original techniques of neutralization were applied to violent criminals by Quint Thurman and later by Robert Agnew.[16] More recently, Jim Mitchell, Richard Dodder, and Terry Norris examined the relationship between self-reported delinquency and church attendance via techniques of neutralization.[17] Stephen Eliason applied the model to poachers and other "wildlife law violators."[18] In this study, Eliason argued, "Sykes and Matza (1957) believed individuals used these techniques both before and after engaging in illegal activity. Thus, they are not justifications simply for involvement after the fact but also serve as important motivations for participation prior to the activity."[19] While these scholars applied Sykes and Matza's original theory to different behaviors, other scholars have posited additional techniques of neutralization to expand the original five-pronged model.[20]

The legacy of scholarship that augmented the original model began with Carl Klockers, who coined an additional neutralization technique, "the metaphor of the ledger."[21] According to Klockers, there are certain individuals who believe that the few bad acts they may find themselves involved in are superseded by their holistic "goodness" and that their deviance is minimized by their belief in themselves as generally good people. Others demonstrated that the metaphor of the ledger was a prominent technique implemented by "dogmen," individuals who train pit bulls for organized fights with other dogs. Beyond the metaphor of the ledger, in his work "The Neutralization of Criminal Offenses," William Minor introduced the "defense of necessity" as an additional means by which deviant actors negotiate a nondeviant perception of self.[22] This approach posits that otherwise immoral behavior can be perceived by the actor as obligatory given certain exigent circumstances. The classic example of this defense of necessity would be a mother who steals bread from a bakery to feed her starving children. While clearly deviant in that the theft constitutes a violation of both social and legal norms, the maliciousness of this act and the subsequent self-identification as deviant could be mitigated by the actor due to the urgent conditions in which she found herself.

The remaining three addenda to Sykes and Matza's original neutralization techniques were posed by James Coleman in his investigation into the causes of white-collar crime.[23] "The denial of the necessity of law" argues that individuals may break a particular law when they believe that law is unjust; "the claim that everybody else is doing it" posits individual deviant acts might be perceived as just, when some critical mass of people are engaged in similar behavior, and "the claim of entitlement" argues that an individual may perceive he or she is entitled to the benefit of some deviant and/or criminal act. While some techniques may have more utility than others, we will move forward using the current ten-pronged techniques of neutralization model in an attempt to better contextualize the mental gymnastics employed by this group of affluent drug dealers.

At the time of his interview, Brad, one of the drug dealers already introduced in Chapter 4, was a twenty-two-year-old business administration major originally from central Florida's Gulf Coast. He could be objectively described as a heavy prescription-drug user and tangentially involved in sales. As we mentioned, Brad denied being involved in prescription-drug sales, yet in the next breath while explaining how he helped bankroll prescription-drug runs to Mexico said, "I've been indirectly involved in the sales side of it." Brad went on to reduce the effect of his own criminal behavior with the excuse "everyone was into it." While his statement unambiguously supports "the claim that everybody else is doing it" neutralization strategy, the majority of these affluent drug dealers mitigate their overt criminality utilizing Klockers's metaphor of the ledger, a process in which individuals somewhat selectively and subjectively tabulate their behavior, as if they were using a ledger. Some degree of deviance or criminality is acceptable, as long as these "calculations" reveal a preponderance of wholesome, norm-abiding behavior. Criminality and deviance are framed as mere periodic transgressions from an otherwise virtuous existence. These mental gymnastics allow these drug dealers to neutralize their criminality when desired and to "drift" between their identities as underworld renegades and their identities as future bastions of social and economic convention.[24] The prevalence of the metaphor of the ledger is made evident through the language employed by these affluent drug dealers to downgrade the seriousness of their criminality, the sheer scope of their illegal businesses, and by their hiding behind a veil of being college students embarking upon legitimate and socially praiseworthy pursuits.

Many of these dealers were being groomed and firmly expected to become future victors in the legitimate economy. Several subjects were already the owners and operators of one or more legitimate small businesses and the subjects in the study were disproportionately current or former business majors. It was common for some members in this network to apply the terminology from the legitimate aspects of their lives, and from their business-school training, to their criminal enterprises. Some subjects routinely used economics or business jargon when discussing the intricacies of their drug-dealing businesses. The words "inventory" and "capital" were light-heartedly used interchangeably with "stash" and "cash" depending on the context and the players in the discussion. It is possible these dealers were using language to veil their illegal businesses with the dressings of a legitimate pursuit, reinforcing virtue by alluding to their scholastic and professional aspirations. While other drug dealers derive status from "clocking," wearing beepers, and flaunting the dealing lifestyle, it seems these affluent dealers consciously downplay their criminal identity when desired.[25] Moreover, as previously discussed, many of these college students made the irrational choice to become drug dealers in part because they steadfastly embraced the spirit of capitalism—either there was a demand for illicit drugs that was not being met or the supply of illegal drugs was so restricted that it artificially inflated the price, and thus the rewards of haphazardly venturing into criminality were dramatically increased. Embracing the spirit of capitalism and using the language of legitimate business pursuits helped intertwine the legitimate and illegitimate aspects of their lives. This impacted the subjective calculations employed in the "metaphor of the ledger" and assisted these drug dealers in neutralizing their own criminal behavior when they saw fit.

In the exchange below, Brice and Ann explicitly blurred the boundaries between legitimate and illegitimate undertakings.

BRICE: Had I continued it I would have completely changed my profile. I would have, ya know, I have seen what is profitable. It seem[s] way smarter to sell ya know larger quantities, that way you get less traffic and less people. It is important to maximize your money per contact, the same thing I try to do in my current job. I try to maximize my commissions per person.

ANN: Fewer people, more of their money.

BRICE: Ya know, so you meet the fewest contacts and make the most from that contact. I think it is important to have people who buy different quantities too, that way you can make a little bit more profits at different levels you know what I mean? Lower levels you can make more profit and at higher levels you can make less profit. If you have a combination of all . . . you have people buying ounces, people buying half ounces, people buying QPs [quarter pounds] that you can get though it, offset it, it's beneficial so you can go through it faster.

Did the business keep you from doing school work or looking for a job, or legitimate stuff?

BRICE: Probably. But I probably would have been doing something else, I really wasn't that motivated. I'm not that type of person. It was on my schedule. The job I have now is on my schedule, sometimes on my client's schedule. I have an 8:30[am] tomorrow. Bitch, I am gonna charge him what we call a P.I.A. fee, pain in the ass fee.

These affluent drug dealers steadfastly maintained a commitment to legitimate pursuits, despite the demands of their illegal businesses. Indeed, it is possible that individual dealers rationalized their illegitimate businesses because they were viewed as secondary to their legitimate pursuits; their core identity remained rooted in conventional norms and their criminality was merely a tangential aspect of a predominantly legitimate identity. This dynamic is further illustrated by the constant struggle of these dealers to keep their illegal businesses a manageable size.

The majority of the illegal businesses within this network had tremendous growth potential. The continual challenge for dealers was limiting their clientele and continued expansion, given the demand for their products among college students. Many of them had all the necessary components to expand their part-time businesses into full-blown industries, with larger quantities of both drugs and profits. And, many had, or had earned, enough capital to finance the purchase of larger quantities of drugs. The few who lacked capital surely had enough rapport to be "fronted" for larger quantities of drugs from which to expand their businesses. Thus, the capital, clientele, and connections were all readily available for substantial business expansion. However, not a single one of the relatively large-scale dealers in the sample chose to become full-time drug dealers and to abandon their legitimate pursuits entirely. Given the apparent absence of logistical restraints, a dedication to the capitalist doctrine of profit maximization, and little fear of the criminal justice system, why would these individuals in the drug-dealing business choose stagnation over expansion? This choice to limit the scope of these illegal businesses is evidence of a reluctance to self-identify exclusively as a drug-dealer. If illegitimate roles were to supersede legitimate ones, dealers would lose their key extenuation tool; they would be forced to recognize themselves as drug dealers first and foremost and not only when they were moved to embody the trappings of cowboy criminality. Using the tabulations prescribed in "the metaphor of the ledger," it is likely that substantial connections to legitimacy allowed these dealers to craft a self-concept that dismissed the severity of their own criminality; despite a criminal stutter-step, their holistic goodness allowed them to maintain a core identity derived from their status as a student, athlete, or professional.

Dealers in this population have substantial opportunities to achieve success in the legitimate world; they are college-educated, typically having a variety of legitimate skills and professional associations. Their illegitimate enterprises exist simultaneously with extensive commitments to the legitimate spheres of their lives. The seemingly temporary, tangential nature of their criminality works in conjunction with dedication to legitimate aspirations to allow dealers to avoid the internalization of a universal deviant self-identity. Indeed, most of our dealers routinely managed some combination of licit and illicit commitments and activities; they juggled school, a legitimate job, daily drug use, and their signature illicit drug-dealing activities. In fact, their drug activities often seemed to be simply spliced into their otherwise ordinary daily lives. Beefy provided a solid example of this phenomenon. He was a full-time student, held down a part-time job as a bank teller, smoked marijuana during virtually every break in his schedule, and also routinely sold marijuana to our networks' users. Despite his substantial drug use, Beefy seemed to function relatively well across all of his vocations and managed to remain focused on a series of long-term legitimate career goals.

> *So do you get pretty good grades?*
> BEEFY: Oh yeah, usually As and Bs. I think cumulative I have like a 3.1 or something like that.
> *What is your major?*
> BEEFY: Sociology.
> *Do you have a minor?*
> BEEFY: Business.
> *You want to stay in [this part of California]?*
> BEEFY: Um, I'd like to stay in California. I am not really partial to [this area]. Either way it depends on where I get a job and how much they are offering to pay.

Similarly, Maria, a white, twenty-one-year-old college student and drug dealer balanced school work and her relatively small drug-dealing business. On several occasions, she was observed multitasking; consuming marijuana and doing homework while waiting for customers to arrive and while they were there sampling her product.

Ashcan also expressed a firm commitment to legitimate long-term goals. Apparently, the restrictions posed by his future scholastic commitments might dictate the extent of his future drug dealing. In other words, as noted in his full quote in Chapter 3, Ashcan very clearly suggested that, during the course of his legitimate aspiration to become a lawyer, he might find it practical to return to drug sales "if I need some money or something."

In contrast with the bulk of drug-dealing organizations document-ed in the criminological literature and those loose organizations that tend to comprise the majority of our nation's jail and prison drug-offender populations, the individuals in this network were not driven by necessity. Nor were they dealing as a means to escape the plagues of social disorganization afflicting our inner cities. Not only did these dealers perceive the existence of legitimate opportunities, they were also poised by the status afforded them by the "accident of birth" to embrace them.[26] It also seems that the shallow commitment to illegitimacy resulting from the existence of legitimate opportunities for success aids in allowing these affluent dealers to minimize perceptions of their own deviance.

While the maintenance of an essential nondeviant self-identity was evident throughout our contacts with the majority of this population, there was one dealer interviewed who presented a glaring exception. LaCoste was the only subject over the course of this study's more than five years who readily identified himself as a criminal and exhibited the boastful nature common in criminological discussions of drug dealers. While many of the affluent drug dealers occasionally flaunted their criminal status, only he seemed to readily embrace criminality as his master status.

LaCoste: I'm a criminal. Yes, I definitely see myself as a criminal . . . Like you walk down the street looking at the birds, and I'm walking down the street and out of the corner of my eye I see an open window.

There are several factors that might account for LaCoste's atypical, flamboyant self-identification as a criminal. His mother had recently gone through a serious bout with cancer; his father's job simultaneously compromised the amount of bonding time while allowing LaCoste the financial wherewithal to run amok; he was struggling to fit in among a student population with as much money as he had at his disposal and from much "cooler" parts of the country than the Midwest; and he had some serious substance abuse issues of his own. It is also clear from his statement and others he made that his deviant self-identification did not derive solely from the use and sale of drugs. Rather, as we note throughout this work, he had more than a passing participatory interest in other types of crime, an interest that clearly differentiated him from the rest of the subjects in this population. Finally, LaCoste was unique in this population because he had carried a gun in the past and is one of the few dealers to regularly sell harder drugs. But, LaCoste is an inimitable exception in this group of drug dealers that only periodically and rather reluctantly self-identified as criminals. Unlike LaCoste, whose tough-guy facade was unrelenting, most of the affluent drug dealers who made up our network only embraced the pseudo-gangsta personas periodically.

Dealer Bio: Cecilia

Cecilia was born and raised in a working-class community in California, not far from where she would ultimately attend college. Despite being a dedicated student, in high school she would routinely host "ditch parties," when her group of friends would ditch school after lunch, drink and party at her house. She noted that drug dealing was ingrained in this local culture, as evidenced by the fact that all the digital and "triple-beam" scales in her high-school science classes were continually being stolen until the administration ultimately chained them to the science lab tables. Unlike the vast majority of the dealers in this study, Cecilia was not "from money." Growing up, she had a series of part-time jobs including working at a local tourist attraction, waitressing at a family-owned Italian restaurant, and as a trainer for professional show horses. She had a genuine love and passion for horses that lead her to pursue a degree in biology with the ultimate goal of attending veterinary school and becoming a large-animal veterinarian.

Cecilia was accustomed to balancing substantial demanding endeavors simultaneously. At the height of her drug-dealing enterprise, she was nearing the completion of a rather rigorous degree program in the natural sciences, training a show horse several times per week, and was the sole proprietor of a substantial marijuana-dealing enterprise moving roughly eight pounds of marijuana per month with a wholesale street value of approximately $32,000. Like most of the other dealers in this study, the profits from her sales were typically spent on partying, supporting friends' partying, gourmet dinner parties, and other champagne tastes that should not have been affordable on a college student's beer budget. Despite these commitments, she remained firmly dedicated to her friends and maintained an active social life, with marijuana and alcohol as central features. Like the vast majority of dealers in this study, Cecilia's social life and "the business" routinely took priority over scholastic commitments and directly facilitated procrastination. Habitually, she would not begin studying for a big exam until

(continues)

118

Dealer Bio: continued

the night before; fueled by strong coffee, she would subsequently pull the infamous "all nighter" in order to prepare. Despite the fact that the majority of her biology-major peers were fiercely attempting to get into medical school, hiring private tutors, were often relentlessly competitive and not distracted by employment (in the underground economy or otherwise)—Cecilia graduated on time and earned fairly good grades in one of the most demanding majors on campus.

After a 2008 follow-up interview, Cecilia laughed vivaciously as she described that she recently learned that some of her friends referred to her college apartment as the "black hole"; there was an abundant supply of marijuana, a constant stream of friends to hang out with, and apparently no visible clocks anywhere in the main room of the apartment. This combination routinely facilitated inadvertently missing classes and other commitments. Cecilia commented that she was surprised that everyone that lived there actually managed to graduate from college. Cecilia reminisced about an event both she and a researcher witnessed years before involving "Sleepy Steve," a regular customer and friend of Cecilia. He had earned the nickname "Sleepy" because, as a veteran marijuana user, the markers of marijuana use were readily apparent on his face (bloodshot eyes, lethargy, etc.). As was his routine, Sleepy Steve entered the apartment, warmly greeted his friends and acquaintances in the room, and proceeded to purchase, consume, and share an eighth of marijuana. A considerable amount of time passed—an hour, if not longer—before he suddenly shot up to his feet and exclaimed a series of good natured, yet self-deprecating profanities. Quite intoxicated, Sleepy Steve struggled to locate his belongings including his keys, wallet, and newly purchased sack of marijuana, while he explained to the group that he was currently on a date! Uncontrolled laugher ensued from everyone in attendance. Apparently, he had only been out with this young woman a few times and she was uncomfortable going with Steve to the drug spot, although bringing a

(continues)

Dealer Bio: continued

friend or significant other to make a purchase was a practice that was common and generally acceptable. Sleepy Steve, undoubtedly fueled by his own intoxication and the environment of the "black hole," had forgotten that his date had been waiting in the car the whole time! Neither Cecilia nor the researcher could recall Steve subsequently going on another date with this young woman.

Surprisingly unique among the dealers in this study, Cecilia's dedication to the marijuana lifestyle was infused with politics and science. For Cecilia, pot was political; she would routinely praise progressive marijuana legislation and the sociobiological benefits of marijuana use, demonstrating both her scientific training and her proclivity for the drug.

Conclusion

If nothing else, the dealers in this affluent California college drug-dealing network vividly illustrate the deficiencies in how we currently contemplate and consider illegal drug activity in the United States today. In the criminal justice system, in broader society, and even in academia's tendency to focus research efforts primarily on the drug-dealing activities of the poor, we seem all too willing to embrace the "dualistic fallacy"—the erroneous assumption that a clear distinction exists between criminals and noncriminals.[27] As explored through the lens of labeling theory and symbolic capital, our network's dealers engaged in mental gymnastics that allowed them to manage two striking contradictions. They demonstrated a disconnect between their tangible and obvious criminal behaviors and their intangible self-identity, and they demonstrated a self-identity that allowed them to "drift" between conformity and criminality. It seems these criminals were able to suppress the deviant components of their self-identity for three reasons. First, a lack of actual law-enforcement consequences contributes to a reciprocal labeling process; they are labeled as nondeviant and thus develop a nondeviant self-concept. Second, common assumptions about drug crime and drug criminals seem to contribute to the erroneous conclusion that their demographic is largely noncriminal. Last, these dealers created their core identity around their legitimate roles and thus minimized their conceptual commitment to criminality. Utilizing the metaphor of the ledger, these dealers can drift back and forth between the sneaky thrills of identifying as drug dealers and reap the material and social benefits of this identity, yet they can also find the comfort of grounding their identity in traditional norms and values. When taken together, these factors provide limiting mechanisms that allow these dealers to minimize perceptions of their own deviant behavior, their own mental gymnastics of denial.

Notes

1. Sykes and Matza, "Techniques of Neutralization," p. 666.
2. According to the biennial survey conducted through the National Judicial Reporting Program on behalf of the US Department of Justice, in 2004 felony marijuana trafficking convictions in state courts totaled 22,180. This figure does not include convictions in federal court or the tens of thousands of felony convictions in state courts stemming from marijuana possession as the most serious offense leading to criminal conviction. US Department of Justice, Bureau of Justice Statistics, *State Court Sentencing of Convicted Felons.*
3. Ibid.
4. Becker, Outsiders.
5. Ibid., p. 9.
6. Lemert, *Human Deviance, Social Problems, and Social Control.*
7. Akers, *Criminological Theories,* p. 122.
8. Ibid.
9. Tannenbaum, *Crime and the Community,* p. 21.
10. Kappeler and Potter, *The Mythology of Crime and Criminal Justice;* Burston, Jones, and Roberson-Sanders, "Drug Use and African Americans."
11. Sykes and Matza, "Techniques of Neutralization."
12. Stankiewicz, "In Search of a Political Philosophy," p. 89.
13. Sykes and Matza, "Techniques of Neutralization."
14. Priest and McGrath, "Techniques of Neutralization."
15. Mannle, "An Empirical Exploration and Interpretation of Neutralization Theory."
16. Thurman, "Deviance and the Neutralization of Moral Commitment"; Agnew, "The Techniques of Neutralization and Violence."
17. Mitchell, Dodder, and Norris, "Neutralization and Delinquency."
18. Eliason, "Illegal Hunting and Angling."

19. Ibid., p. 4.

20. Eliason, "Illegal Hunting and Angling"; Minor, "The Neutralization of Criminal Offense."

21. Klockers, *The Professional Fence.*

22. Minor, "The Neutralization of Criminal Offense."

23. Coleman, *The Criminal Elite.*

24. Sykes and Matza, "Techniques of Neutralization."

25. Anderson, *The Code of the Street.*

26. Language taken from US Supreme Court case *Frontiero v. Richardson,* 411 US 677, 686.

27. Regoli and Hewitt, *Delinquency in Society.*

6

Perceived and Actual Risks for College Drug Dealers: Un-Risky Business

Rooted in classical criminology, deterrence theory suggests that human beings are rational actors who actively and carefully weigh the likely costs and benefits associated with their behavioral choices. When these choices involve unlawful behaviors, adherents to deterrence theory posit that, by ratcheting up punishments and the costs of doing business, potential criminals will opt to conform to societal norms rather than pay the costs associated with running afoul of the legal system. While theoretical explanations of social phenomena are often dismissed as conjecture or "mere empty ruminations—fun, perhaps, but not something for which practical men and women have time," with regard to criminal justice policy these abstract ideas have real social consequences.[1]

Insofar as deterrence theory is concerned, its place as the philosophical foundation for US criminal justice policy has given it near-doctrinal status.[2] This homage to the classical cost/benefits approach can be seen most clearly in US drug policy, particularly those policies that emerged during the 1980s and 1990s "war on drugs." Since the inception of this metaphorical war, the US government has been unyieldingly committed to punitive prohibition strategies that more often target first-time and low-level offenders rather than the drug kingpins for whom the policies ostensibly were intended.[3]

Given these macro-level dynamics, it would seem that only very impulsive or very desperate people would potentially mortgage their freedom and their future by choosing to sell illicit drugs. In other words, the potential costs associated with illegal drug dealing would only be deemed worthwhile by people who saw for themselves no other viable money-making alternatives or people for whom the idea of doing a stretch in the penitentiary did not seem like such a frightening or ignoble fate. However, the affluent drug dealers with whom we came into contact seemed to reject this theoretical paradigm in their determination to make an *irrational choice,* haphazardly bounding into criminality despite the presumably apparent threat of negative criminal and social consequences. Indeed, one of the most perplexing questions we faced in the years we spent interviewing and observing the drug dealers in our network revolved around why affluent, young, predominantly white, college students would even interstitially choose the life of a drug dealer given all that they theoretically should stand to lose. While the substantial costs borne by their urban minority counterparts have proved to be quite real, what we found for our network's dealers was that their choice to sell drugs might not have been so irrational after all. Before going into the particular risks and rewards associated with our network's drug dealers, it is important to put into context the US drug war and the disproportionate burden it has placed on poor and minority drug offenders.

Punitiveness, Paupers, and Pigmentation: Incarceration in the United States

The United States has amassed the largest prison system in the world. As discussed in Chapter 1, currently, over seven million of its adult residents are under some form of correctional supervision. More than 3 percent of the US adult population is either in jail or prison, or being monitored in the community while on probation or parole; 2.3 million of these people are serving time behind bars, locked up in local jails, state prisons, or federal prisons. The result is an incarceration rate in the United States far higher than any other industrialized, democratic nation, but also one substantially higher than many nations ruled by notoriously despotic regimes.[4] While home to roughly 5 percent of the world's population, the United States houses 25 percent of the world's incarcerated population, a statistic that has led some critics to dub the land of the free as the "incarcer*nation.*"

The United States was not always so punitive. Rather, the mid-1970s marked a critical tipping point in the shape and direction of US criminal justice policy. Fueled in part by Robert Martinson's somewhat dubious finding that "nothing works"[5] insofar as criminal rehabilitation programs are concerned, an already receptive pro-punishment polity effectively did away with rehabilitation as a purpose of punishment and focused instead on retribution, deterrence, and incapacitation as the justification for funneling people through the criminal justice system. The corresponding result of this philosophical shift was an increasingly dense web of mandatory minimum sentences, automatic sentence enhancements for particular types of crimes, limitations on habeas relief, and the increased federalization of what once were state criminal justice issues. In all, these shifts ushered in the dawn of the "get tough on crime" era, ultimately facilitating dramatic increases in US rates of incarceration. In fact, between 1980 and 2006, the US incarcerated population ballooned from around 500,000 people to more than two million, an increase of nearly 450 percent.[6] Most significantly, this population escalation was primarily driven by shifts in criminal justice philosophy and policy, not increased rates of offending. In fact, over the second decade of this incarceration boom, the rates of both violent and property crimes in the United States substantially declined.

As it stands today, there are more than 2 million people behind bars in the United States—only three US cities have a population greater than that of the jail and prison system. And if these inmates were transplanted to one central location this new city's inhabitants would rival in numbers that of Houston, Texas.[7] In what is perhaps a more galling tale of the US incarceration tape, the number of people behind bars in the United States is also greater than the number of people who graduate from US colleges each year, double the number of people who graduated from US colleges in 1998, and more than triple the total number of all US soldiers killed in combat since the Revolutionary War.[8] According to the justice-oriented advocacy group, Human Rights Watch, "No functioning democracy has ever governed itself with as large a percentage of its adults incarcerated as the United States."[9]

No segments of the population have felt the pressures of the incarceration boom more than the poor and people of color. At the time this book went to press, the current incarceration rates for African Americans and Hispanics were 3,042 and 1,261 per 100,000 respectively, compared to an incarceration rate of 487 per 100,000 for whites.[10] African Americans currently comprise approximately 13 percent of the US population but constitute over 42 percent of jail and prison inmates.[11] Moreover, more than one in every nine African-American men between the ages of twenty-five and twenty-nine called a US jail or prison "home" in 2006.[12] Assuming a continuation of the status-quo, over his lifetime an African-American baby boy born in 2008 has a one in three chance of serving time in prison and his Hispanic counterpart will have a one in six chance.[13] This dramatic overrepresentation of young men of color in the criminal justice system has profound cumulative effects on US communities[14] and raises fundamental questions about equity, due process, and equal protection in the correctional and judicial systems. Unfortunately, as the US Supreme Court has demonstrated quite clearly over the past twenty-five years in its adoption of doctrines upholding these racial and ethnic inequalities as constitutionally permissible, the answer to these fundamental questions does not seem to bode well for black and brown people in the United States.

In addition to a disproportionate impact on people of color, current punishment policies continue to come largely at the expense of those on the lower rungs of the socioeconomic ladder. As criminologist Jeffrey Reiman writes: "For *the same criminal behavior,* the poor are more likely to be arrested; if arrested, they are more likely to be charged; if charged, more likely to be convicted; if convicted, more likely to be sentenced to prison; and if sentenced, more likely to be given longer prison terms than members of the middle and upper classes."[15]

Reiman further argues that the justice system's targeting of the lower classes and people of color who are grossly overrepresented among the poor creates a distorted picture of the US crime problem. Although the poor are disproportionately represented among those arrested and incarcerated, contrary to many media reports and the general perception of the US public,[16] criminal behavior is not isolated or even heavily concentrated among members of the lower classes. Rather, the overwhelming majority of evidence suggests that formal criminal justice system intervention and punishments are disproportionably meted out against members of the lower socioeconomic classes.

Numerous micro-level and social-structural factors interact to influence the criminal justice system's disproportionate impact on the poor and people of color. Some of these contributory factors include a plea-bargaining process that encourages people of lesser means to avoid trial; the diminished privacy and heightened visibility that corresponds with poverty; the increased reliance on overburdened and resource-poor public defenders by minorities and poorer people; and ongoing racial profiling and the targeting of minority communities by law-enforcement personnel. However, it has been well documented that none of these factors have contributed more to this class and race disparity than the war on drugs.[17]

The War on Drugs

In the summer of 1995, the Discovery Channel hosted an hour-long special titled, "The Cronkite Report—The Drug Dilemma: War or Peace?" News legend Walter Cronkite concluded his program by saying, "We cannot go into tomorrow with the same formulas that are failing today. We must not blindly add to the body count and the terrible cost of the war on drugs only to learn . . . thirty years from now that what we've been doing is wrong, terribly wrong."[18]

By "terribly wrong," Cronkite was likely referring to the very policies that established the foundation of the current drug war and the empirical data that underscore the extent to which this war has been misguided, ineffective, and has overburdened US taxpayers and the justice system. Criminal justice experts attribute nearly 25 percent of the current incarcerated population directly to the punitive drug policies enacted during the Reagan-Bush era and enhanced during the subsequent Clinton and Bush administrations.[19] In 1980, prior to the launching of the war on drugs, drug law violators comprised only 6 percent of state prisoners,[20] a figure that has quadrupled since then. In the decade preceding the launch of the drug war, drug offenders consistently made up about 25 percent of federal prison inmates, a figure that ballooned to over 60 percent by the mid-1990s and remains at well over 50 percent today.[21] Further, drug offenders continue to clog US courts, constituting approximately 35 percent of all felony convictions in both the state and federal systems.[22] Framed in terms of raw numbers, the retributive strategies of the war on drugs are directly responsible for the incarceration of over 500,000 inmates currently housed in US correctional facilities,[23] a more than twelve-fold increase from the 40,000 drug offenders that were incarcerated in 1980. Finally, over the nearly three decades of the US drug war, drug offenders have been the fastest growing sector of the US prison population, primarily a result of increased law-enforcement scrutiny and not that of increased rates of offending.

Since the start of the war on drugs, the state of California has largely mirrored national criminal justice policy trends. In 1983, drug offenders constituted 7 percent of all felony inmates in California; by 2000 that population had bloated to 26 percent.[24] Drug offenders comprised nearly 31 percent of all new felony inmates in the Golden State in 2001, and more than one-third of these inmates were serving time for possession of a controlled substance instead of for more serious drug crimes like distribution and trafficking.[25] While the incarceration of low-level drug offenders is controversial for multiple reasons, the most rational and least controversial objection may be that, on average, it costs nearly $36,000 per year to keep one person behind bars in the state of California and warehousing these predominantly nonviolent drug offenders consumes a considerable portion of the state's nearly $10 billion corrections budget.[26]

With specific regard to the racial and economic disparities that have stemmed from changes in national and state drug laws, and consistent with the effects of the more general get tough model that took hold in the early 1980s, the war on drugs has not affected all groups equally. In fact, most criminologists and sociologists who study crime have held that the war on drugs has brought about dire consequences for already marginalized groups and those traditionally overrepresented among the lower socioeconomic classes. Analyzing Department of Justice data, Phillip Beatty, Amanda Petteruti, and Jason Ziedenberg comment on these disparities in criminal justice policies:

> African Americans are disproportionately incarcerated for drug offenses in the US, though they use and sell drugs at similar rates to whites. As of 2003, twice as many African Americans as whites were incarcerated for drug offenses in state prisons in the US. African Americans made up 13 percent of the total US population, but accounted for 53 percent of sentenced drug offenders in state prisons in 2003.[27]

Criminologist Michael Tonry adds that, with the glaring exception of drug law prison and jail commitments, incarceration rates generally reflect rates of offending rather than racial bias at various stages of the criminal justice process. However, writes Tonry, "Drug law enforcement is the conspicuous exception. Blacks are arrested and confined in numbers grossly out of line with their use or sale of drugs."[28] In their analysis of Department of Justice data, Human

Rights Watch backs Tonry's claim concluding, "Relative to population, Black men are admitted to state prison on drug charges at a rate
that is 13.4 times greater than that of White men . . . primarily the
result of public penal policies and law enforcement priorities, not
different rates of drug offending."[29] And finally, an investigative
report in *USA Today* reached similar conclusions: "Urban Blacks are
being detained in numbers far exceeding their involvement in the
drug trade."[30]

Despite the enormous social and financial costs incurred over the
more than two decades of the war waged on drugs, illegal drugs are
still widely available throughout the United States and recent estimates suggest that roughly twenty million Americans aged twelve
and older are current illicit drug users.[31] According to Judge James P.
Gray, "Our communities remain awash in illegal drugs in spite of
every enforcement effort, and there is no progress in sight."[32] Gray
argues that despite a firm commitment to punitive zero-tolerance
policies, only one law can truly govern drugs in the United States—
the law of supply and demand.

As spending on the drug war continues to increase (in 2009, the
federal cost alone of running the drug war was $14.8 billion),[33] these
massive expenditures have done little to curtail drug use, increase the
relative cost of illicit drugs, or decrease the purity of street drugs
available in US markets.[34] For example, in 2000 the retail cost of one
pure gram of powder cocaine was $149, the lowest price in at least
twelve years; that same year, one pure gram of heroin cost $1,029,
over 66 percent less expensive than in 1988.[35] In addition, a bountiful
supply of marijuana remains available across the nation, particularly
in the US Southwest, and experts agree that the marijuana on today's
market is more potent than it was at the beginning of the drug war.
Additionally, while most marijuana that makes its way into the hands
of US consumers is imported from Mexico, California leads the nation
in both indoor and outdoor domestic marijuana production[36] and, as
we mentioned earlier in this book, decades after the beginning of the
drug war pot has firmly established itself as California's number one
cash crop.[37] According to a 2008 study conducted by Columbia
University's National Center on Addiction and Substance Abuse, after
roughly thirty years of the war on drugs and draconian drug policies
serving as the cornerstone of multiple presidential administrations and
legislative platforms, US teenagers report that it is easier for someone
their age to buy marijuana than it is to buy beer.[38]

The empirical evidence demonstrating the increased prevalence of illicit drugs combined with the glaring racial and socioeconomic disparities that have come as a direct result of contemporary drug war strategies suggest that the war on drugs is not, at its core, about public health or moral platitudes. What this evidence does suggest quite clearly is that, regardless of the existence or absence of discriminatory purpose, the drug war has served the ultimate function of waging war on the poor and people of color. Resting somewhere beneath the surface of it all, the statistical record also exposes an injustice that is conspicuously absent from conversations on Capitol Hill and college hill alike. This injustice centers on the egregious extent to which the war on drugs, in its demonization of the already disenfranchised, has quite conspicuously ignored other key constituents in the domestic drug trade. Our study's primary drug market, composed of affluent college students who heavily use and wheel and deal in illicit street drugs, is one such overlooked constituency. And, as history reveals, the relative immunity of wealthy white people from law enforcement scrutiny is not an anomaly; rather, it is the norm. As Laura Penny rather succinctly summarized in her commentary on the effects of the drug war:

> The War on Some Drugs is largely a war on the poor. The cartels have lawyers and bodyguards and havens to protect themselves from justice. The minor players and users do not. Some drugs are classier than others, but the abjectness of the drug user's condition, and the force of prohibition against them, is dependent on the class of the user, not the effects of the substance itself. Woe betide the collared crackhead from Any Ghetto, who can look forward to a stint in prison. Would that he, like Noelle Bush or Rush Limbaugh, had the resources for revolving-door rehab.[39]

Symbolic Capital: Social Cachet and the Complexion for the Connection

For nearly a century, sociologists and criminologists have commented on the ways the socioeconomic status of an offender influences treatment by actors at various stages of the criminal justice process. As Edwin Sutherland highlighted during his 1939 presidential address to the American Sociological Association, the public, scholars, and the criminal justice system itself all fixate on the crimes committed by the underprivileged and all but ignore those committed by people in positions of high social status. In support of this critique, contemporary criminologists point to the overwhelming extent to which knowledge of criminal behavior and the theories about criminality that ultimately shape public policy are guided by official statistics generated from the criminal justice establishment. In analyses of self-reporting studies, victimization surveys, and virtually every other noncriminal justice source of US crime statistics, these data have been shown to overrepresent, often drastically, lower-class criminality.

The reason for the relative absence of more affluent lawbreakers caught up in the official criminal justice net is no real mystery. As Rosoff, Pontell, and Tillman noted, "Persons of the upper socioeconomic class are more powerful politically and financially and escape arrest and conviction to a greater extent than persons who lack such power."[40] Specific to our current research on college drug dealers, Pierre Bourdieu's framing of "symbolic capital" [41] sheds some additional light on the reasons that actors in the criminal and campus justice systems seemed to overlook or ignore this relatively affluent, largely white college drug using and dealing subculture as well as others around the country with similar characteristics. In moving conversations of social status beyond the relatively simplistic framework of material wealth and social class, Bourdieu reasoned that economic, social, and cultural fields have acquirable "human capital" associated with them, and people are defined by themselves and by others through the amounts of this human capital that they ultimately garner. If any of these three fields alone or in combination with each other are socially recognized as legitimate by others, particularly people in positions of relative power or authority, it becomes transformed into "symbolic capital." That is to say that class and the privileges associated with class are not only matters of objective and quantifiable social structure; they are also matters of "representational" structure and symbolic capital, which Bourdieu defined as a "degree of accumulated prestige, celebrity, consecration or honor and is founded on a dialectic of knowledge and recognition."[42]

Included in this framework is the value of social networks, which Bourdieu further reasoned could be used as cachet to produce or reproduce inequality. In our dealers' encounters with both on- and off-campus agents of formal social control, which included local police, highway patrol, border patrol, campus police, residence hall staff, and others, the social networks to which these dealers belonged, in conjunction with the fact that they did not meet stereotypical, superficial law enforcement drug-dealer criteria, served as a de facto get-out-of-jail-free card. Or better yet, their accumulated symbolic capital served as a "never-go-to-jail-in-the-first-place" card. Again, nearly all of our network's dealers were white or would be perceived as white, and the one or two who were visibly nonwhite certainly "played" white in both how they interacted with their peers and with authority figures. Virtually all of our dealers were raised in and continued to travel in relatively affluent social circles. They demonstrated their privileged backgrounds materially through expensive cars, brand-name clothing, and other symbols of material wealth, as well as through learned cultural conveyances of affluence. And finally, most of them attended a university that was hesitant to rock the proverbial boat because it was dependent upon these students' tuition dollars or, more accurately, their parents' tuition dollars, for its day-to-day operations. Beyond direct tuition stimulus, the university was also reliant on their students' social status for its "brand" reputation, and needed the appearance of affluent homogeneity and safety in its many possible forms in order to recruit future classes of relatively privileged white kids. Accordingly, the dealers in this network had amassed enough symbolic capital to grant them a certain degree of legal immunity in spite of their rampantly illegal drug activities, a fact that most of the dealers we spoke with were quite aware of.

As a test of a similar thesis in the now classic study "The Saints and the Roughnecks," criminologist William J. Chambliss observed two deviant groups of high-school boys and their interactions with their local community and law enforcement. He described the Saints as "Eight promising young men—children of good, stable White upper-middle-class families . . . good pre-college students" and, through his observations, found this group to be "some of the most delinquent boys at Hanibal High School."[43] In contrast, the Roughnecks were "six lower class White boys . . . constantly in trouble with police and community even though their rate of delinquency was about equal with that of the Saints."[44] While committing similar varieties and levels of deviant acts, the community and law enforcement's perceptions of and actions toward these two cliques differed greatly. Over the two years these groups were under observation, no official arrests were made of the Saints. During the same period, each Roughneck was arrested at least once, some several times, and two members of this group were incarcerated in a school for boys for six months. The community perceived the Saints as local leaders who were "sowing their wild oats." In contrast, it was assumed the Roughnecks' current deviance would evolve into more serious forms of criminality. Chambliss's explanations for the differential treatment of these two groups by both the community and law enforcement revolved around their comparative visibility and demeanor, and overt biases in favor of the Saints and against the Roughnecks.

Chambliss reasoned, "Differential visibility was a direct function of the economic standing of the families. The Saints had access to automobiles and were able to remove themselves from the sight of the community."[45] Much of their deviance, therefore, occurred in neighboring communities where they could strategically avoid tarnishing reputations in their hometown. Moreover, the Saints could hide much of their drinking and drug use inside their homes. In contrast, because of economic restrictions, like the lack of transportation, the Roughnecks tended to carry out their deviant acts—primarily theft, drinking, and fighting—in the heart of their community. This visibility or, conversely, invisibility of deviant behavior played a central role in the community's polarity of perceptions regarding these two groups.

According to Chambliss, the perceptual difference between the groups was further compounded by differences in demeanor between members of each gang. For example, when confronted by authority figures, the Saints were consistently "apologetic and penitent," demonstrating their adherence to middle-class norms and feigning respect for authority figures. Their manufactured deference often spared them from prosecution or formal charges being filed against them.[46] Authority figures, even those with a "pleasant" approach, received consistent "hostility and disdain"[47] in their interactions with the Roughnecks.

The final explanatory variable discussed by Chambliss was bias. Undoubtedly fueled by visibility and demeanor, but also likely linked to Bourdieu's notion of social capital, prejudice on the part of the community and law enforcement had drastic consequences for members of the Roughnecks. A predisposition favoring the Saints was apparent in the actions of teachers, administrators, community members, the police, and the parents of the Saints themselves. On the other hand, when a Roughneck was in trouble, often even the boy's parents presented attitudes coinciding with that of the community as a whole, seeming to express that their son was destined for more serious levels of delinquency.

Visibility, demeanor, and bias are "surface variables" that act in combination to explain disparate treatment of people by law enforcement personnel.[48] Chambliss argues that implicit in the behavior of the police is "the class structure of American society and the control of legal institutions by those at the top of the class structure."[49] While engaging in relatively similar levels of deviance, these groups received drastically different treatment partly as a result of the underrepresentation of those of low socioeconomic status at all levels of the US power structure. Chambliss's findings rather well capture what we observed in our interactions with our primary network's dealers, and what they observed of themselves. As Chambliss concluded, "Selective perception and labeling— finding, processing, and punishing some kinds of criminality and not others—means that visible, poor, non-mobile, outspoken, undiplomatic 'tough' kids will be noticed, whether their actions are seriously delinquent or not."[50]

Accordingly, Chambliss and Bourdieu provide an appropriate theoretical framework to guide research questions and areas of inquiry in places where, intuitively and often quite obviously, deviant behavior exists but that behavior goes unrecognized or unpunished. We found our present study to be one of those appropriate places. In terms of demographic distance from their poorer drug-dealing counterparts, the individuals that collectively made up our relatively affluent drug-distribution network were rather similar to the Saints and they had many of the same material and capital advantages and characteristics. Our dealers also had the added advantage of attending a university with a vested interest in projecting a homogeneous and safe image that ran counter to the public's perception of some other area institutions better known for partying than pedagogy.

Rich Kids and the Cops

Much of the criminological literature and most practices of law enforcement officials and criminal justice policymakers presume a clear, yet erroneous, distinction between criminal and noncriminal populations. This so-called dualistic fallacy[51] is overly simplistic in general, but is rendered glaringly naive given the internal and external dynamics within and surrounding the upper-middle-class drug dealing and using population that served as the focus of the present study, an overtly criminal population that existed largely immune to the brunt of the criminal justice system. Despite their brazen illegal business practices, members of this network had relatively few interactions with law enforcement, and these few interactions consistently resulted in either no punishment or relatively minor negative sanctions.

The role and prevalence of law enforcement is central to both the street corner drug-dealing world and criminological literature concerning drug-distribution networks. Both sources identify police as a daily concern for drug dealers who regularly employ and refine the systematic tactics they use in their efforts to avoid arrest.[52] Phillippe Bourgois's description of a crack dealing network in Harlem provides a clear example of this awareness, "There was always a strong undercurrent of anxiety over the risk of arrest . . . Primo, Caesar, and other dealers provided me with dozens of accounts of close calls with the police. They had developed complex, risk-minimization strategies . . . Primo attributed to carelessness the one time he was successfully arrested and convicted."[53] Patricia Adler's groundbreaking study of high-level cocaine dealers and international drug smugglers echoes Bourgois's account of the causes for Primo's arrest and the idea that police intervention is often the consequence of a lack of prevention by street dealers in illicit drugs: "Thus, aside from accident and the collusion of informants, dealers and smugglers attributed most arrests to their own negligence, to their failure to observe routine security precautions . . . Drug traffickers' rules for staying out of legal trouble took the form of three reactive strategies—secrecy, insulation, and manipulation—based on their perceptions of how police operated."[54]

In direct contrast to the world of drug dealing described by Bourgois, Adler, Terry Williams, and virtually everyone else who has studied successful drug syndicates, we found that members of our affluent college student drug-distribution network never extensively interacted with law enforcement, at least not for their illicit drug activities. Related, but perhaps more compelling, our dealers did not perceive the police as a serious threat to their drug activities or way of life in general. In the very few formal interactions between this population and the police, there were relatively minimal consequences that had the direct effect of reinforcing our dealers' perceptions of law enforcement as a negligible danger.

Relatively early in the study, Beefy had been apprehended by campus police and cited for possession of drug paraphernalia. As punishment for violating the campus drug policies as well as state laws, he received a small fine by the university and his case was never brought to anyone's attention beyond the walls of the campus. This may seem to be a normal response for private campus police officers who are often viewed as "fake cops" without full law-enforcement powers. However, on this particular campus, the police officers carry real firearms, conduct searches of vehicles and dorm rooms, and otherwise have full jurisdictional authority in the policing and investigation of crimes committed on campus. The campus is even equipped with its own emergency call center that students and other members of the university community are encouraged to call before alerting off-campus authorities. The city police only respond to campus incidents when they are summoned by campus police, when a 911 call originating from campus is received, or when they are in pursuit of a suspect who flees onto campus property. Therefore, even with crimes that very clearly could be charged as felonies, drug crimes in particular, a deliberate choice is made by campus authorities not to report these crimes to external agencies for formal prosecution.[55] Indeed, in one campus drug incident reported to us by a residence hall staff person, a student was nabbed by campus police for having what was described to us as "a forest" of marijuana growing in his dorm room. In another more recent incident, a student was apprehended by campus authorities while shooting up heroin in a campus bathroom stall. To our knowledge, in neither case were city police or any other external law enforcement authorities notified.

In Beefy's particular case, after his run-in with campus cops, he remained a relatively major dealer, and what he described as essentially a nonevent did not appear to have a specific deterrent effect:

BEEFY: You were supposed to pay a $150 fine and go to like two drug classes and some kind of shit. I never called. They never did anything. There's no block on my account so . . . Pop's probably paid for it. [laughs] Who knows. I never checked any receipts so I don't have any idea of what happened to it. But they've never contacted me to take any of the classes and I've never contacted them so . . .

Beefy's reaction to his rendezvous with the campus cops was reflective of our group's overall nonchalant view of law enforcement, an attitude made further evident by their ongoing reckless drug-dealing activities. Over the course of our observations, we noticed that very few substantial preventative measures were taken to avoid the scrutiny of law enforcement. In fact, in comparison to the strategies employed by typical street-drug dealers, it almost seemed as if our network's dealers were deliberately trying to draw attention to themselves or test social and legal boundaries. Routinely, ounces and even pounds of aromatic marijuana were carelessly tossed into school backpacks, Styrofoam coolers, or simply stuffed into pant pockets as part of everyday drug transactions; sophisticated packaging was rare and most transportation techniques could be characterized as, at best, haphazard. In fact, several dealers reported having ounces of marijuana at a time simply mailed to their campus addresses from their out-of-town sources. And, they often joked that the smell of marijuana was perceptible through the packaging.

Criminological literature archives a bountiful legacy of adult and juvenile drug-dealing organizations that are well schooled in risk-minimization strategies and negotiating inherently high-risk activities with the ever-present possibility of police contact; this affluent drug-dealing network, via its members' collective bungling, was clearly an outlier among the networks of its more sophisticated criminal peers. Drugs and money were rarely kept in back rooms, safes, or alternative locations, as is common in many drug-dealing networks. Rather, the stash house and dope house were one and the same among our network's dealers. For example, pounds of marijuana were observed being stored under the bed of one of the dealers and in the dirty laundry bin of another. In another case, cash was strewn about in both a desk drawer and the sock drawer of one of our major dealers.

As fans of hip-hop music and other thug-life glamorizing media, one might expect that even basic drug-dealing savvy might have seeped into our dealers' daily operations. It did not; there was a near total lack of security, either formal or informal. We witnessed only one case in which subjects utilized a vacuum sealing machine to package their drugs, a drug-dealing industry standard that compresses bulk and reduces the pungency of pot.[56] Most interestingly, especially among college-educated criminal entrepreneurs, there was virtually no discussion about or apparent awareness of core constitutional protections, the Fourth Amendment, probable cause, and other glaringly obvious matters that would seem valuable in minimizing police detection and prosecution.

Principal dealers carelessly operated out of their apartments or from on-campus housing. And, with few exceptions, the majority of their illegal business was on full display and in plain view upon walking through their front door. Legitimate house guests, neighbors, and even the Girl Scout pushing her cookies would regularly have a full look at incriminating evidence and ongoing drug operations. As referred to in an earlier chapter, upon arrival to one of our interview and observation sessions with one of the largest dealers in the sample, it was noticed that ounces of marijuana, scales, large sums of cash, customers, and drug paraphernalia were visible from a relatively busy off-campus beach community street. Another dealer was apparently so mesmerized by a late afternoon three-hour class that he left behind four ounces of marijuana with a street value of about $1,500. Unconcerned that someone may have found the contraband and notified campus police, he casually returned to the classroom later on that evening to find only the sweatshirt in which he had casually "concealed" the drugs.

These events reaffirm the notion that this network, and presumably others like it operating on campuses around the nation, is an ignored anomaly among street-drug dealing organizations documented in the criminological literature and among those historically suffering the brunt of the drug war ire. Given the omnipresence of both law enforcement and stick-up artists looking to prey upon either form of currency usually held by street dopemen—cash and drugs—drug dealers in urban communities would seldom have the luxury of casually cruising around their neighborhood with similar quantities of illegal drugs. In fact, even the rank-and-file corner boys who make up the most visible element in the urban drug scene generally know better than to hold on their person quantities of drugs substantial enough to immediately trigger felony charges. However, for our study's dealers, the pervasive lack of even the most fundamental security precautions suggests that law enforcement is not perceived as a substantial threat within this affluent drug-dealing network or others that may similarly benefit from systemic biases. Another conversation with Beefy addresses the overall lack of concern expressed by most of our dealers when it came to law enforcement:

At the "height" were you afraid of being caught?
BEEFY: It was always in the way back of your mind but not really.
Why not really?

BEEFY: I don't know. You were just kind of in the moment like . . . things would just happen. People would call in the morning before you go to class, people would call like on lunch breaks, people would call after work and after class. It was just constant stuff that you're doing, you don't really have time to worry about that sort of thing. I've never been a really big worrier so . . .

The real and perceived lack of police attention is made further evident in the words and actions of Brice, a former linchpin and major marijuana dealer in this network. At the time he came into the study, Brice, a white upper-class male drug dealer in the network, was twenty-four years old. He sold drugs, primarily marijuana, throughout his college career and, after completing his degree in business and entering the legitimate workforce, he had modified his network status and downsized his dealing enterprise. During his active dealing period, he reported being stopped by the police five times for speeding and on each occasion he was traveling with multiple pounds of marijuana in the car and driving under the drug's influence. But, as was the case for all of our dealers when police officers incidentally encountered them, Brice was never searched or arrested. It seems that the officers' profile and preconceived notion of criminals and drug pushers gave them no reason to suspect that a young man like Brice might also be a big-time drug dealer. Brice's careless actions were typical of operators in this network and indicative of a perception by dealers that law enforcement personnel presumes them to be good kids. Further, as a conversation we had with Brice and his girlfriend Ann indicates, to the extent that they may be involved in illicit activity, our dealers had the quite valid impression that the police view them as a particularly low priority.

Were you ever scared of the police?
BRICE: Yes and no, you are always a little nervous.
ANN: When you have massive amounts like we did when we had it here, there were multiple times when there were multiple cop cars parked out front for other things, not for us.
What measures were taken to avoid the police?
BRICE: I just think that in that environment, in that beach environment, there is so much to and fro traffic.
ANN: It's a college town; people are coming, going, hanging out.

BRICE: It is not conservative you know. I don't know, I just wasn't worried about it. I mean it is always in the back of your mind . . . but I just wasn't worried so much. I think we are a very low priority. We buy a pound and split that up and sell it. The guy we are buying it from ya know buys five to ten [pounds] and the guys he is buying it from fuckin' should be nervous because he is buying like one hundred [pounds].

In spite of California's somewhat liberal marijuana laws, trafficking in pot remains a serious felony in the state and is certainly a serious violation of the federal antidrug laws that have served as the cornerstone of the drug war. The quantity of pot they were selling aside, when asked why they felt that they were such a low law-enforcement priority, Brice and Ann went on to suggest that location, socioeconomic status, and race influence the way this network is perceived by police.

There is so much discretion in law enforcement.
BRICE: Probably has to do with what else you are doing and what you have done prior.
ANN: Probably the cops' just general opinion on you when it happens. I mean if you're a clean-cut suburban kid.
Through the course of doing these interviews, we had a mutual friend of ours who used to live on Precious Street, you know who I am talking about?
BRICE: Uh huh.
I went to his new place on Tropicana Street with Cecilia and was asking him questions and stuff. He had ten people over, everything is in the front room, everybody was smoking, the scale the whole bit and his front door was open to one of those alleyways down there . . . he didn't seem to be too concerned, I got up three times to shut the door, no one else cared. Why do you think that is?
ANN: It is the beach.
BRICE: I think in those beach environments . . .
ANN: It's all college kids . . .
BRICE: Well put it this way, the guy Shindi who got killed [in a car accident unrelated to drug dealing] sold to cops. Obviously the way he broadcast it, the way he delivered to people, pretty much cops would obviously figure that out after years and years and years of operating in [our local area], I mean they are not stupid ya know. I

think number one it's not a priority or number two they are getting paid off, they get some percentage of profit or something . . . I understand there is a lot bigger world out there because as I see it, it is not a priority in certain areas.

ANN: I mean if it was that big of a priority . . .

BRICE: People would have to change their habits.

ANN: I mean if someone really wanted to bust us they could . . .

BRICE: I mean you go through [a particular beach community] and I swear half the fuckin' houses smell like skunk, and there is not that many skunks in that neighborhood. People are growing in their garages and everywhere else.

Cecilia reaffirmed that this group of dealers largely perceived law enforcement as a negligible threat and more of an inconvenience than an obstacle that they were compelled to structure their illegal activities around avoiding. This collective perception fueled a haphazard approach to criminality where even fundamental risk-mitigation strategies like the use of drug euphemisms rather than speaking openly about drugs by name were nonexistent. Cecilia asserted that the "college umbrella" justifiably offered them some degree of protection because, after all, they were students with potential rather than dead-ender street pushers. In her opinion, law enforcement "should be spending their time busting people" that did not have potential to eventually contribute to society in the positive, noncontroversial way as they did.

CECILIA: Oh. Um. Well obviously no one was very careful. Hardly anyone talked with code. There wasn't a whole lot of emphasis placed on being careful in any way whatsoever. It was very sort of . . . I don't know I got the impression in college that you were protected by being in college to some extent . . . That obviously the authorities should be spending their time busting people that are not working toward a potentially better future. So I guess I always felt that there was a safety umbrella over folks in college. And it certainly seemed that once people got out of college and continued to pursue their otherwise endeavors, that [laughs] the law started to make its appearance more.

Clearly, this criminal population is perceived and treated atypically by law enforcement. Or, perhaps more accurately, they seemed to be treated quite typically for people in their socioeconomic group and with their quantity of social and symbolic capital. However, this level of deference and indifference toward the members of our drug-dealing network is not at all characteristic of that afforded everyday Americans by members of the law enforcement community.

Over the course of this research, we became convinced that relative affluence and social status played the primary role in diverting the scrutiny of criminal justice officials from the flagrantly illegal drug activities that characterized our college dealer network. However, money and prestige do not explain every aspect of our dealers' relative immunity from the ire and consequences of the drug war. Indeed there are other contributory factors that may help explain why networks like these, moving in relatively large quantities of illicit drugs and operating in a brazenly public fashion, are not higher up on the law enforcement priority list. Specifically, we have identified six additional extra-status factors that shed light on the de-prioritization of affluent drug dealing networks like the one we examined. We do think it important to stress, though, that many of these factors ultimately have their roots in the luxury and privileges tied to wealth and capital.

No Guns, No Glory

Unlike urban street corner markets where the lack of legitimate opportunity and the perception of "hustling" as the only way to earn a living lead to violent exchanges in battles for drug-dealing turf and to otherwise settle drug-related grievances, affluent drug networks like that which we observed rarely have episodes of violence and therefore might be a low police priority. Indeed, many of the drug-dealing networks in the criminological literature regularly employ violence as a dispute-resolution mechanism and as a means to maintain power hierarchies.[57] As hip-hop artist Jay-Z rapped in one of his not quite suited for radio songs chronicling the street-drug trade of which he was once a part:[58]

> In the underworld we take care of beef ourselves
> And another thing, yo, we police ourselves.
> Either you follow them codes or don't sell cocaine
> This life will swallow you whole so get outta game
> Go to church every Sunday and pray hard
> Drug dealer (haha) don't quit your day job

More academically, Terry Williams's classic study of teenage cocaine dealers in Upper Manhattan corroborated Jay-Z's assessment of the use and prevalence of violence in street-drug markets. As Williams noted, "A persuasive enforcement mechanism is the threat or actual imposition of violence upon those who breach trust and abuse the privileges accorded dealers."[59] Additionally, Bourgois's study of Harlem crack dealers chronicled similar uses of violence among urban drug dealers.

Regular displays of violence are essential for preventing rip offs by colleagues, customers, and professional holdup artists. Indeed, upward mobility in the underground economy of the street-dealing world requires a systematic and effective use of violence against one's colleagues.[60]

Beyond ethnographic accounts of violence in the street-drug trade, in their more quantitative examination of drug-related homicides in New York City, Paul Goldstein, Henry Brownstein, Patrick Ryan, and Patricia Bellucci revealed a nuanced picture of the relationship between illicit drugs and fatal violence. In their examination of 414 homicide events in select New York City police precincts in 1988, presumably one of the peak years and locations for crack-cocaine distribution and use within the United States, 218 (52.7 percent) were somehow tied to illegal drugs. Of these drug-related homicides, 162 were classified as *systemic,* meaning that the "Violence arises from the exigencies of working or doing business in an illicit market—a context in which the monetary stakes can be enormous but where the economic actors have no recourse to the legal system to resolve disputes."[61] Thus, they concluded that 74.3 percent of all drug-related homicides in this New York sample were a direct product of the underground, criminal marketplace and essentially the result of conflicts between drug dealers or between drug dealers and users.

Within the network that served as the foundation of our research, the use of violence, even threats of violence, were conspicuously absent, and our observations and interactions led us to deduce that there were multiple market factors that afforded our dealers this relatively peaceful existence. Not the least important of these factors was the fact that, for the most part, our dealers did not depend on the drug trade for their livelihood. While certainly the selling of illegal drugs was central to their lifestyle, they were not dependent upon drug money for their day-to-day existence like their urban counterparts might be.

Beyond that, because of the sheer expansiveness of the student customer base and the consistent demand for drugs these customers provided, our network's dealers did not have turf disputes or competition over clientele. Rather, the dealers we observed and interviewed often found it necessary to continually implement strategies to minimize their customer base, picking and choosing those whom they felt would be the most reliable and least likely to bring them trouble. This expansive customer base allowed these dealers to avoid what drug expert Peter Reuter calls "competitive violence"[62]—pragmatic violence that dealers employ to establish and maintain their drug territory and customers. As an example of Reuter's concept, in the mid-1980s Congress pressured the District of Columbia government and federal law enforcement agencies to go after drug kingpins largely believed by city officials to be a stabilizing force in the local drug economy and a regulatory mechanism in an otherwise uncontrollable drug scene. While this resulted in the arrest and conviction of notorious DC drug kingpins like Rayful Edmond,[63] this tactic was also directly credited in spawning a multi-year bloodbath as smaller dealers fought over territory serving a relatively limited client base.

Beyond the absence of competitive violence, within the college drug dealing population we studied, dealers and customers generally had very few liaisons with the traditional illegitimate world, further facilitating a lack of violence within this group. Drug networks associated with larger criminal groups, like the Mexican Mafia in California, for example, would undoubtedly lead to increased levels of violence. In "Pattern, Purpose, and Race in the Drug War," Troy Duster examined the initial phases of the war on marijuana. He argued that there were two latent consequences of federal law enforcement's increased scrutiny and pursuit of marijuana. First, the availability and potency of cocaine increased as more drug-dealing networks moved away from trafficking in marijuana and prioritized cocaine. Second, the nature of the US marijuana industry was dramatically altered. Prior to the war on drugs, a substantial portion of marijuana was the product of a "cottage industry" that was not necessarily intertwined with larger, diverse criminal organizations. As the risks of manufacturing and distributing marijuana increased, this cottage industry was largely, but seemingly not entirely, replaced by long-standing, organized criminal groups. Our research revealed that this affluent network seemed to be supplied primarily by independent, regional marijuana cultivators and not by entrenched criminal groups like street gangs or prison gangs. This return to the cottage industry model and the avoidance of larger, more violence-prone criminal organizations contributed to this affluent drug-dealing network's ability to avoid regularly engaging in violence.

Our network's dealers and their clients also had the distinct advantage of not being raised in environments historically subjected to intense law enforcement scrutiny, police brutality, police racism and racial profiling, and other overreaches of police power. Therefore, the inherent mistrust of police that is found in many urban and minority communities is not hard-wired into these dealers. This is not to say that our network's dealers were fond of police. Still, unlike street dealers and other inner-city minority residents whose mistrust of police leads them to handle disputes and conflicts on their own, the dealers we interacted with were apt to call upon the police in a time of personal crisis. Similarly, when they did initiate contact with law enforcement, they could feel relatively confident that the police would not abuse their authority in their interactions with them. This was the case even in circumstances where our affluent dealers showed rather obvious signs of involvement in illegal activity.

In fact, what proved to be among the more audacious undertak-. ings by any our network's dealers revolved around a summoning of police in response to one of the very few acts of drug-related violence experienced within the network over the entire time we studied the drug market. One evening relatively early on in the research process, three armed men forcibly entered the home and operations center shared by three of our network's dealers. At the time, two of the three dealers were home and the third was on campus attending a class. In classic home-invasion robbery form, while holding them at gunpoint, the robbers proceeded to restrain the two dealers with duct tape and rob them of substantial amounts of cash and drugs recklessly strewn about and high-end electronics. Shortly after the robbers fled, the third dealer-roommate arrived home to find his partners still bound up. Rather than retaliate in the style more true to form in the world of drug-dealing gangsters, without a moment's hesitation, these dealers of privilege dialed 911. In quickly putting together the pieces of the robbery, the dealers deduced that the robbers were from another Southern California town approximately two hours drive away. They went on to conclude that the robbers were associates of someone who accompanied a trusted buyer during a drug transaction at their place a week or so earlier. Apparently, this buyer's associate described to his friends and soon to be robbers our dealers' operation as an unfortified drug outlet and easy robbery target.

When the police arrived a few minutes later, the crime victims described the robbery, the people they believed to have perpetrated the crime, and the direction in which they believed the robbers to be headed. They conspicuously left out the fact that they were drug dealers and were robbery targets for this exact reason. And, as one of the robbery victims told us, the police "totally knew what was going on." Nonetheless, the police officers aided the victims by contacting Border Patrol officers stationed at San Onofre, the previously mentioned immigration checkpoint that the robbers would have to pass through on their way home. Based on the description of the perpetrators provided by the dealers, Border Patrol agents easily identified and apprehended the robbers as they attempted to pass through the checkpoint. Per our informant, the dealers were even able to recover their cash and stolen electronics, although they wisely refused to claim ownership of the marijuana also found in the car.

In another instance, one of our network's dealers was threatened with a baseball bat outside of his dorm room by another campus dealer to whom he owed several thousand dollars. Not surprisingly, the only other episodes of mentionable violence ever brought to our attention in the more than five years we spent around this network all involved LaCoste. When asked if he had ever been caught by the police for his drug activity or had any interesting episodes with "weird" customers, LaCoste replied, "We got robbed one time. I got held up before, a couple of different times. I got a buddy who got thrown out of a car naked." Given his mannerisms and overall cocky demeanor, it is difficult to determine whether LaCoste was actually robbed (although he likely was), or whether the robbery and stickups were attributable to his personality traits, his brashness and arrogance as a drug dealer, or some other factors external to his drug dealing.

By and large, as we noted in an earlier chapter, Brice characterized their network as "friendly-like." Accordingly, in times of dispute or disagreement members typically relied on a variety of nonviolent conflict-resolution strategies to sort things out and restore their relationships to their normal state. Indeed, the dealers we interviewed seemed genuinely surprised when we posed questions concerning drug market–related violence. For example, former business major and ounce-quantity pot dealer turned current small business owner, CJ, said that he "never really thought about" violence. Phil, another owner of multiple small businesses and current ounce-quantity marijuana dealer concurred, "Violence, with marijuana, ya know it probably kept me from kicking some ass. If I am in a fight or flight situation I usually will fight, if I am in a flight or fight situation on marijuana, I usually fly." Diamond, the largest dealer in our sample, did not respond and looked somewhat perplexed when he was asked "What about violence?" Attempting to solicit a response, he was prodded further, "Have you ever had to knock anyone out? Resolve anything physically?" He replied, "Nothing like that has ever happened here."

As if he were selling off his medical practice on his road to retirement, when Brice downsized his network in his effort to go at least partially legitimate, he passed the majority of his customers on to Cecilia, who had been providing marijuana to a small network of friends for several years. At the time of the study, she was a senior in college majoring in biology; upon inheriting Brice's business, she became one of the largest drug dealers in the sample. Roughly once a week, she would walk to Diamond's house with $8,000 in cash and would return with two pounds of high-quality marijuana. When she was asked about violence, she responded, "If a guy went with you, that was all the security you would ever think to need. A friendship network."

Certainly, conflicts did arise among dealers and between dealers and customers in this network. However, rather than violence, non-confrontational methods of dispute resolution were the norm and the primary mechanism of social control exercised by dealers in this network was exclusion and ostracism. Similar to Patricia Adler's aforementioned study of upper-level drug dealers and smugglers, group conventions among our dealers were enforced and maintained through segregation from the group. Problem behavior or failure to adhere to established norms of customer conduct often resulted in customers being banned from future purchase. For deviant dealers, similar politics of exclusion came into play by fellow dealers, higher-level suppliers, and customers. While clearly less immediate than the brunt consequences of violence, the specter of ostracism was a commanding norm-regulating mechanism within this network.

As we noted in this and earlier chapters, these affluent college students made the seemingly irrational choice to vault into criminality more for status than material gain. Therefore, they did not face the structural disadvantages that push many into criminality out of necessity, but rather utilized their drug profits largely to bolster their status and to underwrite social and personal expenses. Ostracism is particularly acute precisely because many of these dealers are actively pursuing prestige through gangsterism and their status as drug dealers. Unlike many open-air drug markets where relationships tend to be more anonymous and superficial, these affluent dealers knew their clients directly, or knew someone else who was a friend of their clients. Being excommunicated from the group can amount to a "social death" or, at the very least, the ceremonial removal of their facade of gangsterism. Therefore, relatively mundane informal social control mechanisms like ostracism proved much more effective among these dealers than they would in typical street markets.

Even when conflicts between dealers became heated and, in the context of the streets would have most certainly erupted into violence, alternative dispute resolution strategies that occasionally bordered on the absurd prevailed among members of our network. Take, for example, Brice's account of a money dispute he had with fellow dealer, Dallas. Brice recounted how their long-time partnership dissolved and their continuing disagreements culminated in this incident:

BRICE: Well . . . he came over because he was all pissed off . . . he was pissed off about fuckin' what he received for fuckin' compensation, he didn't get what he thought he should have gotten. He fuckin', he screwed himself over really. He came over here all irate one day, had Ann leave the house and just kinda' fuckin', he was all pissed off. At that particular time I wasn't even sure what his particular reason was, numerous things . . . he was yelling about this and that, that he didn't get what he deserved out of it . . . He caught me at the house and I told him, "I am over this, you are sneaky, you can break in anywhere, I don't even want to see you again. If I even see you again I will do something drastic ya know." I also told him that we had a weapon [a gun], which is true, Ann does, I mean that really has nothing to do with me but I knew it and so I used that as evidence. He's [Dallas] like "you know, fuck it." He pulled out my dad's business card and said "lets just see what your Dad thinks about your new-found interests, let's see what he thinks about your point of view." He held the business card in front of me, eventually when it was all said and done [Brice got the card back] but he said he had another one or something. I wasn't of clear conscious so I would be at fault somehow but I don't think [my dad] would [have] bought into everything Dallas would have said.

It seems that rather than going for the guns, "I'll tell your Daddy" proved to be a more effective weapon in this situation, one of the most heated exchanges we heard of or observed within our campus drug-dealing network.

While we again feel that the lack of violence most decidedly played some role in shielding our network's dealers from law-enforcement attention, it does not come close to completely or adequately explaining the drastic disparities in policing between this population and differently situated drug-dealing populations. In fact, substantial amounts of US correctional resources are allocated to the policing and incarceration of nonviolent offenders. According to Bureau of Justice statistics, nearly one-half of all inmates currently serving time in state prison are incarcerated primarily for nonviolent offenses. In the federal prison system, the percentage of nonviolent offenders is even greater, hovering around 77 percent of the system's nearly 200,000 inmates.[64] With specific regard to drug offenders, in 2003, 72.1 percent of the system's federal drug law violators were nonviolent and 34.4 percent were first time, nonviolent offenders.[65] While it certainly stands to reason that the infusion of violence into the drug markets likely results in increased scrutiny from law enforcement, the data clearly suggest that a lack of violence, particularly among the drug-offending population that currently weighs down every level of our criminal justice system, does not effectively shield groups from law-enforcement scrutiny. Thus, the lack of violence within this group of affluent drug dealers cannot sufficiently explain away the lack of punishment associated with their illegal behavior.

Small Fish in a Vast Narco-Traffic Sea

Given finite law-enforcement resources, it is possible that this affluent drug-dealing network was overlooked or not made a priority because they were comparatively small fish in a vast sea of drug crimes. It could be argued that the scope of these dealers' illegal businesses fall beneath some de facto quantity threshold that does not warrant substantial police and prosecutorial attention. Again, as Cecilia suggested, the police have bigger fish to fry. While perhaps this approach does

Dealer Bio: Dallas

Throughout the course of the study, Dallas proved genuinely brilliant among his college peers, a true renaissance man with a dedication to the illicit drug game that was more deep-rooted, authentic, and multifaceted than any other dealer in our study. Dallas earned his moniker by continually proving to be a survivor, a rugged individualist reminiscent of the renegade cowboy culture of the US Southwest. However, he was continually a source of controversy and consternation, much like the 1980s television drama that bears his name. His individualism and flair for the dramatic were strikingly evident in the story chronicling his initial migration to California.

Dallas grew up in the northern Midwest—some said Minnesota, others Wisconsin—but Dallas was rarely one to give definitive answers. Regardless, his hometown was surely a long way from an elite private school nestled near the Pacific Ocean. According to cultural lore, throughout high school his parents were tired of him regularly coming home drunk and stoned and tried a series of unsuccessful disciplinary strategies to alter his behavior. After a particularly indulgent night of intoxication, Dallas returned home to find his parents waiting up for him and subsequently threatening to not pay for his college education. As the story goes, he immediately responded to their threat by picking up a college guide, flipping through the pages, finding an expensive far away school (the hub campus for this study), and declaring he would be attending that institution and paying for it himself—and continuing to indulge in marijuana and alcohol in the meantime. Thus, Dallas's veracious devotion to both licit and illicit entrepreneurialism was born.

While a business major, Dallas supported himself largely through his experience and virtually unrivaled artistic ability as a glassblower.[a] He would make intricate, high-end marijuana bubblers and glass marijuana storage devices that local headshops[b] would routinely sell for over $2,000. However, he could make roughly $100 per hour doing "production work," blowing

(continues)

Dealer Bio: continued

simple pipes that sold for roughly $10 each. Indicative of his stubborn nature and inability to compromise, Dallas would often refuse to do production work even when he had to take leaves of absence from school and was living on Brice's balcony or in one of his retail spaces. By his own declaration, production work was neither challenging nor artistic and thus of little interest to Dallas. During the course of the study, Dallas rented two spaces in local strip malls to house his glassblowing business. Brice actually invested in one of the enterprises and was learning to blow glass himself. As a consummate rugged individualist, Dallas would do all the construction on these retail spaces himself—often at night and never with the proper permits or safety equipment. He once set off the alarm system early in the morning in his own space attempting to install a makeshift ventilation system for his glassblowing equipment. Dallas was notorious for both partying and procrastinating, thus he would often have to work days on end to make ends meet. While he was a frequent marijuana user, uppers and stimulants were clearly more pragmatic and thus his drugs of choice. Like most veteran professional glassblowers, his arms bear the consequences of working closely with gas-driven welding torches. He claimed that his arms were so used to being burned that they no longer reacted to incidental contact with fire, although his contentious history warrants skepticism.

While always a bit elusive, Dallas was apparently involved in both marijuana cultivation and distribution partnerships. His mantra was the "rule of fours"; a four-by-four-by-four-foot box would yield $4,000 of hydroponic marijuana every four months. Possibly driven by his craftiness and need to make substantial sums of money, his illicit and licit dealings always seemed to involve controversy and disagreement, as made evident in the "daddy's business card" dustup he had with Brice. As another example, Dallas would occasionally travel the West Coast making guest appearances blowing glass at various headshops. One of the researchers visited a headshop in Washington

(continues)

152

Dealer Bio: continued

State where Dallas was rumored to have spent a few weeks. According to one of the clerks, Dallas had arrived and quickly used other people's equipment and materials without permission to craft some pretty nice pieces. Subsequently, Dallas sold them and then left town abruptly without notice and without compensating the shop that hosted him as agreed.

Near the end of the study, Dallas was nearing completion of his business degree despite taking several leaves of absence for financial reasons. He was living with his girlfriend and, since he never owned a car, would routinely ride his skateboard over five miles to campus to attend class. He was also taking a welding class at night and had his final project proudly displayed in his backyard. Dallas had meticulously crafted a tremendously intricate, six-foot-tall metal robot that looked like a militarized figure from Star Wars, complete with arms that would rotate and a nose that resembled a Gatling gun.

One of the most notable moments in the sordid Dallas legacy came one particular Halloween. Indicative of his attention to detail, flair for the dramatic and a dose of diva ideology, Dallas arrived at a Halloween party fashionably late and dressed as famous West Coast rapper-icon Tupac Shakur; for a Midwestern white college student, the resemblance to Tupac on this particular day was absolutely uncanny. His ensemble of sagged jeans, work boots, no shirt, and a blue bandana on his head were dead on. However, it was his willingness to shave his head, bronze his white skin with brown industrial polish and meticulously mimic Tupac's tattoos with black industrial polish that was truly reflective of his spirit and artistry; no one saw Dallas for several days after that Halloween; rumor had it the polish didn't come off for a week.

Notes: a. A craftsperson that fashions molten glass into usable objects and/or art using exhaled air through a long, narrow tube to shape the glass.

   b. Retail store dedicated to selling marijuana paraphernalia and accessories.

explain some of the variance in relative drug-dealer scrutiny, drug arrest and prosecution data demonstrate something quite the opposite. It seems that the majority of people who have fallen prey to the drug-war hawks have not been high-ranking drug distributors. Rather, the drug-war cowboys have disproportionately lassoed first-time, low-level offenders.[66] Recent statistics indicate that more than 80 percent of all arrests for drug crime in the United States are for simple possession of a controlled substance, rather than for more serious drug crimes like trafficking or manufacturing.[67] Moreover, the vast majority of the 19 percent of drug arrests for manufacturing or distribution were of relatively small-time user-dealers, not the notorious drug kingpins that are routinely the subject of the tough-on-crime discourse.[68] Again, it is possible that relative size of operations may play a role in police and policy approaches to drug law enforcement. However, it clearly seems that the raw criminality of this affluent drug-distribution network does not tangibly differentiate this group from the hoards of drug users and drug dealers who are currently filling US jails and prisons as a direct result of three decades of punitive prohibition and the war on drugs.

The Invisible Elite

Data suggest certain dynamics associated with our network's affluent dealer population are once again comparable to those articulated by William Chambliss in "The Saints and the Roughnecks." As previously discussed, both the boys identified as members of the Saints and the Roughnecks engaged in similar levels of deviance, but were perceived and treated quite differently by the community and law enforcement. Of Chambliss's three variables used to explain the differences in treatment between the groups he observed, relative everyday invisibility to law enforcers and bias on behalf of law enforcement could partly explain why so much of our dealers' deviance went undetected or unpunished. In short, with relative affluence comes a practical and expectational level of privacy not afforded members of lower socioeconomic classes.

Some aspects of privacy and invisibility might make the criminal actions of this affluent drug-dealing population less apparent to law enforcement. Specifically, our network's dealers possessed two logistical luxuries over typical street dealers; they operated within private residences and, while large in numbers, their customer base was rather insular. Consequently, our dealers sold their wares behind closed doors (although sometimes with the door wide open) in residences largely immune from police patrols, and they were never pressed to actively push their product or solicit strangers on the street as customers. These factors distinguish this network from the bulk of inner-city networks and to an extent make their activities less susceptible to law-enforcement attention.

When policing drug crime, it is well documented that inner-city drug raids are relatively successful, efficient, and politically safe expenditures of police resources. Inner-city drug dealers operating in open-air market environments are far more likely to have strangers as customers and, in spite of the lengths to which they go to conceal their activities, these dealers are nonetheless certainly more detectible by most standard policing tactics. As crime and punishment expert, Michael Tonry argues:

> Any experienced police official could have predicted that policies of wholesale arrests of dealers would sweep up mostly young minority user-dealers in the cities. This is not necessarily because more members of minorities use or sell drugs, but because arrests are easier to make in disorganized inner-city areas where many more minority dealers operate than do in middle- and working-class neighborhoods where white dealers operate.[69]

In 2002, Court TV aired a program on drug buy-and-bust operations in New York City that demonstrated the efficacy of these policing techniques targeting inner-city, open-air drug markets. A four-person police team, composed of one undercover officer, one spotter, and two uniformed officers in a squad car, easily took down five drug sales suspects in a matter of one hour.[70] As further indicated within the criminological literature, visibility is a component of open-air drug markets that make them more vulnerable to the traditional ways the police enforce the war on drugs and conversely might make affluent dealing populations like that we observed less vulnerable.

Further, police work is a results-oriented endeavor where "collars," "clearances," and the occasional well-publicized big bust serve as the primary barometers of success. As vividly indicated by arrest and incarceration data, particularly in the area of drug-law violations, evenly casting the net of police scrutiny has never been a part of the US criminal justice system. Beyond that, people in the United States have grown accustomed to certain "safe" categories of arrestee, largely poor and minority group members who can be subjected to grossly disproportionate rates of arrest while the public at large seems unwilling to even bat an eye. And, as Brice's comments suggest, this relative invisibility brought about by selective law enforcement and bias was a fact that our network's drug dealers seemed very much aware of and one on which they capitalized. Brice recounted an event in which alcohol and bad judgment conceded any remaining shred of visibility advantage that his residence may have provided, yet he was still able to avoid arrest. It is worth noting that, throughout the course of the research, we made every possible effort to verify the accounts provided by the dealers. In this case, we were able to confirm that Brice was led into his apartment in handcuffs by a police officer and that marijuana and marijuana paraphernalia were visibly displayed in the front room, but the remainder of the following account is based solely on Brice's description of events.

BRICE: I have learned since then, I think we were lucky. I was lucky because a police officer saw my fuckin' setup.
Tell about that.
BRICE: I paid him off, fuckin' I mean, I paid him.
ANN: Nice little clean cut white kid.
BRICE: I think it was 900 bucks total and I think 800 of it went to the girl and the other hundred went to the fuckin' police officer to pay him off. She got the money, she called me and asked what were you on? Ya know, I was loaded. Fuck, I don't remember half of it, I fucked up her car, you know the story. We were drinking at the bars and got real loaded. Somehow while walking home I found a ladder, an extension ladder. I fuckin' had it over my head and I did not like the looks of this Volkswagen Bug. So I threw it right on the fuckin' hood and it went into the windshield. I was pretty proud of that and I just started walking. Three girls came out and started screaming at me . . . all I know is that they surrounded me. I . . . mean ya know, I am not gonna like assault them.
ANN: You could have fuckin' run.
BRICE: All I know is before I fuckin' knew it they had my wallet so obviously I couldn't go anywhere. I wasn't going to leave until I got it back. Then they got a police officer there, the police officer was like "how do you want to handle this?" I'm like, "I got money I'll pay her, let's go to my house right now," knowing I had cash. The whole

house was dark, everyone was asleep, I had the handcuffs on and was with the police officer. We walked all the way up the stairs.

Was there anything in the front room he could have seen?

BRICE: Maybe . . . a couple tubes . . . a few bongs out and maybe like a little jar of like something to smoke, but the lights were off so potentially he could have missed any of it. He was more concerned about watching me, making sure I wasn't doing anything freaky. So we're walking upstairs in the dark, we go all the way into my fuckin' room. Suddenly, it's dark in my room, but fuckin' mad lights on . . . the lights are just going off . . . you know my room. Everything else is off, and it was blatantly obvious there were grow lights in there. Ya know, he never even questioned me, he didn't look at it. He uncuffed my hands so I could get the money. He came in the room, didn't look at anything. He stayed with me, he didn't leave to go. Obviously that did not look normal in a bedroom.

So he stayed with you, you opened the drawer.

BRICE: Yeah, he stayed with me, I opened the drawer. I was lucky there was nothing in the drawer because sometimes I put like the bud in the drawer, it was just the money in the drawer. I pulled out [pause] 900 bucks actually and I am 100 percent positive he took 100 bucks.

Why do you think he did that?

ANN: Less paperwork for him.

BRICE: I couldn't have had another drinking infraction. I had a DUI I needed to get off my record. Any sort of drinking infraction, disturbing the public, whatever they are gonna call it, that infraction would have been a break in my probation. He probably fuckin' saw that ya know . . . after I talked to him and said "I'll fuckin' pay for the damage ya know." He kept askin' "what do you want to do about this? What do you want to do about this?" Like he was gonna take me in or something like that.

ANN: How did you come up with the dollar amount to give him?

BRICE: Well, it was expensive. She gave me a receipt; it was like 50 bucks less than the 800. I think it was agreed upon between the girls and the cop the dollar amount.

But no mechanical expert was there or anything?

ANN: They didn't call the insurance company?

BRICE: No. It was like in the middle of the night at like two or three o'clock in the morning. So that cop he was probably, I don't know, he could have . . .

ANN: Fucked you ova'.

BRICE: Yeah, but he didn't he would rather make him 100 bucks and not have to log in fuckin' whatever.

What could he have busted you for?

BRICE: Well . . . I would assume there was over a half pound of bud in there so I would assume you are over the minimum. I would assume at least a lot of it was bagged up. Obviously there was a scale in the presence . . . that was another thing I was nervous about because . . . I could have put that in the wrong drawer . . . ya know you add those things up and I assume I am going down.

Why didn't he take you in?

BRICE: He fuckin' took the hundred bucks. Once he uncuffed me, I gave him the money, he counted it and left. How is he gonna justify going into some guy's house? Why would he not take me into the police office? I am sure that is breaking protocol, that is all that means. He probably did not know what he was gonna stumble on at all. Guaranteed he had to have known there was a grow room in there. It had to of smelled like pot . . . at that point in time maybe his shift was like over, who knows the reason . . . he definitely charged me over 100 dollars more than the girls charged me. I talked to the girls the next day when I was counting my money and that is pretty much what happened.

While visibility, or lack thereof, usually protected people like Brice and our other dealers from the wrath of the police, occasionally, when visibility broke down, old fashioned bias and, at least in this instance, graft, typically could be relied upon to keep dealers out of real trouble. Still, visibility as the primary explanatory variable is problematic because the ability to operate within a residence is advantageous only to the extent that it is coupled with a perception of risk and commonsensical evasion tactics. As previously discussed, transportation and distribution strategies within this network were generally haphazard and members typically failed to actively employ even fundamental risk-minimization strategies. Our network's dealers did not operate on the street corner, but their nonchalance and bungling, in an equitable world, should have drastically minimized the visibility advantages their relative affluence afforded them. However, it stands to reason that any criminal enterprise is ultimately only as visible as lawmakers and law enforcers desire it to be.

No Friends in Low Places

Existing literature on drug crime has demonstrated that "many drug users and drug dealers avoid detection because they occupy otherwise legitimate social roles and lead basically straight, middle-class lives."[71] Historically, a significant amount of domestic drug distribution is controlled by street gangs, the mafia, motorcycle gangs, prison gangs, and other criminal groups.[72] In comparison, for the most part, our network's dealers were not connected or affiliated with any of these more notorious criminal organizations. As discussed, high-level dealers within the college network we observed typically were supplied by a few independent marijuana cultivators and supplemented that supply with their own growing operations. Aside from their drug-dealing operations, these affluent dealers and their customers lived a somewhat traditional, relatively affluent existence and were therefore less likely to interface with the types of larger criminal organizations more likely to interact with and draw attention from law enforcement. And since most of our network's dealers and users never had direct drug-related encounters with law enforcement, there was never pressure placed upon them to "roll over" on other network dealers as part of plea bargain processes.

It's Not What You Know, It's Who You Know

One of the other obvious advantages of affluence is ready access to the financial and political capital necessary to make criminal matters disappear, to have their severity mitigated, or to prevent them from being detected in the first place. Indeed, substantial legitimate resources and political ties distinguished our network's affluent drug dealers from the masses of other dealers filling US jails and prisons as a result of the war on drugs. Once again, at least one and possibly two traffickers had parents who were elected high-ranking city officials in other states; others had parents who were high-level international and domestic businesspeople, car dealership owners, medical doctors, psychiatrists, and executives for major accounting firms.

In what proved to be quite reasonable conjecture, our dealers seemed to assume these support systems would be at the ready and able to intervene if their drug-dealing activities were ever brought to the fore by law enforcement personnel. As Beefy said when asked how he would arrange for good legal defense if he were to be arrested and prosecuted, "Oh yeah. Just call the parents and come clean with them, and they deal with it." In fact, in the few cases involving the police and one of our dealer's drug operations, the dealer's parents completely financed legal representation and took action to curtail consequences and minimize damage done to their child's reputation. The experiences of LaCoste and Brice provide insights into this parental safety net.

At the time we met him, LaCoste was a college freshman and a relatively large-scale marijuana dealer who dabbled in other drugs including cocaine. Recall that by his own assessment, LaCoste was "untouchably wealthy." He was also one of the few dealers in our network that had been arrested and charged with relatively serious drug and weapons offenses. But, as he explained it, his father was able to intervene, significantly mitigating any formal repercussions.

> *So what actually happened, were you put away at all?*
> LaCoste: Yeah, for like ah . . . I don't know, I got real good lawyers [laughs]. Like real good lawyers . . . and I got a concealed gun charge and a possession over an ounce charge and they were trying to give me some intent to distribute. But I just got a possession ticket that's all and then the weapon and everything else disappeared.
> *How did you pay for these lawyers?*
> LaCoste: Na, that's not me . . . I'm not gonna claim to have paid for those. Turn that off [points to the tape recorder], I don't want to say that [laughs]. No, but that would have to be my dad. Or my parents . . . I can't pay for fucking like six lawyers.
> *Do your parents know what you're up to?*
> LaCoste: Yeah, I mean they understand. They know I smoke lots of weed. They just think I buy the weed though.
> *What does your dad do?*
> LaCoste: He's a partner in [a large accounting firm].
> *And your mom?*
> LaCoste: She kicks it at the house.

The tangible value associated with affluence and the accompanying ability to mobilize legal resources in one's defense was remarkably apparent during what proved to be the most critical legal development of the entire study. This occurred when, after years of being one of the network's biggest drug suppliers, Brice was arrested and faced drug charges that could have landed him in prison for six and a half years. At the time of his arrest, Brice had been renting a two-bedroom apartment with a garage for the sole purpose of cultivating marijuana. As was typical for Brice and most of the other dealers we observed, risk-minimization strategies were once again lacking. No one lived in the residence, it was furnished only minimally and Brice, Ann, and others only came and went in the evening. Eventually neighbors became suspicious and notified the police of what they suspected to be an illegal drug operation. DEA and local police officers initiated a surveillance operation on the residence and, one evening when he came to check on his crops, Brice was busted.

Brice's arrest yielded over one hundred marijuana plants and an estimated $30,000 in marijuana-cultivation equipment. Ultimately, Brice was charged with the cultivation of marijuana and intent to distribute a controlled substance. Given the number of plants seized, the cultivation charge alone carried with it a five-year, federal mandatory minimum prison sentence, and the intent to distribute charge would tack on an additional sixteen months in federal prison. It seemed that the law of averages as it related to this network's extensive criminality and its membership's collective nonchalance was finally going to result in substantial criminal justice consequences. Beyond that, Brice's case had the potential to create a reverberation throughout the network as Brice was one of the key suppliers and losing him stood to significantly interrupt the inflow of marijuana. And finally, if convicted, one might reasonably conclude that the notion of general deterrence that rests as the philosophical foundation of Western criminal law would finally have the potential to take hold within our network as it would bring to light the very real consequences of being caught dealing.

However, as Brice's case unfolded, it vividly illustrated many of the theoretical and substantive critiques of the justice system and put a tangible face on the concepts of symbolic capital and privilege. His case also further underscores some of the additional explanations for the lack of law-enforcement scrutiny into the drug-dealing lives of our relatively affluent college students. Despite the seemingly unyielding punitiveness of the drug war, despite having a previous DUI conviction, despite facing six and a half years in prison, access to resources and knowing or being related to the right people ultimately allowed Brice to avoid long-term consequences for his rampant criminality.

Immediately after his arrest, Brice turned to his parents who bankrolled the hiring of a high-profile private criminal defense attorney and a number of other experts[73] to advocate on behalf of their son. As Brice informed us via a series of e-mails after his case was closed, the value of resources and connection is undeniable.

BRICE (E-MAIL APRIL 2004): Just signed a deal yesterday! . . . Basically, they dropped the big charge, and the other will not be on my record within 18 months. I have to do 100 hours community service, lose my 4th Amendment, get drug tested, and have to remain in therapy for at least 6 months. However, once it's all over I can answer that I've never been arrested, and nothing will ever be on my record. Even now, it's not recorded anywhere since they never made a judgment against me. Kind of like the diversion program, but better, because I have no parole or probation counselor. I am free to leave the state any time I want, I just cannot get any misdemeanor offences otherwise I break the terms of the deal.

BRICE (E-MAIL NOVEMBER 2005): My follow up Court date was this morning at 8:30. Everything [has] been dismissed. No longer on any probation and everything is expunged from my record! Anyway today is a very good day.

Bias

Given the well-established consequences of the war on drugs for underrepresented populations and the lack of law-enforcement scrutiny of this affluent population, an exploration of the dynamics within and surrounding this network would be incomplete without a discussion of police bias. The collective carelessness exhibited by this network's members is indicative of a perception that largely dismisses the possibility of facing criminal justice consequences as a result of their illegal behavior. It is rather likely that the pervasive lack of concern within this network is a manifestation of the disproportionate impact of drug policies on poor, urban, minority youth. This network operates largely immune from any substantial consequences of its members' illegal behavior, in part because of differential treatment by the criminal justice system. Tonry, Clarence Lusane, and other drug policy experts generally agree that bias is one of several factors that account for the disproportionate impact of the war on drugs on traditionally underrepresented populations. This disparity fosters a reciprocal effect that then exempts groups of affluent, primarily Caucasian, high social status criminals from facing substantial consequences for their behavior. In *The Police and the Black Male,* Elijah Anderson writes,

> The police are primarily agents of the middle class who are working to make the area more hospitable to middle-class people at the expense of the lower classes. It is obvious that the police assume Whites in the community are at least middle class and are trustworthy on the streets. Hence the police may be seen primarily as protecting "law abiding" middle-class Whites against anonymous "criminal" Black males.[74]

When It Is All Said and Done

While the particular characteristics that define our network might very well be unique, it is safe to assume that our drug network is not an anomaly. In February 2002, police made six arrests on the American University campus in Washington, DC, seizing ecstasy, marijuana, and $15,000. This network was organized by affluent, twenty-year-old, Caucasian college student Ben Gelt who distributed drugs to several Washington area colleges. At the time of his arrest, Susan Barnes-Gelt, Ben's mother, was a Denver, Colorado, city councilwoman whose name had been tossed around as a legitimate mayoral candidate, and his father was a well-known attorney and former chairman of the Denver Democratic Party. Despite the seriousness of the offense, Gelt pleaded guilty to only a marijuana charge and the remaining members of this network had their files sealed as part of a plea agreement involving only misdemeanor charges.[75] Such precedents of leniency for affluent, college drug crimes are ironic given the potential impact of criminal justice consequences.[76]

Though not at all a plea for increased policing of college campuses and heightened scrutiny of college drug networks like the one we spent the past several years observing, it is nonetheless logical to assume that a greater law-enforcement presence in this population would have a drastic impact on the membership's willingness and capacity to traffic in illegal drugs. A single dealer in this network, serving substantial criminal justice consequences, would probably have a reverberating effect causing many dealers to abandon their illegitimate businesses completely. Individual dealers might slide along the continuum away from their deviant roles and align themselves completely with nondeviant society. This argument is supported generally by criminological theory and speculation and supported specifically by social scientist Alfred Blumstein, who argues, "The threat of a lengthy prison sentence is undoubtedly very effective at deterring white-collar crimes that tend to be committed by middle class individuals."[77]

Of course, dealing in street drugs is not white collar crime in any sense of the term. However, it is possible to extrapolate from this statement that substantial consequences are likely to be an effective deterrent in this population of drug dealers and those like it because of the dealers' relative affluence. Being sent to prison for a common street crime would surely not be a status symbol among this set, but more likely a source of shame and a marker that would compromise many existing legitimate opportunities for success. In the relatively few cases of law-enforcement intervention in affluent college drug-dealing organizations, minimal consequences have resulted. Blumstein infers, and we would contend, that real consequences would disrupt these types of organizations and set a precedent that might well deter similarly situated criminality.

Still, the fact that crimes committed by people in certain social positions go unpunished is not what we see as the central problem. The real issue is that, all too often, an individual's social position results in excessive scrutiny or, conversely, excessive leniency on behalf of the criminal justice system. The US contemporary commitment to punitive incarceration policies (for the poor) makes the United States an anomaly among our peer nations. Our incarceration rates dwarf those of other western democracies, as well as nations that we typically criticize on a variety of human rights fronts. While this punitive approach to criminal justice is not limited to combating illicit drug use and distribution, particularly among the lower echelons of the US socioeconomic strata, it is beyond contestation that the drug war has been the single most significant catalyst to the incarceration explosion in the United States over the latter two decades of the twentieth century. Experts highlight the dramatic effect of the war on drugs on our prison population, and especially its impact on traditionally marginalized populations.

Existing in the midst of this drug-war reality was our Southern Californian upper-class marijuana dealing network. Over the years that we studied this network and today, this primarily Caucasian population has remained immune to the brunt of the war on drugs, and law enforcement has been a very minimal presence in their lives. While in the year following the conclusion of this study there was a major state college drug bust in the region, the circle of dealers that remained in our network and the dealers that took the place of those who had matriculated out of the drug game and into more conforming occupations carried on unaffected. Rampant criminal behavior did not result in significant formal consequences and law enforcement did not perceptually align this group of criminals with the "enemy" in a three-decades-old "war" on drugs. This population serves as but one example of the disproportionate impact of the war on drugs on traditionally underrepresented populations and the relative immunity from criminal-justice scrutiny enjoyed by many relatively affluent individuals who participate in what would otherwise be perceived as common street crime. This relative immunity distorts the true nature of their behavior and contributes to the cumulative series of injustices and public misperception perpetrated by US failing drug policies.

Notes

1. Lilly, Cullen, and Ball, *Criminological Theory,* p. 6.
2. Akers and Sellers, *Criminological Theories.*
3. Kappeler and Potter, *The Mythology of Crime and Criminal Justice.*
4. According to a November 2006 report from the National Council on Crime and Delinquency, the United States incarcerates at a rate 4 to 7 times higher than its Western peers in the UK (145), France (88), Germany (95), and Italy (102). More telling, US incarceration rates are still unrivaled by undemocratic nations such as Iran (206), Zimbabwe (139), China (118), Cuba (487), and Russia (607). See Hartney, "US Rates of Incarceration."
5. In "What Works? Questions and Answers About Prison Reform," Martinson evaluated 231 criminal justice rehabilitation programs with varying scopes, designs, and goals. While the results of his study were appropriately complex, his "nothing works" statement was taken by many to represent the totality of his findings and used to facilitate a broad policy shift away from rehabilitation programming. Palmer ("Martinson Revisited") conducted a replication study with less stringent evaluation criteria and found that 48 percent of these same 231 rehabilitation programs did contribute to the rehabilitation of offenders. In 1979, Martinson officially withdrew his original findings, but his work had already made an indelible mark on public policy. Tragically, the impact and controversy of his study lead Martinson to commit suicide in 1980.
6. US Department of Justice, Bureau of Justice Statistics, "Key Facts at a Glance: Correctional Populations."

7. US Census Bureau, "Population Estimates, 2000–2007."

8. Dynamic Data, How Many People?

9. Fellner, *Punishment and Prejudice.*

10. US Department of Justice, Bureau of Justice Statistics, *Prisoners in 2006,* p. 23, Appendix Table 8.

11. US Census Bureau, "American Community Survey"; US Department of Justice, Bureau of Justice Statistics, "Key Facts at a Glance: Correctional Populations."

12. US Department of Justice, Bureau of Justice Statistics, *Prison Inmates at Midyear 2007.*

13. Mauer and King, *Uneven Justice.*

14. Lusane, *Pipe Dream Blues.*

15. Reiman, *The Rich Get Richer and the Poor Get Prison,* p. 112, emphasis in original.

16. Dorfman and Schiraldi, *Off Balance*; Burston, Jones, and Roberson-Sanders, "Drug Use and African Americans."

17. Beatty, Petteruti, and Ziedenberg, *The Vortex*; Mauer and King, *Uneven Justice*; Gray, *Why Our Drug Laws Have Failed and What We Can Do About It*; Fellner, *Punishment and Prejudice*; Currie, *Crime and Punishment in America*; Duster, "Pattern, Purpose and Race in the Drug War"; Baum, *Smoke and Mirrors*; Duke, "Drug Prohibition"; Tonry, *Malign Neglect.*

18. Gray, *Why Our Drug Laws Have Failed and What We Can Do About It.*

19. US Department of Justice, Bureau of Justice Statistics, "Key Facts at a Glance: Correctional Populations"; Fellner, *Punishment and Prejudice.*

20. Fellner, *Punishment and Prejudice.*

21. US Department of Justice, Federal Bureau of Prisons, "Quick Facts About the Bureau of Prisons."

22. US Department of Justice, Bureau of Justice Statistics, *Felony Sentences in State Courts,* 2004.

23. Beatty, Petteruti, and Ziedenberg, *The Vortex.*

24. California Department of Corrections and Rehabilitation, "California Prisoners and Parolees."

25. Ibid.

26. California Department of Corrections and Rehabilitation, "Fourth Quarter 2007 Facts and Figures."

27. Beatty, Petteruti, and Ziedenberg, *The Vortex,* p. 2.

28. Tonry, *Malign Neglect,* p. 49.

29. Fellner, *Punishment and Prejudice.*

30. Baum, *Smoke and Mirrors,* p. 323.

31. US Department of Health and Human Services, Substance Abuse and Mental Health Services Administration, "Results from the 2007 National Survey on Drug Use and Health: National Findings."

32. Gray, *Why Our Drug Laws Have Failed and What We Can Do About It,* p. 93.

33. Office of National Drug Control Policy, "Budget Summary"; Office of National Drug Control Policy, *National Drug Control Budget.*

34. Nadelmann, "Addicted to Failure."

35. Office of National Drug Control Policy, "What American Users Spend on Drugs," Table 6—Retail Prices Per Pure Gram for Cocaine and Heroin, 1988–2000.

36. US Department of Justice, Drug Enforcement Administration, "Drug Trafficking in the United States."

37. California marijuana crops pull in an estimated annual yield of $3.8 to $8.26 billion. Grapes are the state's second largest cash crop with an annual yield of $2.63 billion.

38. "National Survey of American Attitudes on Substance Abuse XII: Teens and Parents." 2007.

39. Penny, *Your Call Is Important to Us: The Truth About Bullshit,* p. 118.

40. Rosoff, Pontell, and Tillman, *Profit Without Honor,* p. 2.

41. Bourdieu, "The Forms of Capital."

42. Bourdieu, "The Field of Cultural Production."

43. Chambliss, "The Saints and the Roughnecks," p. 24.

44. Ibid.

45. Ibid., p. 29.

46. Ibid., p. 30.

47. Ibid.

48. Ibid.

49. Ibid.

50. Chambliss, "The Saints and the Roughnecks," p. 31.

51. Regoli and Hewitt, *Delinquency in Society.*

52. Williams, *The Cocaine Kids.*

53. Bourgois, *In Search of Respect,* pp. 37, 110, 111.

54. Adler, *Wheeling and Dealing,* pp. 100–111.

55. By way of a consent agreement with the city police department, campus police and the university officials to whom the campus police chief reports have complete discretion on matters that would otherwise be charged as misdemeanor offenses in off-campus environments. With regard to the possession of marijuana and marijuana paraphernalia, campus protocol for first-time offenders requires no referral to city police. Rather, the sanctions include parental notification, a $150 fine, a meeting with a drug and alcohol counselor, and, if the student lives on campus, a year of "housing probation" in which if the student is written up for any other drug or alcohol offense, he or she will be removed from on-campus housing.

56. Vacuum sealing machines create an air-tight seal around contents by removing the air from a plastic sheath and then using heat to seal the open end of the bag. They are legal, widely available, inexpensive (typically costing between $40 and $220) and commonplace in the illicit drug game.

57. Anderson, *The Code of the Street*; Williams, *The Cocaine Kids*; Bourgois, *In Search of Respect.*

58. D.J. Clue featuring Jay-Z and Ja Rule, "Gangsta Shit."

59. Williams, *The Cocaine Kids,* p. 33.

60. Bourgois, *In Search of Respect.*

61. Goldstein, Brownstein, Ryan, and Bellucci, "Crack and Homicide in New York City," p. 116.

62. Reuter, *Disorganized Crime.*

63. Rayful Edmond was a notorious Washington, DC, drug kingpin who, in 1989 at the age of 24, was charged with multiple federal drug and drug-related charges. "DC's version of John Gotti," Edmond was largely credited with spearheading the introduction of crack into Washington, DC, drug markets and was alleged to move thousands of kilograms of cocaine into the DC area every month. He was ultimately convicted and sentenced to life in prison. Interestingly, years after his conviction, he found himself again before a judge for charges stemming from his involvement in brokering street-drug deals from behind bars.

64. US Department of Justice, Bureau of Justice Statistics, "Key Facts at a Glance: Correctional Populations."

65. Sentencing Project, "The Federal Prison Population."

66. Kappeler and Potter, *The Mythology of Crime and Criminal Justice.*

67. US Department of Justice, Sourcebook of Criminal Justice Statistics, "Percent Distribution of Arrests for Drug Abuse Violations."

68. Kappeler and Potter, *The Mythology of Crime and Criminal Justice*; Reuter, MacCoun, and Murphy, *Money from Crime.*

69. Tonry, *Malign Neglect,* p. 42.

70. Elias and Houts, *Brooklyn North.*

71. Granfield and Cloud, "The Elephant That No One Sees," p. 441, paraphrasing Biernaki, *Pathways from Heroin Addiction.*

72. Lyman and Potter, *Drugs in Society.*

73. During the course of Brice's case, his legal team was in contact with at least one horticultural and biological science expert and various psychiatrists to serve as expert witnesses on his behalf.

74. Anderson, *The Code of the Street,* p. 142.

75. Jellinek, "Curriculum of Crime."

76. See Chapter 7 in this volume for full details of a recent undercover drug operation at San Diego State University that yielded a total of seventy-five student arrests.

77. Blumstein, "Prisons," p. 480.

7
Conclusions and Epilogue: No Dreams Deferred

On Tuesday May 6, 2008, the spotlight of the national news media trained onto the campus of San Diego State University (SDSU) and, at least momentarily, the issue of illicit drug markets on college campuses would have a central position in public discourse. Dubbed "Operation Sudden Fall," a multi-agency yearlong undercover operation by the Drug Enforcement Administration and the San Diego State University Police Department yielded a total of 130 undercover drug purchases and 125 arrests, including ninety-five current students at SDSU.[1] With noticeable fanfare, the DEA utilized Cox Arena, SDSU's indoor multipurpose events building, which seats thirteen thousand, to stage, interrogate, and process suspects taken down in the sting.

In total, Operation Sudden Fall led to the seizure of $60,000 in cash, fifty pounds of marijuana, forty-eight marijuana plants, thirty bottles of hashish oil, four pounds of cocaine, 350 Ecstasy pills, and various types of drug paraphernalia. Given the quality and quantities of substances involved, the San Diego District Attorney's Office estimated the total street value of the seized illicit drugs at over $100,000.[2] In addition, agents and officers seized a shotgun and three semiautomatic handguns. Immediately following the first wave of arrests, many of these seized items were prominently displayed at a press conference featuring SDSU president, Stephen Weber. The choice of May 6 for this grand showing of police force—the raids, the arrests, and the press conference—was quite deliberate. One year earlier, on May 6, 2007, SDSU student Jenny Poliakoff fatally overdosed on a combination of alcohol and cocaine

169

following a sorority dance and celebration that some sources suggest capped off a multiday drinking and drug binge. Poliakoff, a young, pretty, white, nineteen-year-old freshman and member of the Alpha Phi sorority, has since been Homerically dubbed "the face that launched a thousand narcs" as it is largely believed that her highly publicized overdose prompted campus and San Diego authorities to initiate the sting operation.

The extent of charged criminality among the arrested students varied substantially. According to published reports, the bulk of the students involved were likely purchasing drugs for their personal use or to divide the drugs among a few friends.[3] In total, forty-one of the students arrested were not discovered via the undercover operation, but rather as the result of "normal police work over a period of months, and many of those arrested involved small amounts of marijuana."[4] However, these facts notwithstanding, many of the arrested students were classified as "mid-level distributors" by Damon Mosler, the narcotics division chief of the San Diego County District Attorney's Office.[5] Members of seven officially recognized SDSU fraternities were prominent among the arrested drug dealers and, ultimately, six fraternities were initially suspended from campus by the university. Notably, Operation Sudden Fall also yielded to authorities a student majoring in criminal justice who was charged with gun violations and possession of 500 grams of cocaine. In an additional ironic twist, one student arrested and charged with distributing cocaine was scheduled to receive a master's degree in Homeland Security in June of that year and has served as a Student Community Service Officer for the SDSU Campus Police.

According to published reports, many of the SDSU drug dealers were not well-honed, strategic criminal entrepreneurs skilled in the art of the drug hustle. Similar to the haphazard approach employed by the dealers in our network sample, these SDSU dealers committed a series of blunders that made them easy prey for undercover operatives once the university decided it wanted to take action. Based on evidence from the undercover operation, Mosler concluded, "They weren't picky about who they sold to"[6] and that, routinely, undercover operatives faced little scrutiny when they telephoned suspected drug dealers attempting to make an initial drug buy. According to Moser the undercover agents would simply ask, "'Hey, I heard you deal. Will you sell to me?' And they did."[7] Most brazen were the sales and advertising tactics employed by members of the Theta Chi fraternity, which was described as a "hub of cocaine dealing" on the San Diego State University campus.[8] Similar to the ignorance, bravado, and total lack of concern for law enforcement displayed by our network's dealers, one nineteen-year-old SDSU student sent a mass out-of-office text message to his "faithful customers" explicitly advertising discounted prices on various quantities of illegal drugs. This text message was later posted on the DEA website and cited as critical evidence in Operation Sudden Fall:

> Attn faithful customers both myself and my associates will be in vegas this coming weekend bad news is we will not be here to complete sales good news is from [n]ow until midnight thursday gs [grams] are 35 eights [one-eighth of an ounce] 110 quads [one-quarter of an ounce] 210 so stock up we will be back sunday night.[9]

In addition to allegedly being an instrumental figure in SDSU's illicit drug network, this student had a prominent and respected legitimate position within the campus community. He served as a spokesperson on the San Diego State website for a program titled "Compact for Success," a partnership with the South Bay region of San Diego that guarantees students that graduate regional high schools with a grade point average of B or better will be automatically admitted to SDSU.

The scope of the operation, along with the subsequent publicity, led to a variety of public reactions from the campus community and the San Diego region. Alex Kreit, a law professor at Thomas Jefferson School of Law, located in nearby downtown San Diego, penned a compelling article published in the *San Diego Union Tribune*. In "What SDSU Drug Bust Won't Achieve," Kreit speculated that Operation Sudden Fall will have a minimal and fleeting impact on the supply of illicit drugs on the San Diego State University campus. He criticized the zero-tolerance approach toward illicit drugs employed by many college campuses and argued that SDSU's purported goal of a "drug-free learning environment" is wholly unrealistic. Rather than the get tough tactics that have mired the past several decades of drug control policy, Kreit advocated for an official "Good Samaritan Policy" on the San Diego State University campus that would encourage students to seek medical help during emergencies related to drugs and alcohol by shielding them, in these cases, from formal punishment. Indeed, Kreit cited a 2006 policy evaluation of Cornell University's Good

Samaritan Policy that suggests that these policies are "incredibly effective at encouraging students to seek help in such circumstances"[10] and are likely to substantially reduce the harms associated with legal and illegal drug use and abuse. In the wake of the drug bust, SDSU's Students for a Sensible Drug Policy went to significant lengths to advocate for a Good Samaritan Policy as an integral component of an overarching harm-reduction approach to drug use and abuse on campus. As part of their advocacy, these students staged a mock graduation ceremony with seventy-seven chairs, commemorating the seventy-five students who had been arrested to date, along with the two fatal overdoses on the SDSU campus over the past calendar year.

In an attempt to minimize the damage done to its reputation by the sting or perhaps to spin into a positive the campus's extensive drug use and sales revealed by the operation, SDSU initiated a "public-relations blitz" shortly after the culmination of Operation Sudden Fall themed "We're Prouder Than Ever."[11] This campaign featured prominent members of the local community and alumni from SDSU in radio, television, and print ads. We're Prouder Than Ever emphasized the safety of the campus, the value of a degree from the university, and the employability of past and present SDSU students. While somewhat short lived, San Diego stand-up comedian David Feingold mounted an advertising campaign of his own, immortalizing the event on a t-shirt. To our knowledge, the shirt has yet to be actually produced and was apparently intended as "parody and satire." However, Feingold's online advertisement featured a mockup of a black t-shirt with the SDSU logo along with the text "XTC 08" embedded in a graphic representing an ecstasy pill. The advertisement read: "Get the shirt seen 'round the world . . . This is a high quality T Shirt commemorating the BEST YEAR EVER at SDSU. Where were you when the drug bust went down? Did you know anyone arrested? Did you party this year?"[12]

Drug-Life Goes On

This high profile case notwithstanding, most college drug dealers do not get caught. In spite of the highly publicized zero tolerance rhetoric revolving around the SDSU bust and the get tough jargon that has come to identify the drug war era, over the entire course of our study of college drug dealers, no dreams were taken away. In fact, no dreams were even deferred as a result of our dealers' involvement in the drug game. It seems that for most of our network's drug dealers, illicit drug sales was a temporary indulgence en route to traditional pathways of success, pathways made substantially easier by the leg up they were given from the accident of birth and the collective blind eye turned toward their illegal activities.

Because of the relationships we established with some of the dealers and other informants within our study's network, we were fortunately able to remain in contact with or otherwise keep track of several of the dealers profiled throughout this book. For those that we were able to contact directly, even though they had mostly left drug dealing in their past, they were largely willing to consent to follow-up interviews. In a couple of other instances, we were not able to speak directly to the former dealers, but were able to receive an update on their lives after college from friends and associates. Across the board, none of those with whom we were able to speak or otherwise keep tabs on is presently involved in illicit drug sales, at least not in any substantial way. Some of our former dealers still use marijuana with some degree of regularity, but without the excess characteristic of their earlier days as collegiate drug entrepreneurs. Additionally, a few dealers routinely buy moderate quantities of marijuana and split it among friends to help offset the costs of their continued personal use of the drug. We did find that at least one of our study's dealers periodically cultivates small quantities of marijuana for his personal consumption, but none to sell. With these comparatively inconsequential exceptions, it seems, like most youthful offenders irrespective of race or class, the majority of our former dealers have matured out of crime and are living the "traditional" lives they, their families, and society at large always assumed they would fall into. Unquestionably, this maturation process was made far easier by their lack of formal interaction with the criminal justice system and being formally labeled a drug dealer.

Interestingly though, the entrepreneurial savvy and spirit of capitalism that were essential assets in many of their illicit businesses are currently evident in their endeavors as they have crossed over to become full-time actors in the lawful economy. After the culmination of his court case, Brice became quite successful in the legitimate world spending several years as a licensed real estate agent working for a moderately sized, well-established firm. He and Ann then relocated to Brice's home state with plans to marry in 2009. Ann is currently unemployed, but firmly dedicated to their recently acquired home, a three-bedroom, two-bath rambler on an acre of land. Brice chose to relocate to his home state largely because of the business opportunities facilitated by his family, who apparently held no grudge against him for his earlier transgressions. In fact, his father ushered him into a management position in a regional branch of a transnational distribution corporation. Brice has since held both management and sales positions within this company and he seems poised and content to settle into his current domestic and professional situations for the indefinite future.

In a follow-up interview, Brice was asked about his decision to abandon his illicit enterprise and fully dedicate himself to the legitimate world. While he admitted that the prospect of cultivating marijuana is still tempting, he is deterred from further criminality because it could potentially jeopardize his current professional position.

BRICE: But dealing with all that kind of stuff, I really would have no desire to do that again. I would tell ya quite open and honestly that I would love it, it was so much fun cultivating, I would love to do that in my spare time. As like a hobby. [I] could like play around with a few plants here, little ornamental treats. Now because of the situation, because it is illegal, and because I have a lot at stake. It could effect like my ownership in my company [and] my control to my company and all that kind of stuff. I could never do it. It would just . . . the risk would far far outweigh what I would ever get from it. That would be a thing that I would say I would miss. That was the fun part. I mean . . . watching something from the start to the finish. Ya know, you get to do all processes in between and you have a finished product when you are finally done.

Brice also added that logistical difficulties associated with living out of state and away from the network he had once mastered facilitated his decision to abandon his criminality. Being spatially isolated from his former suppliers and customers would demand establishing new inroads into the underground drug-dealing economy. Soliciting a new customer base is routine in urban open-air drug markets. However, as we have already described, markets like that in which Brice served as a major player for several years are largely closed to outside dealers. And as Brice knew all too well, as an outsider, trying to tap into the marijuana demand stream and beat the bushes for clients in a new market hundreds of miles from where he once made a name for himself would expose him to risks that he was unwilling to take. In our final formal conversation with Brice, he offered the following remarks:

Is there anything that I didn't ask you that you would like to include?

BRICE: Well . . . Uh . . . I think that to a certain extent one reason for me logistically, I couldn't keep the business end up of it is because of living in a different state too. That would mean then having to market to people, and I certainly would never do that at this stage of the game. Ya know. I could see the draw if I was in [our network's old Southern California city] and in contact with all the original people we were in contact with, I could easily see the draw of continuing. Like okay, it would be really, really hard for me to be in Cecilia's situation [still back in Southern California] and shut up shop. I think that would be much harder . . . than when I, ya know, when I was getting . . . I was just like "well shoot," "well fuck" I see that I work full time and I see that I would not have time to do this. But I wanna do other things, like other things that I like, like cultivating and stuff like that.

As we noted in an earlier discussion, when Brice downsized his network status, he passed on the majority of his customers, along with his suppliers, to Cecilia and she instantly became one of the network's largest drug dealers. Currently, she too has largely abandoned her illegitimate pursuits and has experienced some success in the legitimate world. Almost immediately after completing her BA degree in biology, Cecilia was hired as an entry-level administrator for an institution of higher learning in California. She quickly was promoted to a managerial position and seems well entrenched in the community, both professionally and socially. She is also applying her training in biology, attending night school and working toward certification in alternative medicine. In a 2008 follow-up interview, Cecilia commented that the transition from college into the professional world provided built-in incentives for her to abandon the underground economy. These incentives revolved around an increased awareness of risk, her professional aspirations that did not coincide with drug dealing, and, echoing Brice, losses in readily accessible clientele.

OK. Why did you stop, or at least downsize substantially?
CECILIA: Well because, like I keep referring to the umbrella of
college . . . and I definitely felt like um, I hadn't been busted while
I was in college. I think that the consequences would have been
different [after college], I felt like they would have been more
severe. I also felt like I sort of existed [in] the childhood of college
and trying to emerge as an adult in some type of a career field.
That that [dealing drugs] is not really the thing you know . . . so
you kinda start to think that you should separate yourself and then
naturally you also don't have all of those college friends so the
demand also decreases.

Like Cecilia, Dallas also remained in our network's home city
and, shortly after graduation, he too abandoned his illegitimate
endeavors. After completing an undergraduate degree in business,
Dallas segued into the real estate industry and seemed to be doing
well as a reformed drug dealer. While we were unable to contact
Dallas directly, we were able to get an update on how his life has progressed from Brice.

BRICE: Dallas is a mortgage [broker] . . . well last I saw and I don't
know because if the downturn in the economy that changed anything
. . . but he was in home loans. He was working for a broker down in
[the network's local area].

Diamond, the largest dealer in our sample, has also apparently
gone straight. He completed an undergraduate degree in business, left
the area, and relocated to Hawaii. He currently works in a management capacity for a construction company owned by his older brother. Pretty Boy, an ounce marijuana dealer in the sample, initially
worked in an administrative capacity for an athletic organization
coordinating vendors and managing corporate sponsors and promo-
tions for a venue serving as home to various sports teams. Pretty Boy
is now working full time for a former college classmate who
designed and patented an innovative type of skateboard. They are
currently selling the product nationwide and are in the process of
negotiating with some national sports retail chains. Brice commented
that this was a true entrepreneurial "success story."
Rasta, one of the few nonwhite dealers in our network, has also
continued on with his education and entrepreneurship. When we

last spoke with him, he was finishing his master's degree in a social science field and was still catering to college students through a legitimate small business he started with a friend from college. In regard to Ashcan, after graduating from the network's hub university, he attended and successfully graduated from a prestigious law school and is currently a staff attorney at a large law firm. One final dealer in the sample who was only observed but never formally interviewed also went into the real estate business after completing an undergraduate degree in business. Presently, he has two children and is a homeowner near where he at one time set up shop as a drug dealer.

The Monopoly's postcollege endeavors continue the theme of criminal desistance. However, his present legitimate pursuits are humorously reminiscent of his drug-dealing days as he still makes his living selling expensive, mind-altering, potentially addictive substances for profit. After completing his business degree, the Monopoly indeed went "straight" and abandoned his substantial illegal drug-dealing enterprise. However, the skills that he honed as a drug dealer translated directly to his future legitimate endeavors as a high-end wine salesman in his home town.

Of all of the dealers we were able to track down in the years since we first interviewed and observed them, the only success story anomaly is LaCoste. As we noted in Chapter 3 in his dealer bio, LaCoste was academically disqualified after his freshman year from our network's primary university. And, like our other dealers who remained true to their perceptions of self, LaCoste remained true to his self-identified criminal status. After his academic disqualification, LaCoste moved back to the Midwest where, upon last report from an informant, he was facing a series of felony charges, the nature of which we are unsure.

One of the most consistent and universal findings in all of criminology is the relationship that exists between the age of offenders and their propensity for criminal behavior. While there is disagreement about the significance of other intervening variables, there is a general consensus that individuals are less likely to commit all types of crime as they get older. This trend is often referred to as "the maturation effect" or "aging out" of crime.[13] We asked Brice why he thought all the former drug dealers in this network, who were positioned to expand their illicit businesses into full-blown industries, chose to go straight. His response suggests that criminality often correlates with the lifestyle and lack of responsibility affiliated with youth, and it also reaffirms many of the dynamics described in the maturation and social bonds literature.

So why do you think . . . it seems that most people were positioned to be full-time, career drug dealers. They had enough customers, they could pay all their bills, but everybody seemed to go straight. Why do you think that is?

BRICE: I don't know if anyone chose it as a career path you know. I mean . . . I mean it was something to do when you are young and allowed for a . . . for a . . . fun lifestyle. It allowed for . . . I would just say the lifestyle more or less ya' know . . . Um . . . And ya know, we were all in school or just out of school and primarily . . . I mean I don't think anyone did that as their career path. I just think it was something that they were doing at that time. ·

The Paradox of Policy: A Glance Toward the Future

Midway through Operation Sudden Fall, Kurt Baker, a student at nearby Mesa College, also fatally overdosed on a combination of alcohol and oxycodone at a San Diego State fraternity house. While Poliakoff and Baker's deaths are undoubtedly tragic and warrant the public and institutional attention they received, they do raise significant questions about resource allocation decisions by local, state, and federal law enforcement agencies. Specifically, given the approximately twenty thousand fatal unintentional drug overdoses each year in the United States, how often do these various agencies, particularly at the federal level, initiate extensive undercover operations in response to a single fatal drug overdose? Furthermore, what role do extra-incident criteria like visibility, institutional affiliation, and individual characteristics like the race, class, and "appeal" of the overdose victims play in law enforcement's decision to launch long-term and resource-sapping sting operations?

Seemingly based primarily on Poliakoff's death, a pretty, white, middle-class young woman, the Drug Enforcement Administration committed undercover operatives to San Diego State University for an entire year and in a fashion that seems to contradict the administration's own stated objectives. According to DEA's mission statement, the "primary responsibilities" of the agency are to disrupt "major violators of controlled substance laws operating at interstate and international levels" and engage in cooperative efforts with foreign and transnational law enforcement agencies to combat multinational organized criminal groups.[14] Carrying out the mandates contained within this mission statement would seem to locate the fraternity-centered drug dealers at San Diego State University and similar set-ups on other college campuses well below the scope of operations that are central to the charge of the agency.

Moreover, the evidence suggests that a year-long, multiagency undercover operation is an atypical response by law enforcement to a single known overdose fatality involving illegal drugs. Put simply, the sheer mass of unintentional drug overdose fatalities experienced by Americans each year would likely prevent unleashing the resources demanded by Operation Sudden Fall in every case, or even the vast majority of cases. In 2005, the Drug Abuse Warning Network (DAWN) collected and analyzed data from coroners and medical examiners offices located in 386 jurisdictions across the United States.[15] Utilizing these data, DAWN has fashioned an encompassing and comparative picture of drug-related mortality in the United States in their report *Area Profiles of Drug-Related Mortality*. According to this report, in San Diego County during the 2005 calendar year there were 314 known accidental deaths attributable to the misuse of legal or illegal drugs. There were an additional 60 suicide fatalities as a result of legal or illegal drug overdoses. Of the 314 deaths, there were only a few cases in which alcohol was the sole agent that caused the fatality. In the overwhelming majority of fatalities, multiple drugs were consumed simultaneously. This means that in nearly all of the 314 deaths illegal street-drugs or the criminal nonmedical use of prescription drugs contributed to the overdose fatality. Tragically, fatal overdoses involving illegal drugs are an almost daily occurrence in San Diego County. The mission of the DEA and the frequency of drug fatalities in the region both seem to suggest that Operation Sudden Fall was an atypical response by law enforcement to a tragically typical drug overdose. Further, it is not illogical to conclude that related factors extending beyond an overdose event, factors like race, class, the perceived attractiveness of the victim, institutional affiliation, and other superficial elements that contribute to determinations of newsworthiness, played a more central role in the decision to launch the SDSU sting operation in the wake of Poliakoff's death than did any real objective assessment of harm.

Throughout this book, we have criticized the lack of law enforcement attention on our sample of affluent drug dealers and the hyperattention of the war on drugs on the socially, economically, and politically marginalized. Now, it may seem as though we are shifting the critical lens toward the motivations of the DEA when SDSU drug dealers, who by definition enjoy some degree of symbolic capital, are facing formal consequences for their criminal activities. On the contrary, given the historic disproportionate impact of the war on drugs on traditionally underrepresented groups, we applaud law enforcement for actively targeting criminals of higher socioeconomic standing that more closely resemble the *boys next door* than they do the *boyz in the hood*. Nonetheless, it is unsettling that the investigation was driven by a single drug-related fatality, particularly considering that none of the hundreds of other area drug overdoses that same year received similar attention. In an ideal world, law enforcement would respond universally to drug-related harms rather than being pushed to action by the visibility, socioeconomic status, institutional affiliation, or other measures of symbolic capital associated with a victim.

The behaviors and dynamics of the San Diego State University drug dealers unearthed through Operation Sudden Fall have some implications for our own research. While our sample and the SDSU drug dealers probably differ in some significant ways, there are issues beyond their mutual status as college students that clearly dovetail with the findings of our study. First, it seems that at least some of the SDSU drug dealers exhibited the carelessness and haphazard approach that were characteristic of our group of affluent drug dealers. Many of the SDSU drug dealers did not vet potential customers and would commonly sell their wares to strangers who called them on their telephone; a few of these strangers turned out to be undercover DEA agents. The SDSU student mentioned above exhibited extreme negligence and a total lack of risk minimization when he sent his mass text message advertising "sale" prices of illegal drugs. These and other factors suggest that the lack of fundamental, commonsensical criminal tactics was not limited exclusively to our sample.

Second, this group of SDSU drug dealers was not selling drugs as a result of financial desperation; they were likely not pushed into the underground economy by extreme poverty or bleak structural opportunities for legitimate success. By definition, college students are engaging in the conformist[16] behavior that is largely held to be the most reliable pathway to upward social mobility. There is also some evidence to suggest that at least some of these dealers possessed substantial financial means. According to the *San Diego Union Tribune,* undercover agents allegedly purchased $400 of powder cocaine from another SDSU student. The deal reportedly took place while he was sitting in a Lexus that was registered to his father.[17] It seems that at least some of these SDSU drug dealers were motivated by a combination of the material and nonmaterial benefits of being a collegiate drug entrepreneur.

Third, these collegiate drug dealers also maintained a seemingly substantial commitment to both legitimate and illegitimate roles. Most obviously, they all played the role of drug dealer and college student simultaneously. However, many of the students were also involved in a series of other noncriminal endeavors. As discussed, members of officially recognized fraternities were apparently cornerstones of the drug-dealing networks that were detected during Operation Sudden Fall. Moreover, arrestees included students who were employed by campus police, earning postgraduate degrees, and working with community outreach groups on campus. It is possible that many of these San Diego State drug dealers were engaged in the mental gymnastics and identity contradictions produced by balancing substantial criminal and noncriminal endeavors.

Last, the remarkable publicity of the SDSU drug busts will hopefully help to correct many popular myths about archetypical drug dealers and users. In her 2008 follow-up interview, Cecilia speculated that the SDSU case will help reveal to the public that illicit drugs are seemingly a ubiquitous element of college culture.

CECILIA: Now that they had that giant bust at [SDSU] and they implicated all those fraternities and they kind of shed some light, opened the door to a whole culture that really only college kids and people who have anything to do with college in general are aware of.

Bonnie Dumanis, a San Diego district attorney, noted that this event "shows how accessible and pervasive illegal drugs continue to be on our college campuses, and how common it is for students to be selling to other students."[18] David Mosler further noted that a similarly structured drug sting would likely have yielded results on college campuses across the nation. But, "Oftentimes administrations don't want us to do this stuff and that's unfortunate . . . I think it's important to do this every now and then to wake people up. It raises everyone's awareness to the dangers of drugs."[19] Mosler's observation seems to further suggest that a college institution provides some degree of protection and administrators are willing to tolerate some degree of criminality.

Indicative of the historic lack of attention to or unwillingness to acknowledge middle- and upper-class criminality by members of the law enforcement and academic communities, some officials have openly stated that the SDSU drug bust was an aberration and suggested that the scope of the drug trade on that campus was an anomaly. Garrison Courtney, a public relations official in the Drug Enforcement Administration, was quoted in the *San Diego Union Tribune* arguing that drug-dealing networks rooted on college campuses are rare. "We know there's drug use in college . . . but when you have an organization that's actually based out of a college area, that's a whole different thing . . . You just don't see that."[20] With all due respect to Mr. Courtney, we saw it everyday, hidden in plain sight.

It seems reasonable, then, to conclude that those in positions to define particular behaviors as criminal and those who construct the overall agenda of the law enforcement community prefer to continue to cast the US drug problem as one primarily located among groups of people different from them, specifically, the minority poor. Yet, the dealers and activities we discussed throughout this book directly rebut this fiction and speak to the extent to which the US drug problem knows no racial or class boundaries, yet continues to be constructed as if it does.

It is not our intention to have this study serve as a call to arms to wage a drug war on our college campuses. On the contrary, it is our sincere hope that this ethnographic investigation of affluent collegiate drug dealers contributes in some small way to dispelling the myth that participation in substantial drug crimes is reserved exclusively for the marginalized, minority, poor, and undereducated members of our society. And we further hope that our work can spark a conversation about a more reasonable, equitable, and balanced set of domestic drug policies as we move forward in the new millennium.

Notes

1. Perry, "San Diego State Launches Public-Relations Effort."
2. CNN, "College Drug Sting."
3. Kreit, "What SDSU Drug Bust Won't Achieve."
4. Perry, "San Diego State Launches Public-Relations Effort."
5. CNN, "College Drug Sting."
6. Ibid.
7. Ibid.
8. McDonald, Saavedra, and Sierra, "Major SDSU Drug Probe Nets 96 Arrests in Raids."
9. US Department of Justice, Drug Enforcement Administration, "Major Operations."
10. Kreit, "What SDSU Drug Bust Won't Achieve."
11. Perry, "San Diego State Launches Public-Relations Effort."
12. SDSU 08.
13. Piquero, Farrington, and Blumstein, "The Criminal Career Paradigm."
14. According to the full DEA mission statement, "In carrying out its mission as the agency responsible for enforcing the controlled substances laws and regulations of the United States, the DEA's primary responsibilities include: investigation and preparation for the prosecution of major violators of controlled substance laws operating at interstate and international levels; investigation and preparation for prosecution of criminals and drug gangs who perpetrate violence in our communities and terrorize citizens through fear and intimidation; management of a national drug intelligence program in cooperation with federal, state, local, and foreign officials to collect, analyze, and disseminate strategic and operational drug intelligence information; seizure and forfeiture of assets derived from, traceable to, or intended to be used for illicit drug trafficking; enforcement of the provisions of the Controlled Substances Act as they pertain to the manufacture, distribution, and dispensing of legally produced controlled substances; coordination and cooperation with federal, state, and local law enforcement officials on mutual drug enforcement efforts and enhancement of such efforts through exploitation of potential interstate and international investigations beyond local or limited federal jurisdictions and resources; coordination and cooperation with federal, state, and local agencies, and with foreign governments, in programs designed to reduce the availability of illicit abuse-type drugs on the United States market through nonenforcement methods such as crop eradication, crop substitution, and training of foreign officials; responsibility, under the policy guidance of the Secretary of State and US Ambassadors, for all programs associated with drug law enforcement counterparts in foreign countries; [and] liaison with the United Nations, Interpol, and other organizations on matters relating to international drug control programs" (US Department of Justice, Drug Enforcement Administration, "DEA Mission Statement").

15. Drug Abuse Warning Network, *Area Profiles of Drug-Related Mortality.*

16. Merton, "Social Structure and Anomie."

17. McDonald, Saavedra, and Sierra, "Major SDSU Drug Probe Nets 96 Arrests in Raids."

18. Kreit, "What SDSU Drug Bust Won't Achieve."

19. McDonald, Saavedra, and Sierra, "Major SDSU Drug Probe Nets 96 Arrests in Raids."

20. Ibid.

Bibliography

Adler, P. *Wheeling and Dealing.* New York: Columbia University Press, 1985.

Advertising Age Marketer Trees 2008. Available at http://adage.com/marketertrees08/index.php?marketer=93#93 (accessed September 23, 2008).

Agnew, R. "The Techniques of Neutralization and Violence." *Criminology* 32 (1994): 555–580.

Akers, R. *Criminological Theories.* Los Angeles: Roxbury, 2000.

Akers, R., and C. Sellers. *Criminological Theories: Introduction, Evaluation, and Application,* 5th ed. New York: Oxford University Press, 2008.

Allen, M. "Pharmacies a Popular Source of Illegal Drugs in Nevada." *Las Vegas Sun,* August 30, 2008. Available at http://m.rgj.com/news.jsp?key=100589 (accessed June 22, 2009).

Anderson, E. *The Code of the Street.* New York: W. W. Norton, 1999.

Associated Press. "Teen-Agers Say Marijuana Is Easier to Buy Than Beer." *North County Times,* August 20, 2002. Available at http://cannabisnews.com/news/13/thread13814.shtml (accessed June 22, 2009).

Bailey, E. "Pot Is Called Biggest Cash Crop." *Los Angeles Times,* December 8, 2006. Available at http://articles.latimes.com/2006/dec/18/local/me-pot18 (accessed June 22, 2009).

Baum, D. *Smoke and Mirrors.* Boston: Little Brown, 1997.

Beatty, P., A. Petteruti, and J. Ziedenberg. *The Vortex: The Concentrated Racial Impact of Drug Imprisonment and the Characteristics of Punitive Counties.* Washington, DC: Justice Policy Institute, 2007.

Becker, H. "Marijuana Use and Social Control." In *Social Deviance: Readings in Theory and Research,* edited by H. Pontell, pp. 238–246. Englewood Cliffs, NJ: Prentice Hall, 1993.

———. *Outsiders.* New York: Free Press, 1963.

Berger, J., M. Free, and P. Searles. *Crime, Justice, and Society.* Boulder, CO: Lynne Rienner, 2005.

Biernacki, P. *Pathways from Heroin Addiction.* Philadelphia: Temple University Press, 1986.

Blackman, S. *Chilling Out: The Cultural Politics of Substance Consumption, Youth and Drug Policy.* New York: Open University Press, 2004.

Blumstein, A. "Prisons: A Policy Challenge." In *Crime: Public Policies for Crime Control,* edited by J. Q. Wilson and J. Petersilia, pp. 451–482. Oakland: ICS, 2002.

Bourdieu, P. *The Field of Cultural Production: Essays on Art and Literature.* Edited and introduced by R. Johnson. Cambridge, UK: Polity, 1993.

———. "The Forms of Capital." In *The Handbook of Theory and Research for the Sociology of Education,* edited by J. Richardson, pp. 241–258. New York: Greenwood, 1986.

Bourgois, P. *In Search of Respect.* New York: Cambridge University Press, 1995.

Broder, J. "California Ending Use of Minor Traffic Stops as Search Pretext." *New York Times,* February 28, 2003. Available at http://query.nytimes.com/gst/fullpage.html?res=9A04E3D9133CF93BA15751C0A9659C8B63 (accessed September 10, 2008).

Burston, B. W., D. Jones, and P. Roberson-Sanders. "Drug Use and African Americans." *Journal of Alcohol and Drug Education* 40 (1995): 19–39.

California Border Alliance Group. *Drug Market Analysis,* May 2008. Washington, DC: National Drug Intelligence Center, US Department of Justice, 2008. Available at www.usdoj.gov/ndic/pubs27/27487/index.htm (accessed June 22, 2009).

California Department of Corrections and Rehabilitation. "California Prisoners and Parolees." 2004. Available at www.cdcr.ca.gov/Reports_Research/offender_information_services_branch/annual/calpris/calprisd2004.pdf (accessed June 22, 2009).

California Department of Corrections and Rehabilitation. "Fourth Quarter 2007 Facts and Figures." 2007. Available at www.cdcr.ca.gov/Divisions_Boards/Adult_Operations/Facts_and_Figures.htm l (accessed July 4, 2008).

Chambliss, W. "The Saints and the Roughnecks." *Society* 11 (1973): 24–31.

CNN. "College Drug Sting Snags Justice, Security Majors, Scores of Others." Available at www.cnn.com/2008/CRIME/05/06/sdsu.bust/ index.html?iref=newssearch (accessed July 28, 2008).

Coleman, J. W. *The Criminal Elite: The Sociology of White-Collar Crime.* New York: St. Martin's, 1994.

Conrad, P., and D. Potter. "From Hyperactive Children to ADHD Adults: Observations on the Expansion of Medical Categories." *Social Problems* 47, no. 4 (November 2000): 559–582. Published by University of California Press on behalf of the Society for the Study of Social Problems.

Currie, E. *Crime and Punishment in America.* New York: Henry Holt, 1998.

Dorfman, L., and V. Schiraldi. *Off Balance: Youth, Race and Crime in the News. Building Blocks for Youth.* Washington, DC: Justice Policy Institute, 2001.

Downton, J., and P. Wehr. "Persistent Pacifism." *Journal of Peace Research* 35 (1998): 531–550.

Drug Abuse Warning Network. *Area Profiles of Drug-Related Mortality.* Rockville, MD: SAMHSA, Office of Applied Studies, 2009.

Drug Abuse Warning Network. *National Estimates of Drug-Related Emergency Department Visits.* DHHS Publication Number 08-4339. Rockville, MD: 2008. Available at http://dawninfo.samhsa.gov/ files/ED2006/DAWN2K6ED.htm#High1 (accessed June 22, 2009).

Drug Policy Alliance. "Race and the Criminal Justice System." Available at www.drugpolicy.org/communities/race/criminaljust (accessed June 12, 2008).

Duke, S. "Drug Prohibition." *Connecticut Law Review* 27 (1995): 569–697.

Duster, T. "Pattern, Purpose and Race in the Drug War." In *Crack in America,* edited by C. Reinarman and H. Levine, pp. 260–287. Berkeley: University of California Press, 1997.

Dynamic Data: How Many People. Available at www.360degrees .org/360degrees.html (accessed June 2008).

The Economist. "Marijuana: Home-grown." October 18, 2007. Available at www.economist.com/world/unitedstates/displaystory.cfm?story _id=10000884 (accessed May 19, 2008).

Elias, D., and D. Houts. *Brooklyn North,* television broadcast, October 27, 2002. Huntington Beach, CA: Court TV.

Eliason, S. "Illegal Hunting and Angling: The Neutralization of Wildlife Law Violations." *Society and Animals* 11 (2003): 225–243.

Faludi, S. *Stiffed.* NewYork: Harper Collins, 1999.

Fellner, J. *Punishment and Prejudice: Racial Disparities in the War on Drugs.* New York: Human Rights Watch, 2000.

Fortune Magazine. "Global 500: Our Annual Ranking of the World's Largest Corporations." Available at http://money.cnn.com/magazines/fortune/global500/2008 (accessed September 23, 2008).

Geertz, C. *Interpretation of Cultures.* New York: Basic Books, 1973.

Goldstein, P., H. Brownstein, P. Ryan, and P. Bellucci. "Crack and Homicide in New York City." In *Crack in America,* edited by C. Reinarman and H. Levine, pp. 113–130. Berkeley, CA: University of California Press, 1997.

Goodhue, R., R. Green, D. Heien, and P. Martin. *Current Economic Trends in the California Wine Industry.* Giannini Foundation of Agricultural Economics, University of California, April 2008. Available at www.agmrc.org/media/cms/v11n4_2_AOF001 ECODOA3.pdf (accessed June 22, 2009).

Graham, J. "Amphetamine Politics on Capitol Hill." *Society* 9 (1972): 13–23.

Granfield, R., and W. Cloud. "The Elephant That No One Sees." In *The American Drug Scene,* edited by J. Inciardi and K. McElrath, pp. 440–451. New York: Oxford University Press, 1996.

Gray, J. *Why Our Drug Laws Have Failed and What We Can Do About It.* Philadelphia: Temple University Press, 2001.

Greene, J. "Attention to 'Details': Etiquette and the Pharmaceutical Salesman in Postwar American." *Social Studies of Science* 34 (2004): 271–292.

Halnon, K. "The Power of 420." In *The American Drug Scene,* edited by J. Inciardi and K. McElrath. New York: Oxford University Press, 2003.

Hartney, Christopher. "US Rates of Incarceration: A Global Perspective." Research from the National Council on Crime and Delinquency, November 2006. Available at www.nccd-crc.org/nccd/pubs/2006nov_factsheet_incarceration.pdf (accessed June 22, 2009).

Hughes, T., and D. Wilson. *Reentry Trends in the United States.* Washington, DC: Bureau of Justice Statistics, United States Department of Justice, 2003.

Inciardi, J., H. Surratt, and S. Kurtz. "African-Americans, Crack, and the Federal Sentencing Guidelines." In *The American Drug Scene,* edited by J. Inciardi and K. McElrath, pp. 214–224. New York: Oxford University Press, 2007.

International Centre for Prison Studies. *World Prison Brief: Prison Brief for the United States of America.* Camden, London: King's College of London, 2008.

Jellinek, J. "Curriculum of Crime." *Rolling Stone,* February 2003, pp. 54–55.

Joralemon, J. "Coca in History and Political Economy." *American Anthropologist* 97 (1995): 799–800.

Kappeler, V., and G. Potter. *The Mythology of Crime and Criminal Justice,* 4th ed. Long Grove, IL: Waveland, 2005.

Karch, S. *A Brief History of Cocaine.* Boca Raton, FL: CRC Press, 1998.

Katz, J. *Seductions of Crime.* New York: Basic Books, 1988.

Kentucky Senate Judiciary Committee. Testimony of Secretary J. Michael Brown. *The Lexington Herald-Leader.* January 24, 2008. Available at http://www.pewcenteronthestates.org/uploadedfiles/one%20in%20100.pdf (accessed June 22, 2009).

Klockers, C. *The Professional Fence.* New York: Free Press, 1974.

Kreit, A. "What SDSU Drug Bust Won't Achieve." *San Diego Union Tribune,* May 8, 2008. Available at http://cfx.signonsandiego.com/uniontrib/20080508/news_lz1e8kreit.html (accessed June 22, 2009).

Lambert, C. "OxyContin Rushes into State's Drug Lexicon." *San Francisco Examiner,* October 7, 2003. Available at http://opioids.com/oxycodone/rushlimbaugh.html (accessed September 21, 2008).

Lawson, W. "ADHD: Diagnosis Dilemma—Mental Health Experts Debate Definitions of Adult Attention Deficit Hyperactivity Disorder and Patterns of Diagnosis and Medication by Socioeconomic Class." *Psychology Today,* September/October 2004. Available at www.usdoj.gov/dea/pubs/cngrtest/ct062408.html (accessed June 22, 2009).

Leiby, R. "A Crack in the System." *Washington Post,* February 20, 1994, pp. F1, F4–F5.

Lemert, E. *Human Deviance, Social Problems, and Social Control.* Englewood Cliffs, NJ: Prentice Hall, 1967.

Lilly, R., F. Cullen, and R. Ball. *Criminological Theory: Context and Consequences,* 2nd ed. London: Sage, 1995.

Little Hoover Commission, Testimony of Judge James P. Gray. (n.d.). Available at www.lhc.ca.gov/lhcdir/drug/GraySep26.pdf (accessed July 4, 2008).

Lusane, C. *Pipe Dream Blues.* Boston: South End, 1991.

Lyman, M., and G. Potter. *Drugs in Society.* Cincinnati: Anderson Publishing, 1991.

Lyng, S. "Crime, Edgework and Corporeal Transaction." *Theoretical Criminology* 8 (2004): 359–375.

Mann, R. *Grass: A Documentary History of Marijuana Criminalization in the US,* videotape. Santa Monica, CA: Sphinx Productions, 1999.

Mannle, H. "An Empirical Exploration and Interpretation of Neutralization Theory Predicted upon Sexual Differences in the

Socialization Process." Ph.D. dissertation, Florida State University, Tallahassee, 1972.

Martinson, R. "What Works? Questions and Answers About Prison Reform." *Public Interest* 35 (1974): 22–54.

Mauer, M., and R. King. *Sentencing with Discretion: Crack Cocaine Sentencing After Booker.* Washington, DC: The Sentencing Project, 2006.

———. *Uneven Justice: State Rates of Incarceration.* Washington, DC: The Sentencing Project, 2007.

McDonald, J., S. Saavedra, and T. Sierra. "Major SDSU Drug Probe Nets 96 Arrests in Raids." *San Diego Union Tribune,* May 7, 2008. Available at www.signonsandiego.com/news/education/20080507 -9999-1n7drugs.html (accessed June 22, 2008).

Merton, R. "Social Structure and Anomie." *American Sociological Review* 3 (1938): 672–682.

Miller, Daniel. *Capitalism: An Ethnographic Approach.* Oxford: Berg, 1997.

Minor, W. "The Neutralization of Criminal Offense." *Criminology* 18 (1980): 103–120.

Mitchell, J., R. Dodder, and T. Norris. "Neutralization and Delinquency: A Comparison by Sex and Ethnicity." *Adolescence* 25 (1990): 487–497.

Mohamed, A. R., and E. Fritsvold. "Damn It Feels Good to Be a Gangsta: The Social Organization of the Illicit Drug Trade Servicing a Private College Campus." *Deviant Behavior* 27 (2006): 97–125.

Moskos, P. *Cop in the Hood: My Year Policing Baltimore's Eastern District.* Princeton, NJ: Princeton University Press, 2008.

Moynihan, R., and A. Cassels. "A Disease for Every Pill." *The Nation,* September 29, 2005. Available at www.thenation.com/doc/ 20051017/moynihan (accessed September 1, 2008).

Musto, D. *The American Disease.* New York: Oxford University Press, 1999.

Nadelmann, E. "Addicted to Failure." *Foreign Policy* 137 (2003): 94–95.

"National Survey of American Attitudes on Substance Abuse XII: Teens and Parents." The National Center on Addiction and Substance Abuse at Columbia University, August 2007. Available at www.casacolumbia .org/absolutenm/articlefiles/380-2007%20Teen%20Survey%20xii.pdf (accessed June 22, 2009).

Office of National Drug Control Policy (ONDCP). *National Drug Control Budget: FY2010 Budget Funding Highlights.* Available at www.whitehousedrugpolicy.gov/publications/policy/10budget highlight/fy10budget.pdf (accessed June 22, 2009).

———. "What American Users Spend on Drugs," Table 6: Retail Prices per Pure Gram for Cocaine and Heroin, 1988–2000. Available at www.whitehousedrugpolicy.gov/publications/drugfact/american%5F users%5Fspend/table6.html (accessed August 19, 2008).

Palmer, T. "Martinson Revisited." *Journal of Research in Crime and Delinquency* 12 (1975): 133–152.

Penny, Laura. *Your Call Is Important to Us: The Truth About Bullshit.* New York: Random House, 2005.

Perry, Tony. "San Diego State Launches Public-Relations Effort After Huge Drug Bust." *Los Angeles Times,* May 16, 2008. Available at http://articles.latimes.com/2008/may/16/local/me-drugbust16.

Petersilia, J. "Prisoner Reentry and Criminological Knowledge." *Criminologist,* The American Society of Criminology, March–April 2003, pp. 1–5.

Piquero, A., D. Farrington, and A. Blumstein. "The Criminal Career Paradigm." *Crime and Justice, A Review of Research* 30 (2003): 359–506.

Priest, T. B., and J. McGrath. "Techniques of Neutralization: Young Adult Marijuana Smokers." *Criminology* 8 (1970): 185–194.

Regoli, R., and J. Hewitt. *Delinquency in Society,* 6th ed. Columbus, OH: McGraw-Hill, 2005.

Reiman, J. *The Rich Get Richer and the Poor Get Prison,* 8th ed. Boston: Allyn and Bacon, 2007.

Reinarman, C., and H. Levine. *Crack in America.* Berkeley, CA: University of California Press, 1997.

Reuter, P. *Disorganized Crime.* Cambridge, MA: MIT Press, 1983.

Reuter, P., R. MacCoun, and P. Murphy. *Money from Crime: A Study of the Economics of Drug Dealing in Washington, DC.* Santa Monica, CA: The Rand Corporation, 1990.

Rosoff, S., H. Pontell, and R. Tillman. *Profit Without Honor.* Upper Saddle River, NJ: Prentice Hall, 2002.

Ryan, Harriet. "Attorney General Calls Anna Nicole Smith's Boyfriend Her 'Principal Enabler.'" *Los Angeles Times,* Saturday, March 14, 2009, A8.

Sampson, R. *Drug Dealing in Privately Owned Apartment Complexes.* Washington, DC: US Department of Justice, Office of Community Oriented Policing Services, 2001.

Scully, D., and J. Marolla. "Convicted Rapists' Vocabulary of Motive." *Social Problems* 31 (1984): 530–544.

SDSU 08. "SDSU 08 T Shirt Men." Available at http://sdsu08.com/ 2008/05/sdsu-08-commemerative-shirt (accessed July 21, 2008).

The Sentencing Project. "The Federal Prison Population: A Statistical Analysis." 2004. Available at www.sentencingproject.org/Admin/ Documents/publications/inc_federalprisonpop.pdf (accessed August 19, 2008).

————. "Felony Disenfranchisement Laws in the United States." 2008. Available at www.sentencingproject.org/Admin%5CDocuments% 5Cpublications%5Cfd_bs_fdlawsinus.pdf (accessed September 10, 2008).

Stankiewicz, W. *In Search of a Political Philosophy.* New York: Taylor and Francis, 1993.

Sykes, G., and D. Matza. "Techniques of Neutralization: A Theory of Delinquency." *American Sociological Review* 22, no. 6 (1957): 664–670.

Tannenbaum, F. *Crime and the Community.* Boston: Ginn, 1938.

Tewksbury, R., and E. Mustaine. "Lifestyles of the Wheelers and Dealers." *Journal of Crime and Justice* 21 (1998): 37–56.

Thompson, C. "A New Vision of Masculinity." In *New Men, New Minds,* edited by A. Franklin, pp. 630–636. Freedom, CA: Crossing Press, 1987.

Thurman, Q. "Deviance and the Neutralization of Moral Commitment: An Empirical Analysis." *Deviant Behavior* 5 (1984): 291–304.

Tonry, M. *Malign Neglect.* New York: Oxford University Press, 1995.

US Attorney, District of Nevada, US Department of Justice. "Las Vegas Pharmacist Charged with Health Care Fraud and Unlawful Distribution," press release, 2007. Available at http://lasvegas .fbi.gov/dojpressrel/pressrel07/healthcarefraud022307.htm (accessed September 23, 2008).

US Census Bureau. "Population Estimates, 2000–2004." Available at www.census.gov/popest/cities/sub-est2007.html (accessed June 22, 2009).

US Department of Health and Human Services, Substance Abuse and Mental Health Services Administration. "Results from the 2007 National Survey on Drug Use and Health: National Findings." Office of Applied Studies, NSDUH Series H-34, DHHS Publication No. SMA 08-4343. Rockville, MD, 2008. Available at www.oas.samhsa.gov/NSDUH/2K7NSDUH/2K7results.cfm (accessed August 20, 2009).

US Department of Justice, Bureau of Justice Statistics. "Felony Sentences in State Courts, 2004." Bulletin NCJ 215646. Washington, DC: United States Department of Justice, 2007. Available at www.ojp.usdoj.gov/bjs/pub/pdf/fssc04.pdf.

US Department of Justice, Bureau of Justice Statistics. "Key Crime and Justice Facts at a Glance: Correctional Populations." Washington, DC: United States Department of Justice, 2006. Available at www.ojp.usdoj.gov/bjs/glance.htm (accessed June 22, 2009).

US Department of Justice, Bureau of Justice Statistics. *Prison and Jail Inmates at Midyear 2006,* Bulletin NCJ 217675, p. 15. Washington, DC: US Department of Justice, 2007.

US Department of Justice, Bureau of Justice Statistics. *Prisoners in 2006,* Bulletin NCJ 219416. Washington, DC: US Department of Justice, 2007.

US Department of Justice, Bureau of Justice Statistics. *Prison Inmates at Midyear 2007,* Bulletin NCJ 221944. Washington, DC: US Department of Justice, June 2008.

US Department of Justice, Bureau of Justice Statistics. Sourcebook of Criminal Justice Statistics. "Number and Rate (per 100,000 US residents) of Persons in State and Federal Prisons and Local Jails." Available at www.albany.edu/sourcebook/pdf/t6132007.pdf (accessed July 15, 2008).

US Department of Justice, Bureau of Justice Statistics. "State Court Sentencing of Convicted Felons, 2004 Statistical Tables," Table 1.1, NCJ 217995, 2007. Available at www.ojp.usdoj.gov/bjs/abstract/scscf04st.htm (accessed August 8, 2007).

US Department of Justice, Drug Enforcement Administration. "DEA Mission Statement." Available at www.usdoj.gov/dea/agency/mission.htm (accessed July 21, 2008).

US Department of Justice, Drug Enforcement Administration. "Drug Trafficking in the United States." Available at www.usdoj.gov/dea/pubs/state_factsheets.html (accessed June 22, 2009).

US Department of Justice, Drug Enforcement Administration, Joseph T. Rannazzisi, Deputy Assistant Administrator, Office of Diversion Control. "Online Pharmacies and the Problem of Internet Drug Abuse." Testimony before the House Judiciary Committee, Subcommittee on Crime, Terrorism, and Homeland Security. June 24, 2008. Available at www.usdoj.gov/dea/pubs/cngrtest/ct062408.html (accessed August 22, 2008).

US Department of Justice, Drug Enforcement Administration. "Major Operations." Available at www.usdoj.gov/dea/images_major_operations.html#2008 (accessed July 21, 2008).

US Department of Justice, Federal Bureau of Prisons. "Quick Facts About the Bureau of Prisons." www.bop.gov/about/facts.jsp#4 (accessed June 22, 2009).

US Department of Justice, Sourcebook of Criminal Justice Statistics. "Percent Distribution of Arrests for Drug Abuse Violations." 2006. Available at www.albany.edu/sourcebook/pdf/t4292006.pdf (accessed June 22, 2009).

US House of Representatives, Testimony of Leonard J. Paulozzi, M.D., M.P.H., Medical Epidemiologist, National Center for Injury Prevention and Control. Centers for Disease Control and Prevention. Testimony before the US House of Representatives on trends in unintentional drug poisoning deaths. October 24, 2007. Available at www.hhs.gov/asl/testify/2007/10/t20071024a.html (accessed September 2, 2008).

Van Nostrand, L. M., and R. Tewksbury. "The Motives and Mechanics of Operating an Illegal Drug Enterprise." *Deviant Behavior* 20 (1999): 57–83.

Venkatesh, S. *Gang Leader for a Day.* New York: Penguin, 2008.

Williams, T. *The Cocaine Kids.* New York: Perseus, 1989.

Index

About the Book

Why do affluent, upwardly mobile college students—who have everything to lose and little to gain—choose to sell drugs? Why do law enforcement officers largely overlook drug dealing on college campuses?

With rich, lively details, A. Rafik Mohamed and Erik Fritsvold deliver unprecedented insight into the world of college drug dealers—and offer an important corrective to the traditional distorted view of the US drug trade as primarily involving poor minorities. Drawing on six years of fieldwork at a predominately white private university, their exceptional ethnography skillfully explores issues of deviance, race, and stratification in the US war on drugs.

A. Rafik Mohamed is chair of social sciences at Clayton State University. **Erik D. Fritsvold** is assistant professor of sociology at the University of San Diego.